D0759649

Poetic Memory

Poetic Memory

The Forgotten Self in Plath, Howe, Hinsey, and Glück

Uta Gosmann

FARLEIGH DICKINSON UNIVERSITY PRESS
Madison • Teaneck

Published by Farleigh Dickinson University Press
Co-published with The Rowman & Littlefield Publishing Group, Inc.
4501 Forbes Boulevard, Suite 200, Lanham, Maryland 20706
http://www.rowmanlittlefield.com

Estover Road, Plymouth PL6 7PY, United Kingdom

British Library Cataloguing in Publication Information Available

Library of Congress Cataloging-in-Publication Data

Gosmann, Uta.
Poetic memory : the forgotten self in Plath, Howe, Hinsey, and Glück / Uta Gosmann.
p. cm.
Includes bibliographical references and index.
ISBN 978-1-61147-036-9 (cloth : alk. paper) -- ISBN 978-1-61147-037-6 (electronic)
1. Plath, Sylvia—Criticism and interpretation. 2. Howe, Susan, 1937– —Criticism and interpret-
ation. 3. Hinsey, Ellen, 1960– —Criticism and interpretation. 4. Glück, Louise, 1943– —Criti-
cism and interpretation. 5. American poetry—20th century—History and criticism. I. Title.
PS323.5.G67 2012
811'.509—dc22
2011014540

Printed in the United States of America

For Lanny

Contents

Acknowledgments

I am grateful for some intensely poetic and memorable hours spent with Louise Glück, Ellen Hinsey, and Susan Howe. Their enthusiasm for this book was invigorating, and their friendship made my work all the more meaningful.

At various stages, Aleida Assmann, Marc Chénetier, Shoshana Felman, and Sabine Sielke provided constructive criticism and illuminating commentary on poetic and theoretical matters. Annette Kuhn was a source of unfaltering optimism. James Longenbach's sensitive reading helped the book to its present shape.

The German Academic Exchange Service (DAAD) funded my research at Yale University.

I am grateful to my husband Langdon Hammer whose encouragement helped this book to see the light of day.

An earlier version of chapter 1 was published in *Memory, Haunting, Discourse*, edited by Maria Holmgren Troy and Elisabeth Wennö. Parts are reprinted by permission of Karlstad University Press. The first part of chapter 3 appeared in *Common Knowledge* and is reprinted by permission of the publisher, Duke University Press.

The poem "Words" from *Collected Poems* by Sylvia Plath, copyright © 1966 by Ted Hughes, is reprinted by permission of HarperCollins Publishers. The poem "The Approach of War" from *Cities of Memory* by Ellen Hinsey, copyright © 1996 by Yale University Press, is reprinted by permission of the publisher.

I want to express particular gratitude to Gerhard Richter for granting permission to reproduce his "Abstract Painting, 1990 (CR 726)," copyright © Tate, London 2010, on the cover of this book.

Abbreviations

AV	Glück, Louise. *Averno*. New York: Farrar, Straus and Giroux, 2006.
BM	Howe, Susan. *The Birth-mark: Unsettling the Wilderness in American Literary History*. Hanover, NH: University of New England Press, 1993.
CM	Hinsey, Ellen. *Cities of Memory*. New Haven, CT: Yale University Press, 1996.
CP	Plath, Sylvia. *Collected Poems*. New York: Harper Collins, 1992.
EB	Howe, Susan. "A Bibliography of the King's Book or, Eikon Basilike." In *The Nonconformist's Memorial*, 45–82. New York: New Directions, 1993.
J	Plath, Sylvia. *The Journals of Sylvia Plath 1950–1962*. Edited by Karen V. Kukil. London: Faber and Faber, 2000.
K	Keller, Lynn. "An Interview with Susan Howe." *Contemporary Literature* 36.1 (1995): 1–34.
MM	Howe, Susan. "Melville's Marginalia." In *The Nonconformist's Memorial*, 83–150.
MR	Howe, Susan. "The Captivity and Restoration of Mrs. Mary Rowlandson." In *The Birth-mark*, 89–130.
NM	Howe, Susan. "The Nonconformist's Memorial." In *The Nonconformist's Memorial*, 3–33.
SM	Howe, Susan. "Submarginalia." In *The Birth-mark*, 26–42.
SWS	Howe, Susan. "Silence Wager Stories." In *The Nonconformist's Memorial*, 34–42.
TI	Howe, Susan. "Talisman Interview, with Edward Foster." In *The Birth-mark*, 155–81.

Introduction

[The soul] . . . is and becomes what it remembers.
 —Plotinus, *Enneads*

POETIC AND HISTORIC MEMORY

In Sylvia Plath's famously ruthless elegy "Daddy," the speaker confesses to the absent father, "I used to pray to recover you." Daddy is dead, but the speaker tries to resuscitate him in her memory. Remembering him is so uncertain but critical an enterprise, she implores the gods in prayer to help her. Yet her attempts at remembering Daddy only deliver increasingly distorted and horrible images of the father, who turns from a "head in the freakish Atlantic" into a Nazi "panzer-man" and a "vampire," and she must "kill" him—or kill all memory of him—to survive. She concludes vengefully, but also with an air of relief, "Daddy, daddy, you bastard, I'm through."

These two lines from "Daddy" lead me to the questions about memory I investigate in my chapters on the work of Sylvia Plath, Susan Howe, Ellen Hinsey, and Louise Glück. I close read these poets in order to understand what it means for Plath's speaker to be "through," or, to put it differently, to have moved beyond attempts at factual forms of memory through which one construes and fails to construe a sense of self by narrating the events of one's life. I argue that these poets ground subjectivity on alternative practices of memory that are distinctly poetic, and I subsume them under the term "poetic memory." What I call "historic memory" presupposes that the self is constituted by the conscious, recollectable experiences of the past. Poetic memory, in contrast, posits that the self is more than the compound of a person's remembered biography. Poetic memory does not depend on the accuracy, linearity, causality, or coherence of historic memory, and it reaches beyond the accountable facts of a life toward the notion of a self that is dynamic, expansive, and full of potential.

1

In the ancient world, Plutarch and Plotinus represent conceptions of memory related to the ones I call historic and poetic. Plutarch presupposes that, to have an identity, one must use one's memory to tell a narrative of one's life. His view that, to some extent, we create ourselves appears modern, and so does his idea that memory has a part in that creation.[1] In his essay "On Tranquility," Plutarch elaborates his views on memory that are implicit in his *Lives* and that drive his work as a biographer and a historian:

> Foolish people overlook and neglect even present goods because they are always intent in their thoughts on the future. But wise people make even what no longer exists to exist vividly for themselves by the use of memory. The present, which allows contact with only the smallest portion of time and then escapes observation, no longer seems to the foolish to be anything to us or to be ours. But just as the man pictured in Hades plaiting a rope allows a grazing donkey to consume what he is plaiting, so forgetfulness, unaware of most things and ungrateful, snatches and overruns things, obliterating every action and right act, every pleasant discussion, meeting, or enjoyment, and does not allow our life to be unified, through the past being woven together with the future. Whatever happens, it immediately consigns it to what has not happened by forgetfulness, and divides yesterday's life from today's as something different, and tomorrow's similarly as not the same as today's. Those in the schools who refute the fact of growth on the grounds that substance is perpetually flowing make each of us in theory ever different from himself. But those who do not preserve or retrieve the past in memory, but allow it to flow away from under them, make themselves needy every day in actual fact, and empty and dependent on tomorrow, as if last year and yesterday and the day before were nothing to them and had not actually happened to them.[2]

Plutarch makes a strong statement for the virtues of historic memory: he depicts remembering as a method to own the present, which otherwise is a fleeting temporality. Through memory, the existence of the present is prolonged—although it "no longer exists," it exists "vividly"—and it can be savored belatedly. Not remembering amounts to leaving the plaited rope to the donkey: memory is compared to the results or fruits of one's labor, which must not be wasted. Just as forgetfulness is "unaware of most things," remembering fosters awareness of one's life. Memory can prevent chaos and fragmentation of experience and provide unification and coherence. "Today's" life is related to "yesterday's" through memory, and rather than finding ourselves alienated from the person we were the day before, we can feel at one with ourselves. Practicing memory saves us from being too hungry for new events in the present and grants us existential tranquility. Plutarch's ideas of memory raise many questions for the postmodern reader: Who does the storytelling? Is the self in place while the story is being told, or does it only come into existence as a result of the telling? Is the self in the story still the one who had the experience? And is the story a true account or only one fiction among others? Nonetheless, Plutarch's ideas represent an important axiom of thinking the relation between memory, language, and subjectivity.

Poetic memory does not reject historic memory. It also is not intended as a critique of history or historiography as a highly varied and theoretically sophisticated discipline. But poetic memory is aware of the limitations that derive from a self grounded in a narrative of its past. It is dissatisfied with the naiveté of such historic narrative, and historiography shares this dissatisfaction. Plotinus, the founder of Neoplatonism, represents an alternative to this Plutarchian vision of memory. Plotinus believes we have a "diviner soul, which makes us what we are,"[3] and he lays out the dangers that the soul faces when it forgets its origins while in its embodied state:

> What is it, then, which has made the souls forget their father, God, and be ignorant of themselves and him, even though they are parts which come from his higher world and altogether belong to it? The beginning of evil for them was audacity and coming to birth and the first otherness and the wishing to belong to themselves. Since they were clearly delighted with their own independence, and made great use of self-movement, running the opposite course and getting as far away as possible, they were ignorant even that they themselves came from that world; just as children who are immediately torn from their parents and brought up far away do not know who they themselves or their parents are. Since they do not any more see their father or themselves, they despise themselves through ignorance of their birth and honour other things, admiring everything rather than themselves, and astonished and delighted by and dependent on these [earthly] things, they broke themselves loose as far as they could in contempt of that from which they turned away; so that their honour for these things here and their contempt for themselves is the cause of their utter ignorance of God.[4]

If the soul forgets its divine origin, Plotinus argues, it forgets its own nature; it disrespects itself and overly credits what Plato calls the sensible world. Overestimating material and sensually perceptible things in turn reinforces the soul's ignorance of God. Plotinus compares a soul that is ignorant of its relation to God to a child who has forgotten about his parents because he was brought up apart from them. Plotinus pleads for a kind of memory that exceeds memory of experiences related only to the sensible world. Suggesting that the soul retains memories from before birth, Plotinus evokes Plato's theory of *anamnesis*, according to which learning on earth is actually remembering what the soul knew before it took on the body.[5] Plath, Howe, Hinsey, and Glück do not necessarily embrace Plotinus's particular metaphysics, but they sense, like Plotinus, that our views of the self are impoverished, and they seek to enhance our vision by enriching our memory. By practicing poetic memory, these poets expand our ideas of who we are.

I trace poetic memory back to Plotinus, but one could also find related ideas in other traditions of thought. Christian doctrine admonishes its believers to remember the divine descent of man, God's boundless love that redeems man's sinful condition, and man's restoration to his rightful place in heaven. A modern formulation of a larger, yet forgotten self is the psychoanalytic theory of infantile amnesia. While Plotinus explains people's ignorance of themselves by their alienation from their divine origin, Freud emphasizes the loss of memory of life's beginnings. Freud points out the paradox that although "there is no period at which the capacity for receiving and reproducing impressions is greater than precisely during the years of childhood," nothing but a few memory fragments from that period up to six years of age remain. Other people may tell us about those first passionate years of our lives from their memory, yet our own recollections are rudimentary at best. Freud concludes that this "prehistoric epoch" is the beginning of sexuality and falls victim to repression. But although we become oblivious to the contents of our experience, "the very same impressions that we have forgotten have none the less left the deepest traces on our minds and have had a determining effect upon the whole of our later development."[6] To a romantic poet like Wordsworth, as I will discuss, the sense of having become estranged from his inner child produces "intimations" of a truer, unknown self.[7]

Other psychoanalytic theorists like Jung, Lacan, or Winnicott describe the formation of a "false self." Winnicott attributes to the mother's face the function of a mirror, in which the child can see and recognize himself or herself. "Many babies, however," Winnicott writes, "do have to have a long experience of not getting back what they are giving. They look and they do not see themselves."[8] What they will introject instead is the mother's mood or the mother's defenses. This process lays the foundation of a false self.

The detriments to being and knowing oneself, however, are balanced by certain capacities of the mind that facilitate poetic memory. The mind naturally engages in fantasy and related mental processes such as dreaming, reverie, and imagination. Freud discovered that infants use fantasy to satisfy their hunger temporarily when the mother's breast is not available. He writes in *Totem and Taboo*: "In a hallucinatory manner, that is, they create a satisfying situation by means of centrifugal excitations of their sense organs."[9] According to psychoanalysis, residues of this archaic mental process can be found in all of us. What the child achieves by employing its bodily sensations, the adult does by means of the will.[10] Fantasy is crucial to poetic memory because it constitutes an essential mental mechanism aiming at transcending factual experience. It testifies to the mind's drive to outgrow itself.

MEMORY IN POETRY

This book is part of two contexts of investigation: the study of poetry and the study of memory. It explores how questions about memory promote understanding of poetry and how poetry complicates studies of memory. Poetry is a *medium* of memory and has been used to preserve memories since ancient times. Preliterary cultures framed their narratives in poetic form to facilitate memorization and oral transmission. Poetry is also a *system* of memory: poems are written from within poetic traditions, positioned in an intertextual context, and they manifest choices regarding poetic form, prosody, and aesthetics that transmit those traditions. Finally, poetry *represents* and *thematizes* memory, its contents and functioning.[11] My concepts of historic and poetic memory provide distinction within the third category, yet they also may have implications for the others. If a poem represents the utterances of a subject who constitutes herself by invoking mythical or literary characters, the poem simultaneously becomes a storage place for these contents and processes of remembering, and references, for example, the Modernist technique of mythical and literary allusion. Often, the categories of memory in literature cannot be neatly separated, and representations of memory (function three) will overlap with practices of memory (functions one and two) and vice versa.

William Wordsworth's and T. S. Eliot's poems are landmarks of the uses of poetic memory in English poetry, and they provide a context and a tradition for Plath, Howe, Hinsey, and Glück. In English literature, Wordsworth discovers personal memory as a topic for poetry. Commenting on his *Prelude*, Wordsworth writes that it was "a thing unprecedented in literary history that a man should talk so much about himself."[12] In his poems, "the workings of memory make their first fully subjective appearance."[13] His "Ode: Intimations of Immortality from Recollections of Early Childhood"[14] figures as the ideal Plotinian memory poem:

> Our birth is but a sleep and a forgetting:
> The Soul that rises with us, our life's Star,
> > Hath had elsewhere its setting,
> > > And cometh from afar:
> > Not in entire forgetfulness,
> > And not in utter nakedness,
> But trailing clouds of glory do we come
> > From God, who is our home:
> Heaven lies about us in our infancy!
> Shades of the prison-house begin to close
> > Upon the growing Boy,
> But He beholds the light, and whence it flows,
> > He sees it in his joy;
> The Youth, who daily farther from the east
> > Must travel, still is Nature's Priest,
> > And by the vision splendid
> > Is on his way attended;
> At length the Man perceives it die away,
> And fade into the light of common day.
> > (V, 58–76)

These meditations on man's preexistence can be interpreted as a trope for a nonempirical self that Wordsworth considers to be a person's true identity. The poet points out a paradox of the human condition: our birth into life on earth is simultaneously the diminishment of another existence and marked by "sleep" and "forgetting" of our "home" with "God." Like Plotinus, Wordsworth attributes to childhood an important function in this process of estrangement. Childhood, for Wordsworth, is a transitory state in which memories of preexistence are still prominent, for the "shades of the prison-house" have not yet entirely closed on the growing person. Plotinus also implies that children still know the parent, God, but are then "snatched . . . from their parents" and so become "unaware of themselves and their parents because of their lengthy upbringing away from them." Both Plotinus and Wordsworth believe memory has the power to retrieve lost knowledge and to restore fullness of being. While Plotinus blames man's alienation from his self on his "arrogance" and his "willing to belong to himself," Wordsworth thinks of it as an unavoidable loss that occurs once the soul has left "its setting" "elsewhere." To Wordsworth, self-estrangement becomes manifest in one's alienation from nature; in the "Immortality" ode, the speaker's perception of nature becomes deficient, while nature itself does not change. The poem begins:

> There was a time when meadow, grove, and stream,
> The earth, and every common sight,
>> To me did seem
>> Apparelled in celestial light,
> The glory and the freshness of a dream.
> It is not now as it hath been of yore;—
>> Turn wheresoe'er I may,
>> By night or day,
> The things which I have seen I now can see no more.
> (I, 1–9)

To regain fullness of being, a person must heal his relationship to nature. Nature is the great rememberer, and this insight makes the speaker exclaim: "O joy! that in our embers / Is something that doth live, / That nature yet remembers / What was so fugitive!" (IX, 129–32).

To the Romantic poet, it is nature that restores a person's memory and helps him recover intimations of his origins and true self.[15] The Wordsworthian poet learns to read the shadows, which initially were an impediment to seeing, but now become the source of it:

> But for those first affections,
>> Those shadowy recollections,
>> Which, be they what they may,
> Are yet the fountain light of all our day,
> Are yet a master light of all our seeing;
>> (IX, 148–52)   [16]

From a Wordsworthian point of view, the Modernist Eliot has lost touch with his childhood self and ceded trust in intimations of "preexistence." *The Waste Land*, [17] composed 120 years after the "Immortality" ode, testifies to a state of profound disenchantment and gnawing despair over life alternating with the ineradicable hope for its renewal. The speaker assembles memories in the form of a great number of literary quotations and references, like the "dry bones" of a past civilization, and arranges them into a poem, the representation of a "waste land." "April is the cruellest month," so the famous beginning of *The Waste Land* reads, because the resurgence of life in spring will only add another cycle of dying: "He who was living is now dead / We who were living are now dying / With a little patience" (328–30). Destiny is indifferently left to the fortune teller "Madame Sosostris, famous clairvoyante," who pulls well-known cards from a "wicked pack": "Here, said she / Is your card, the drowned Phoenician Sailor" (45–6). A sentiment of fatigued despair over the endless repetitions of history pervades the poem. Tiresias, the Greek prophet, can tell the future from taking a glance at the present, because the present continuously repeats the past. "I Tiresias, old man with wrinkled dugs / Perceived the scene, and foretold the rest—" (228–9), is his commentary on the typist's rendezvous with the "young man carbuncular." Culture is no longer a source of mnemonic nourishment, nor is nature. Delirious from thirst, the wanderer in the fifth section, "What the Thunder Said," stumbles along in language:

> Here is no water but only rock
> Rock and no water and the sandy road
> The road winding above among the mountains
> Which are mountains of rock without water
> If there were water we should stop and drink
> Amongst the rock one cannot stop or think
> Sweat is dry and feet are in the sand
> If there were only water amongst the rock
> Dead mountain mouth of carious teeth that cannot spit
> Here one can neither stand nor lie nor sit
> There is not even silence in the mountains
> But dry sterile thunder without rain
> There is not even solitude in the mountains
> But red sullen faces sneer and snarl
> From doors of mudcracked houses
> (331–45)

These are the breathless and repetitive words of a starving self who never knew Wordsworth's "fountain light." There is nothing to drink, nothing to think, nowhere to rest; in this landscape of death, and under this thundering sky, not even silence or solitude will soothe the wanderer gone astray. And yet, from the ruins he reaches "the empty chapel" (389) where "dry bones can harm no one" (391). A lightning and a gust announce the rain, and the thunder speaks "DA," signifying the Sanskrit words "Datta" (402), "Dayadhvam" (412), and "Damyata" (419), or, in translation, "Give, sympathise, control."[18] The recovery of the source of languages implies the manifestation of the divine. The final stanza of *The Waste Land* confirms its ambivalent professions. "These fragments I have shored against my ruins" (431), the speaker concludes. On one hand, memory only grants insufficient "fragments" that aggravate his ruined state. On the other hand, these "fragments" do have the capacity of "shoring" or supporting the self. Eliot evokes a state of decomposition of the self, which memory cannot heal, but which it can enrich.

Wordsworth and Eliot practice different modalities of poetic memory. For the Romantic, memory is an instrument promoting the wholeness of being, while for the Modernist, it also has a decentering and disintegrating effect.[19] Wordsworth's idealization of childhood expresses his desire to recover that lost origin of the self. Analogous to the preverbal child that precedes the speaking and remembering child, nature precedes culture. Wordsworth's invocation of nature represents the attempt to reach back to the origins of being and recover a primary self. Intimations of a lost self lead him to envision and celebrate the possibility of a larger, more authentic self. To Eliot, exploiting memory and nearing its foundations, Freud's "prehistoric epoch," are also hazardous enterprises. Fragmentation of memory reveals the psychotic core, the incoherent mind, a state of disintegration, a world in chaos, a place without meaning or destination. But while Eliot constantly shifts levels between the mythical and the commonplace, the personal and the collective, the glue connecting these fragments is the poet's associating consciousness in the present moment. The fragments of memory are employed as monads that imply the whole and need the whole to acquire meaning.[20] The poem's apocalyptic despair is counterbalanced by its hope for the unifying powers of a greater, divine consciousness. Despite his recognition of memory's negative potential, Eliot draws on the creative and redemptive force of that memory which exceeds the empirical self.

Literary critics have observed in Eliot and other Modernists "hostility towards history" and a resolute turning away from the past to "make it new"; or, particularly in more recent studies, they have argued the oppo-site and found an acute interest in the past, if not an obsession with it in Modernist writing.[21] These two seemingly contradictory views are not irreconcilable, for both require memory. Pound's slogan "make it new" was a phrase translated from the ancient Chinese, and the *Cantos*, from which it comes, he called "a poem including history."[22] Eliot writes about memory in "Little Gidding," the last of the *Four Quartets*: "This is the use of memory: / For liberation—not less of love but expanding / Of love beyond desire, and so liberation / From the future as well as the past." Eliot continues, "See, now they vanish, / The faces and places, with the self which, as it could, loved them, / To become renewed, transfigured, in another pattern."[23] Eliot wants memory to liberate the self from the repe-tition of the past in the future. In addition to the "faces and places" it "loved," the self needs to "renew" and "transfigure" itself and expand beyond repetition. Such possibility of outgrowing the past, however, de-mands deep immersion in it. It requires the frightening decomposition of history into the many "timeless moments"[24] that had been fixed in a stable pattern. *The Waste Land* is the poem powerfully testifying to such undoing.

POETRY IN MEMORY

Besides traditions of memory in poetry, the other context for this study is provided by recent transdisciplinary inquiries into the nature and func-tions of memory. Memory is a highly commercialized cultural subject, and the so-called memory industry it gave rise to, Kerwin Lee Klein writes, "ranges from the museum trade to the legal battles over repressed memory and on to the market for academic books and articles that invoke *memory* as key word."[25] Memory is discussed in a great variety of histori-cal, cultural, and epistemological contexts, of which I will only point out a few.

From a historical point of view, landmark traumata, such as the Holo-caust, are sufficiently remote in time to lose the immediate witnesses who used to guarantee their remembrance.[26] Major museums, such as the United States Holocaust Memorial Museum in Washington, the Los An-geles Museum of the Holocaust, the Museum of Jewish Heritage in New York, and the *Jüdisches Museum* in Berlin, have been founded to ward off oblivion.[27] Besides the Jewish people, other religious, ethnic, and cultural groups seek to consolidate their group identities by narrating and preserving their collective memories. This is experienced as a pressing concern by groups with a history of oppression, be it in postcolonial or U.S. contexts. Whereas the colonizers "wrote History," the formerly colonized hope that memory will help them regain their past. Memory is viewed as an appealing concept because it is flexible enough to avoid ideological homogenization but closed enough to enable communal or ethnic identification.[28] Also, an increasingly globalized economy is often seen as producing political and cultural homogenization, and social groups react to this perception by wanting to consolidate and preserve their distinctiveness through a culture of memory.

Critics of contemporary culture warn that technology and the media increasingly usurp everyday experience. They ascribe to memory the power to slow down the pace of information processing [29] in a culture of high-speed technology, simulated realities, and information overflow. Just as Plutarch suggests, memory is evoked as a means to experience the present more fully. "Memory," Geoffrey Hartman argues, "is not simply an afterbirth of experience, a secondary formation: it *enables* experiencing, it allows what we call the real to enter consciousness and word-presentation."[30] Opposed to an "age of mechanical reproduction" and consequently to a culture where experience per se seems at risk, the increasing interest in memory seeks authenticity by assembling a life's experience.

As Andreas Huyssen points out, current memory debates reiterate, to some extent, Nietzsche's argument, elaborated in his 1874 essay "On the Uses and Disadvantages of History for Life,"[31] in which the philosopher contends that history is only useful when it is made serviceable to the life of the rememberer. Nietzsche diagnosed late nineteenth-century German society as suffering from "a fever of history"[32] and criticized the loss of purpose and proportion in what he considered archival frenzy. Huyssen suggests that "the privileging of memory can be seen as our contemporary version of Nietzsche's attack on archival history, a perhaps justified critique of an academic apparatus producing historical knowledge for its own sake, but often having trouble maintaining its vital links with the surrounding culture."[33] Gabrielle Spiegel shares Huyssen's awareness of the anthropological need for the links between past and present, which, she believes, is a need neglected by poststructuralism. Instead of positing memory as an approach to the past that satisfies postmodern exigencies, Spiegel interprets the upsurge of memory in academic and nonacademic debates as the *rejection* of postmodern attacks on the accessibility of the past. "I believe that the turn to memory so pervasive in academic circles today," Spiegel writes, "forms part of an attempt to recuperate presence in history—a form of backlash against postmodernist/poststructuralist thought, with its insistence on the mediated, indeed constructed, nature of all knowledge, and most especially knowledge of the past. In this sense, I am tempted to claim that memory has displaced deconstruction as the *lingua franca* of cultural studies."[34] On the other hand, present memory debates also derive from postmodern sensibilities and are, for example, motivated by a discontent with historical master narratives. In the context of these epistemological debates, "the shift from history to memory," Huyssen writes, "represents a welcome critique of compromised teleological notions of history rather than being simply anti-historical, relativistic, or subjective."[35]

Nietzsche's views on the usefulness of history for life resonate with my distinction between poetic and historic memory. In fact, Nietzsche, the historian, suggests making "poetic" use of history, and he distinguishes three different modes: the "monumental," "antiquarian," and "critical." A powerful and important man may find in history the "monuments" or "models, teachers, comforters . . . [he] cannot find . . . among his contemporaries."[36] The antiquarian wants "to preserve for those who shall come into existence after him the conditions under which he himself came into existence," and therefore concerns himself with history for the purpose of life. He preserves things in a way that gives his soul a "home," and "the history of his city becomes for him the history of himself."[37] Sometimes, however, history becomes a burden, and "if he is to live, man must possess and from time to time employ the strength to break up and dissolve a part of the past: he does this by bringing it before the tribunal, scrupulously examining it and finally condemning it."[38] Nietzsche is concerned with collective history, but he recommends adjusting it to the personal scope. In each case, history enlarges and enriches the personal narrative and historic sense of self: it provides the possibility of identification with great men and with the past on a larger scale. It provides an ampler home, extended over time, for the self. And should history turn out to be too narrow and burdensome a space, it must be destroyed. Nietzsche sides with the poets when privileging the subjective and singular over the objective and plural, and demanding that the individual pull the collective historical legacy into his orbit and remake it according to his or her own need and desire.

The epistemological, cultural, and historiopolitical advocates of memory understand, with Nietzsche, that it is memory that makes us human and distinguishes us from Nietzsche's grazing cows, whose lack of memory makes them happy but also incapable of explaining their happiness to the questioner.[39] On one hand, the memory advocates follow the Nietzschean impulse of putting history back into the service of life: consolidating and preserving group memories and identities are arguably based on antiquarian motivations. Using memory to insulate the mind against external overstimulation protects our mental existence in an extended temporality. Finding alternative ways of relating to the past besides the historical also serves the fullness of being. On the other hand, one could argue that such mnemonic occupation always runs the risk of slipping into an obsessional automatism resulting in the archival mode so despised by Nietzsche. The risk of obsession is particularly acute when the interest in the past is driven by fear, an undeniable factor in the contemporary upsurge of discourses on memory. Loss of memory leads to an increasingly fragmented and precarious sense of self, as it has been so forcefully described by Eliot, and practicing memory of the historic type is intended to remedy the condition. From this perspective, the "mnemonic turn" essentially follows a conservative impulse. It seeks to reestablish the faltering Plutarchian axiom of identity gained from working and reworking a narrative of the past.

At the same time, one might question whether it is possible, or even desirable, to give in to the Plutarchian impulse. Arguably, well-being can be derived from forgetting just as much as it rests on remembering. Huyssen claims that the fervent interest in memory in contemporary popular and academic culture is a "mnemonic fever . . . caused by the virus of amnesia."[40] Calling this cultural phenomenon a "fever" raises the question of what causes the excess of "heat" that turns a passion into a pathology. The fever could, indeed, be interpreted as a conversion symptom, to evoke what Freud identified as the core indicator of hysteria, pointing to the repression of an impossible idea. This would explain the expenditure of excess energy on the level of the psychic economy. It might be a defensive maneuver aimed at the repression of the thought that much of our self and subjectivity eludes our knowledge and control. Being strangers to ourselves is an always existent source of unease, and it is aggravated by our zeitgeist.

Plath, Howe, Hinsey, and Glück, who are my exemplary practitioners of poetic memory, acknowledge the always existent uncertainty of who we are. A poet like Plath may take a more sardonic stance toward this uncertainty than Howe, Hinsey, and Glück, who engage with it as a form of potential and possibility. These poets all exploit poetry and its generic characteristics to generate alternative modes of memory, which do not share the defensiveness of some historic practices. Poetic memory does not rest on the existence of coherent historic narratives and, liberated from such standards, expresses and constitutes the subjective in different ways.

Memory is an interdisciplinary research subject investigated not only by literary, historical, and cultural research, but also by the sciences. Neuroscience has greatly contributed to the debates about memory by locating different kinds of memory processes in the brain. The amygdala and the hippocampus are believed to be the organs enabling so-called implicit, nondeclarative, and explicit, declarative memory. Explicit memory is conscious and deliberate and comprises autobiographical or personal memory. It is a "conscious awareness of past happenings, to be distinguished from dreaming, imaging and problem solving."[41] These characteristics of explicit memory evoke my concept of historic memory, which provides a sense of self via the narrated facts of a life. Implicit, nondeclarative memory is more elusive. It has been characterized as unconscious, automatic, procedural, and relied on when a person performs routine procedures, such as, to give very concrete examples, playing the piano or driving a car. The amygdala, which is associated with implicit memory, is seen as the recipient of emotional states as well as sensory and motor experiences.[42] Here, memories are triggered by immediate sensual stimuli, rather than associative context. Psychologist Daniel Schacter relates explicit and implicit memory to identity formation when he suggests that "while our sense of self and identity is highly dependent on explicit memory for past episodes and autobiographical facts, our personalities may be more closely tied to implicit memory processes."[43] Schacter distinguishes between a conscious and consciously constructed sense of self and a less conscious self, which, however, may be truer to "our personalities." Poetic memory is neither what neuroscientists call explicit, nor what they call implicit memory; but Plotinus emphasizes the forgotten and unconscious nature of poetic memory, which would associate it with the implicit unconscious memory of neuroscience. Suzanne Nalbantian, in her study of the relationship between literature and neuroscientific memory research, concludes that "literary writers provide beacons particularly into the dark corridors of unconscious memory yet to be explored."[44]

PLATH, HOWE, HINSEY, GLÜCK

If Wordsworth's celebration of the unknown spaces of memory and Eliot's skepticism of mnemonic fragmentation are landmarks for the subject of memory in English poetry, what kinds of poetic memory do poets practice in our day? In which ways do they alter and enlarge notions of what memory is and does in the times of the "memory fever"? What kinds of selves do these poetic rememberers project?

I am drawn toward female poets because historic memory, as laid out by Plutarch, is also the patriarchal model of memory in which the genetic and linear depiction of facts and deeds serves the construction of an essential and enduring "I." One of the earliest forms of historiography was the history of "great men," which Nietzsche recommends to those ambitious men who look for models and ideals. This kind of historical consciousness had repercussions not only on the content of mnemonic practice, but also on its manner—not only on the *what* but also on the *how* of memory—and it instigated the tradition of constituting the self by means of linear, coherent, objective, and teleological narratives. The "I" whose demise Eliot laments in *The Waste Land* is the construct of historic memory. Yet its demise facilitates alternative practices of memory and revisions of subjectivity, and Plath, Howe, Hinsey, and Glück make use of it in diverse creative ways. The subject of poetic memory, as it becomes manifest in their poetry, allows for intimations, associations, and surprise; it is malleable, dynamic, expansive, and inclusive; it also comprises the excluded, repressed, and forgotten. All four poets conceive of their work as feminist; yet the feminist element in their approaches to poetic memory varies. Plath is the iconoclast of collective memory; Howe's practice of poetic memory is antinomian; Hinsey reintroduces space and subjective experience to common ways of imagining the past; and Glück rewrites female archetypes.

To present a wide array of poetic memories, I have chosen poets who represent both traditional and experimentalist strands of American poetry and who write at different moments in the past fifty years, thus absorbing changing cultural climates from the 1960s to the present. Plath has been classified as a confessional poet, and Howe as an experimentalist; Hinsey writes in the European tradition of a poetry of witness, and Glück can be described as postconfessional. The poets' divergent mnemonics require me to resort to the different theoretical approaches to memory provided by sociologists, historians, and psychoanalysts, rather than reading all poets within the same theoretical framework. I am not only interested in reading poetry in the light of specific theories but also in uncovering how the poets diverge from these theories and make their own contributions to our ideas and practices of memory. I treat the poets as theorists of memory in their own right. For this reason, my primary method of exploring the poems is close reading.

Plath, Howe, Hinsey, and Glück make space for poetic memory by countering but, in more subtle ways, also using, expanding, subverting, and ironizing forces of historic memory. These poets' resistance to historic memory is fueled by the memory of a more expansive self than that constituted by its conscious life account. In Plath's work, this influence is visible in the formally classical, rhetorically controlled, and mythologically ornamented style of the poems collected in *The Colossus* (1960), her first book of poetry.[45] By the time she wrote the *Ariel* (1965) poems, Plath had grown fully into her distinctively edgy, blunt, and provocative voice. Although she never deviates from the principle of "constriction and tension,"[46] she draws on a larger variety of registers in the *Ariel* poems, among which the popular prevails over the academic, and the historical often substitutes for the mythological. In her poems from the early 1960s, in the aftermath of the Holocaust, Plath's speakers face the impossibility of remembering "properly," a failure of historic memory, and they discover that the memory of the "father" has been fragmented, shattered, and lost. Historical and pop culture clichés intrude or are invited to fill that void, and such intrusion legitimates the speakers' need to free themselves from having to remember "Daddy." I will read Plath's poems in light of Maurice Halbwachs's theory of conflicts between personal and collective memory. In response to the flaws of historic memory, Plath's speakers become the wild, cruel, vengeful, clever "ladies Lazarus" and killers of daddy, but also their dreamy, contemplative, self-diffusive counterparts in a poem like "Words."

Susan Howe, experimentalist poet-historian, is aware of the conditioning forces of historic memory and questions conventional ways of historic memory formation. Resonating with the poststructuralist critique of historical master narratives, her poems ironize American history writing, which, Howe would claim, legitimates existing power structures by erasing marginal or "nonconformist" figures or by standardizing their writing. Their eccentricities, incoherences, and silences are the very grounds that enable the poet to inhabit the past. While Plath struggles with the "dry bones" of tradition, as Eliot refers to them, Howe experiments with them joyfully in a poetics of disjunction and fragmentation on the space of the page. She emphasizes the influence of the female Modernists Marianne Moore, Gertrude Stein, and, if one wants to consider her as such, Emily Dickinson. Howe, who is Plath's elder by five years but only started writing in the 1970s, is influenced by Charles Olson's and Robert Creeley's notion of the space of the page as representative of the space of American geography and history. Due to the priority she sometimes grants the word over other elements of poetry, such as syntax and conventional poetic form, she is counted among the avant-gardist "language poets." Howe remembers nonconformists and figures from cultural oblivion: representatives of the self's otherness, its multiplicity, and its open, mysterious, and uncharted potential. Sigmund Freud, Julia Kristeva, and Jacques Lacan, all theorists of the more inaccessible domains of memory and the psyche, will contribute to my reading of Howe's *Nonconformist's Memorial*.

Ellen Hinsey, who in 1995 won the Yale Series of Younger Poets with her book *Cities of Memory* and who has published two other collections of poetry titled *The White Fire of Time* (2002) and *Update on the Descent* (2009), writes in the predominantly European tradition of poetry of witness. Poetry of witness, according to Carolyn Forché, originates in a "space between the state and the supposedly safe havens of the personal."[47] Hinsey's poems locate the personal within the historical and the historical within the personal, enhancing the significance of both. Her *Cities of Memory* resonates in interesting ways with Walter Benjamin's historical thinking. Although Benjamin and Hinsey participate in the discourses of different historical periods, they employ comparable strategies when attempting to shift the paradigms of our historical consciousness. Both, for example, neglect the event-structure of conventional historiography or, in Benjaminian terms, the "beads" on the "rosary" of history to investigate the past in terms of the "before" and "after" of events or in terms of the imprint time has left on space. Hinsey's poems resuscitate the past in the spaces of the present and offer places in which the living past prevails over the deadening reiteration of the same history. The spatialized past and its poetic representations become an inexhaustible resource.

Louise Glück is one of the most prominent figures in contemporary American poetry, and her numerous awards and honors—she was the U.S. Poet Laureate in 2003 and 2004 and has won both the Pulitzer Prize (for *The Wild Iris* in 1993) and the Bollingen Prize (2001)—testify to her central, representative position. Her poetry feeds on the personal while it remains detached from it and rooted in an objectifying stance; this is why it has been described as "post-confessional."[48] Contrary to the confessional poets of the 1950s and 1960s, her speakers' unreliable and depersonalized stance is reminiscent of that in poems by Eliot. Like the works of Eliot and the confessional poets, her poetry is psychoanalytic: it is concerned with mental process, free association, and memory. Yet while poets like Plath, Lowell, and Sexton relish the revelations of the intimate, an air of fatigue toward the almost too familiar, the too well known hovers above Glück's poems. She is interested in exploring raw experience for the deep psychic structures underlying it. In this manner, she does not embrace Eliot's attitude of tempered scorn toward the personal, nor does she remain entirely immersed in it. Rather, she searches the intimate for the general, and she explores personal memory to fathom its mythical and archetypal foundations. *Averno* (2006), her book at the center of my chapter, is a prime example of this. In *Averno*, Glück engages with the myth of Persephone, its transmitted form as well as what she fathoms as the repressed, unconscious dimension of the narrative. Persephone can come back to life once her repetition of aimless wandering between the world and the underworld is broken. Glück recreates Persephone by combining personal with mythical memory. By transposing the archetypal patterns of the myth onto personal memory, she integrates and enlarges the self.

When Plath, Howe, Hinsey, and Glück look at the past, they see its flawed representations, its lack of certainty, its margins and gaps, its traces in space, its deep marks in the psyche. They share an intuitive certainty of self as being other and as being that which eludes historic memory, and they look in different places to find what was split off, forgotten, and psychically lost. They use words, which are complex bits of memory, to push against encrusted structures or apparent boundaries of the mind and seek to represent more fluid states of consciousness. To recall Plotinus's aphorism, this is how the soul "is and becomes what it remembers."

NOTES

1. Richard Sorabji, *Self: Ancient and Modern Insights about Individuality, Life, and Death* (Chicago: University of Chicago Press, 2006), 173.

2. Quoted in and translated by Sorabji, *Self*, 174–75.

3. Plotinus, *Enneads* 4.3.27 (1–25), quoted in Sorabji, *Self*, 103, and translated by Barrie Fleet.

4. Plotinus, *Enneads* 5.1, ed. Jeffrey Henderson, trans. A. H. Armstrong, Loeb Classical Library (Cambridge, MA: Harvard University Press, 1984), 11–12.

5. Plato, "Phaedo," in *Complete Works*, ed. John M. Cooper, trans. G. M. A. Grube (Indianapolis, IN: Hackett, 1997), 63. "For us learning is not other than recollection. According to this, we must at some previous time have learned what we now recollect. This is possible only if our soul existed somewhere before it took on this human shape. So according to this theory too, the soul is likely to be something immortal" ("Phaedo" 72e–73a).

6. Sigmund Freud, *The Standard Edition of the Complete Psychological Works of Sigmund Freud* (hereafter, *Standard Edition*), trans. James Strachey, vol. 7, *Three Essays on the Theory of Sexuality* (London: Hogarth Press, 1953), 175.

7. Poetic language has an inherent mnemonic dimension that registers how language was acquired as a part of the subject's coming into being. This is what Mutlu Blasing argues when she reflects on the relationship between "poetic" memory and the preverbal child of psychoanalysis from the perspective of poetry criticism: "Poetic language remembers the history of the process of language acquisition." Mutlu Konuk Blasing, *Lyric Poetry: The Pain and the Pleasure of Words* (Princeton, NJ: Princeton University Press, 2007), 47.

8. D. H. Winnicott, *Playing and Reality*, 1971 (London: Routledge, 2005), 151.

9. Sigmund Freud, *Standard Edition*, trans. James Strachey, vol. 13, *Totem and Taboo* (London: Hogarth Press, 1955), 84.

10. Ibid.

11. I derive this classification of memory in *poetry* from Erll's and Nünning's classification of memory in *literature*. They distinguish between Renate Lachmann's concept of "memory of literature" (literature as a system of intertextuality, including conventions of genre, form, register, literary allusion, and so forth), "memory in literature" (representation of the content and functioning of memory in literature), and "literature as a medium" (or storage place) of memory. Astrid Erll and Ansgar Nünning, eds., *Gedächtniskonzepte der Literaturwissenschaft: Theoretische Grundlegung und Anwendungsperspektiven* (Berlin: Walter de Gruyter, 2005).

12. William Wordsworth, *The Early Letters of William and Dorothy Wordsworth (1787–1805)*, ed. Ernest de Selincourt (Oxford: Clarendon Press, 1935), 489.

13. Christopher Salvesen, *The Landscape of Memory: A Study of Wordsworth's Poetry* (Lincoln: University of Nebraska Press, 1965), 1.

14. William Wordsworth, *Selected Poems and Prefaces,* ed. Jack Stillinger (Boston: Houghton Mifflin, 1965), 186–91.

15. Salvesen, 123. Salvesen elaborates on the mnemonic powers of nature: "Nature, more permanent than the growing boy, than the man bound to human time, may be thought of as a kind of reservoir, a source of mystically diffused memory, helping the poet in his recovery of earlier years, helping, by her good influence, to intensify his own experience and his own memory of it. This kind of transcendent memory maintains poetic memory: 'shadowy recollections' though they may be, they are still 'the fountain light of all our day.' . . . [I]t is poetic memory which answers to the near-oblivion of pre-existence, which returns the sense of immortality."

16. Critics differ in their understanding of how pessimistic or optimistic Wordsworth's appreciation of memory is. Geoffrey Hartman emphasizes the representation of "forgetfulness of Being" in Wordsworth's ode. He argues that "perhaps nowhere else in English is the sentiment of non-being so powerfully addressed as in Wordsworth's ode" (202). Hartman questions how moments of poetic remembering, which are "no more than intimations" can be powerful enough to function as "the fountain of light of all our day . . . the masterlight of all our seeing" (202). He wants to read the ode as a poem about the loss of being rather than possibilities of its recovery, and he argues that "the poet depicts the flux and reflux of a mind aware of a loss that cannot be fixed precisely, a thinking which is always already a grieving, as if thought and grief had an immemorial connection" (203). Geoffrey H. Hartman, *The Unremarkable Wordsworth* (Minneapolis: University of Minnesota Press, 1987).

In *Landscape of Memory*, Christopher Salvesen, in contrast, views the "shadowy recollections," as the "glass half full" rather than "half empty": "something out of the past, a 'shadowy recollection,' remains with the poet and creates a worthwhile future—some thing is left towards which he must work. . . . The future, no less than the past, is given value by poetic memory" (120–21). He writes that "enough has been remembered to give temporal life to the workings of memory: while certainly enough has been forgotten to create a genuine future towards which, and in which, memory, though further from its source, will continue to work. This is the real joy which Wordsworth expresses" (122).

17. T. S. Eliot, *The Complete Poems and Plays 1909–1950* (New York: Harcourt, Brace and World, 1971), 37–55.

18. Ibid., 54.

19. Affirming Eliot's mystical view of history, James Longenbach argues that, ultimately, "*The Waste Land* vacillates between the assurance of transcendental vision and a skepticism that threatens to obliterate the possibility of knowledge altogether." James Longenbach, *Modernist Poetics of History: Pound, Eliot, and the Sense of the Past* (Princeton, NJ: Princeton University Press), 237.

20. Ibid., 201.

21. Gabrielle McIntire, *Modernism, Memory and Desire: T. S. Eliot and Virginia Woolf* (Cambridge: Cambridge University Press, 2008), 4–5.

22. Pound first used this phrase in "Date Line" (1934). Ezra Pound, *Literary Essays of Ezra Pound*, ed. T. S. Eliot (New York: New Directions, 1968), 86.

23. Eliot, *Complete Poems and Plays*, 142.

24. Ibid., 144.

25. Kerwin Lee Klein, "On the Emergence of Memory in Historical Discourse," *Representations* 69, no. 1 (2000): 127.

26. The sudden rise of academic and popular discourses on memory has been explained as "the belated response to the great trauma of modernity, the Shoah." Kerwin Lee Klein finds this interpretation in Saul Friedlander's *Memory, History, and the Extermination of the Jews of Europe* (1993), Michael Roth's *Ironist's Cage: Memory, Trauma, and the Construction of History* (1995), and Dominick LaCapra's *History and Memory after Auschwitz* (1998). Klein, "On the Emergence of Memory in Historical Discourse," 139–43.

27. Amy Hungerford writes a compelling critique of "personifying texts," a practice embraced, she finds, by the United States Holocaust Memorial Museum. The museum does not primarily make the visitor learn about history, she argues, but encourages identification with its victims. He is enabled to "experience" it, rather than reflect on it, and brought "into a personal and emotional relation with the events the exhibits describe." Amy Hungerford, *The Holocaust of Texts: Genocide, Literature, and Personification* (Chicago: University of Chicago Press, 2003), 82.

28. Klein, 137.

29. Andreas Huyssen, *Twilight Memories: Marking Time in a Culture of Amnesia* (New York: Routledge, 1995), 7. Huyssen argues that memory "represents the attempt to slow down information processing, to resist the dissolution of time in the synchronicity of the archive, to recover a mode of contemplation outside the universe of simulation and fast-speed information and cable networks, to claim some anchoring space in a world of puzzling and often threatening heterogeneity, non-synchronicity, and information overload."

30. Geoffrey Hartman, *The Longest Shadow: In the Aftermath of the Holocaust* (Bloomington: Indiana University Press, 1996), 158–59.

31. Friedrich Nietzsche, "On the Uses and Disadvantages of History for Life," in *Untimely Meditations*, ed. Daniel Breazeale, trans. R. J. Hollingdale (Cambridge: Cambridge University Press, 1997), 57–124.

32. Ibid., 60.

33. Huyssen, 6.

34. Gabrielle M. Spiegel, "Memory and History: Liturgical Time and Historical Time," *History and Theory* 41 (2002): 149.

35. Huyssen, 6.

36. Nietzsche, 67.

37. Ibid., 73.

38. Ibid., 75.

39. Ibid., 60–61.

40. Huyssen, 7.

41. Suzanne Nalbantian, *Memory in Literature: From Rousseau to Neuroscience* (Houndmills, UK: Palgrave Macmillan, 2003), 136.

42. Nalbantian, 136.

43. Daniel Schacter, *Searching for Memory: The Brain, the Mind, and the Past* (New York: Basic Books, 1996), 233.

44. Nalbantian, 152.

45. Particularly in *The Colossus*, Plath writes in the tradition of Modernist gentility. She uses classical poetic forms, among which the terza rima dominates in poems such as "Sow," "Lorelei," "Full Fathom Five," "Man in Black," "Snakecharmer," and "Me-

dallion." Plath also writes rime royale ("The Eye-Mote"), couplets ("The Thin People"), sonnets ("Sonnet to Eva" from the juvenilia poems), sestinas ("Yadwigha, on a Red Couch, Among Lilies," a poem from 1958 not included in *The Colossus*), and villanelles ("To Eva Descending the Stair," another "juvenile" poem). Plath imitates what T. S. Eliot called the "mythic method" of the Modernists. Her texts abound with figures from ancient mythology (for example, Persephone, the dryads, Perseus, Godiva, and Electra) and other literature (for example, *Vanity Fair*, Lorelei, and *The Tempest*). Sylvia Plath, *The Colossus and Other Poems* (London: Heinemann, 1960).

46. Interview by Lee Anderson, quoted in J. D. McClatchy, "Short Circuits and Folding Mirrors," in *Sylvia Plath: New Views on the Poetry*, ed. Gary Lane (Baltimore: Johns Hopkins University Press, 1979), 21.

47. Carolyn Forché, "Twentieth Century Poetry of Witness," *American Poetry Review* 22, no. 2 (March–April 1993): 9.

48. Daniel Morris, *The Poetry of Louise Glück: A Thematic Introduction* (Columbia: University of Missouri Press, 2006), 21–35.

ONE

Sylvia Plath

Re-membering the Colossus

A "confessional" poet, according to early Plath criticism,[1] is one who makes the matters of her private life her predominant poetic concern and her poems, once deciphered, lead back to the poet's life. Such views of poetry ignore the transformative interventions of memory in the writing process. Rather, in line with the principles of historic memory, it is assumed that memory is true to biography, and that biographical memory is then reproduced in poetic form. But Plath's poems reveal that there is no such thing as purely personal memory that could constitute the source of intimate confessions. Personal memory is always permeated and distorted by varieties of "collective memory." The poems I discuss dramatize this conflict and are driven by the poet's desire to unmask, exploit, and subvert the imposition of collective memory.

In Maurice Halbwachs's theory of collective memory,[2] personal memory, precarious by itself, is fortified by the interventions of collective memory: a person, according to Halbwachs, remembers about his life what is repeated to him by the community. Besides the contents of his memory, which he needs to be collectively reinforced, his memory also adapts to the paradigms of collective memory. In other words, he does not only remember more easily *what* the collective remembers, but also *how* it remembers. Both aspects of collective memory affect the more personal format of historic memory. The collective mode of memory — its linear, objective, and causal characteristics — is also Plutarch's.

Plath practices poetic memory by revealing the pervasive influence of collective memory and by finding methods to subvert it. I will first suggest that a sense of feeble personal or historic memory pervades some of Plath's poems and that this sense of impaired memory is concomitant with an extensive reliance on "literary memory," which is a term referring to literature as an intertextual system of memory and as a section of collective memory. In "The Colossus," the speaker oscillates between her dependence on collective memory and the desire to cast this influence off. The speaker's memory of "Daddy" is gradually taken over by historical and popular modes of collective memory, and this invasion is ambivalently evoked as a disaster and a relief. The "I" in "Lady Lazarus" takes on a series of erotically provocative, yet morally dubious identities borrowed from the storehouse of collective memory, historical and popular. Her mirroring of her audience's hidden desire becomes a sardonic parody of the assaulting nature of collective memory. In "Words," a more contemplative "I" indulges in the associative flow of words and images, the carriers of memory, and feels soothed rather than threatened by the malleability of subjectivity. My choice of these already extensively read poems is deliberate, for discussing them as memory poems will complicate our understanding of them and revise ideas of confessional poetry.

THE PRECARIOUSNESS OF PERSONAL MEMORY

In "Full Fathom Five" (*CP* 92–93), a poem from Plath's first published book, *The Colossus* (1960), the speaker is situated on the seashore. She scans the water surface for the outlines of an "old man" risen from the bottom of the sea. Images of him come and disappear with the fog and vapors:

> Old man, you surface seldom.
> Then you come in with the tide's coming
> When seas wash cold, foam-
>
> Capped: white hair, white beard, far-flung,
> A dragnet, rising, falling, as waves
> Crest and trough. Miles long
>
> Extend the radial sheaves
> Of your spread hair

The speaker expresses her desire for an encounter by metaphorically alleviating the separation between the realms of land and sea. The old man's face, although its features are extracted from the surface of the sea, is described as one would characterize a field, as "grained" and marked by "archaic trenched lines":

> The muddy rumors
>
> Of your burial move me
> To half-believe: your reappearance
> Proves rumors shallow,
>
> For the archaic trenched lines
> Of your grained face shed time in runnels:
> Ages beat like rains
>
> On the unbeaten channels
> Of the ocean.

The signifier *grain* semantically encompasses the realms of land and sea because it is a synonym of *corn* and, in its archaic meaning, also refers to tint or color—in this case, maybe the color of the sea. The expression "grained face" makes us think of uneven skin; *grain* also contains *rain*. The combination of the "grained face" and the surface of the sea evokes the image of the ocean beaten by rain. Thus, the word *grain* makes the imagination glide smoothly from the earth via the face to the sea. The vehicle "trenched lines" refers to three tenors. The image stands for the marked wrinkles in the face of the "old man," thus associating his features with archaic ages also reminiscent of the timeless quality of the ocean. Secondly, it carries the militant connotations of war trenches, linking him to a bellicose past. Finally, the metaphor mends the realms of land and sea because the "trenched lines" (of his face) refer both to agricultural furrows and to the rifts in a stormy sea. Although the old man's element is the water, the speaker lends her vision verisimilitude by describing him in earthen, solidifying metaphors. In her imagination, the speaker alleviates the separation between land and sea, I and You. Although time and space separate them, the poet experiments with their reunion by means of language.

Despite the speaker's verbal powers and poetic charms, the sea and the old man remain indifferent to her efforts and pleas. The "You" resists any attempt to be tracked down. When the speaker intensifies her efforts to see clearly, the apparition of the old man fades: "I / Cannot look much but your form suffers / Some strange injury // And seems to die: so vapors / Ravel to clearness on the dawn sea." Any attempt at grasping the "You" "injures" it and makes it disappear. The sea remains unaffected by time or weather, and "Ages beat like rains / On the unbeaten channels / Of the ocean." The military connotation of "trenched" is continued in the belligerent confrontation between rain and sea. The contrast between the drumming though powerless rain and the indifferent ocean is sharpened by the play of "beat" and "unbeaten." The rain performs an aggressive yet futile attack on the sea to uncover what it hides. The ocean only epitomizes its indifference in an expression of "sage humor and / Durance."

The impossibility of benevolently approaching the "You" or belligerently attacking it upsets the speaker:

> Such sage humor and
> Durance are whirlpools
>
> To make away with the ground-
> Work of the earth and the sky's ridgepole.
> Waist down, you may wind
>
> One labyrinthine tangle
> To root deep among knuckles, shinbones,
> Skulls. Inscrutable,
>
> Below shoulders not once
> Seen by any man who kept his head,
> You defy questions;
>
> You defy other godhood.
> I walk dry on your kingdom's border
> Exiled to no good.
>
> Your shelled bed I remember.
> Father, this thick air is murderous.
> I would breathe water.

The sea's authoritative equanimity is anything but reassuring, but undoes, for the speaker, all dimensional order. Top and bottom, ground and sky are confused. The "You" additionally undermines the stability of the ground with its "labyrinthine tangle." Like ancient catacombs, this destabilizing maze holds "knuckles, shinbones, / Skulls." The bottom of the sea, as the speaker says in the final stanza, is the "father's" "shelled bed," that is, a bed made of shells or a bed, to continue the military connotations, that has been "shelled" or bombed into ruins. The father is associated with the "old myth of origins / Unimaginable," and this "shelled graveyard" is another image the speaker ventures to picture the "unimaginable." She implies that her yearning for the old man in the sea is grounded on her quest for her "origins" and her early memory.

At the end of the poem, the speaker describes an impossible choice between land and water: "I walk dry on your kingdom's border / Exiled to no good. // Your shelled bed I remember. / Father, this thick air is murderous. / I would breathe water." Plath puns on "walking dry" by evoking its literal sense, walking on land, and its figurative sense, walking without life. Without its complementation by the sea, the land is lethal and its "thick air is murderous." Yet the sea is at least as threatening to her subjectivity as the land. In stanzas 4 and 5, the speaker compares the "old man" to an iceberg "to be steered clear / Of, not fathomed," and she also betrays her fear of a possible collision: "Your dangers are many." She knows that reunification with the "old man" would signify "breathing water" and thus her annihilation. Plath lets her readers determine whether the speaker ponders "breathing water" in a desirous tone or as a deterring consequence of her desire for unification. The line can be read as a main clause meaning that the speaker would *like* to breathe water, or it can be read as a conditional construction in which the subordinate clause is left out. With the missing conditional clause added, the sentence could read: if she went into the sea, if she yielded to her yearning for the "shelled bed," if she were caught by his dragnet, or if she attempted to recover him, she "would [consequently] breathe water." The modal verb *would* thus makes "breathing water" both willed (she would like to breathe water) and unwilled (if a certain condition were fulfilled, the consequence would be breathing water, which would take away her breath), under her own control and controlled by outer conditions or forces. The speaker remains in her state of suspension and non-belonging, and again, the oxymoronic expression "breathing water" points out the perfect but impossible symbiosis: surmounting the separation of the elements, uniting air (breathing) and water, merging "I" and "You."

"Full Fathom Five" is a poem about memory on at least three levels. It can be interpreted as a poem about the difficulty of personal memory. Second, it is a markedly "intertextual" poem that strongly draws on—and thus remembers and reworks—other literature of memory, such as Shakespeare's *Tempest* and, in a less direct way, Proust's *In Search of Lost Time*. Both levels of memory are related, for the speaker's struggle for personal memory is compensated by her reliance on literary memory. Third, the discursive positions of subjectivity in the poem—the "I" and the "You"—are, as I will argue, positions related by memory.

"Full Fathom Five" is an allegory of memory, if one reads the speaker's attempt to approach and grasp the "old man" as a labor of remembrance. The sea is an image for the totality of memory, its depth and boundlessness enticing exploration, and the "You" is the desired object of memory. Plath affirms the connection between the sea image and processes of remembering not only in her poems but also in her journals. She writes that thinking about the sea is like "digging into the reaches of my deep submerged head" (*J* 223). The sea metaphor in Plath's imagination is a motor instigating and driving mnemonic practice. In "Full Fathom Five," the sea represents the mass of an undifferentiated, blurred past that the speaker sounds for the "You" or for the clearer contours of a memory. From the surface of the sea, the speaker imaginatively penetrates into its depth and fathoms potential danger. The image of the iceberg implies that only the tip of memory is visible and that collision with its bottom may prove lethal. The terms used to describe the speaker's mnemonic labor—*surfacing, coming in with the tide, dragnet, floating near, obscurity*, and *disappearing*—depict the vagueness of personal memory. The attempt to extract images of the lost, beloved "old man" from the shapes of the sea leads only to very precarious results. Trying too eagerly to decipher the form of the "father," it suddenly "suffers / some strange injury" and "die[s]." Even if unconscious memories approach consciousness as the tides reach for the land, the tide sucks back into itself, and the mnemonic images retreat before conscious knowledge. Metaphorically and formally, memories fluctuate like the sea and steadily move and change shape. The fifteen stanzas of the poem are written in terza rima with syllabic verse; the first line of every stanza has seven; the second, nine; and the third, five syllables. So the lines visually imitate the waves' rise and fall as well as their constant movement. The sea is intrinsically "vague," a word that refers both to the wave and a state of uncertainty.

Simultaneously, the unchanging shape of the stanzas (hence, the visual effect of repetition) imitates the sea's indifference toward the speaker's pleas. In stark contrast with the speaker's inner upheaval in the poem, its lines stoically continue the pattern.

As an allegory of mnemonic labor, "Full Fathom Five" depicts the quest for personal memory as an uncertain, possibly risky enterprise. At the end, the speaker's survival may be threatened precisely because it cannot be grounded on personal memory. Her labors of memory remain crowned with only dubitable success: that which the speaker almost "sees" on the surface of the sea disappears the moment she thinks she can grasp it, and her imagination takes over picturing the "old man" as roaming on the bottom of the ocean. The speaker's inability to remember results in the ambivalent desire to cut loose from her mnemonic obsession and to become one with the ocean. What are the reasons for the failure of personal memory? On one hand, it may be an expression of Plath's actual sense of a flawed personal memory, for which I will provide some biographical and textual hints. On the other hand, and particularly when looking at her poems as highly self-conscious and staged projections of subjectivity, the lamentation of poor memory may, in fact, be concomitant with the relief of forgetting. The sense of the precariousness of personal memory may also be conditioned by difficulties lying in the concept of personal memory itself, which, as I will argue, is undermined by the interference of collective memory.

Sylvia Plath had a pervasive sense of "poor memory." Her mnemonic self-consciousness exceeded the average recognition of mnemonic imperfection. The early death of Plath's father and the mother's attempts to protect the children from it may have produced the feeling of an absent past. In her autobiographical novel *The Bell Jar*, Plath writes, "My mother hadn't let us come to his funeral because we were only children then, and he had died in the hospital, so the graveyard and even his death had always seemed unreal to me." The protagonist Esther Greenwood decides to "take on a mourning my mother had never bothered with."[3] The electroshock treatment that Plath underwent after her suicide attempt at the age of twenty-one may have contributed to the fear of memory losses, a frequent side effect of this kind of "therapy." Esther Greenwood describes the mental numbness that follows an electroshock session: "Sitting in the front seat, between Dodo and my mother, I felt dumb and subdued. Every time I tried to concentrate, my mind glided off, like a

skater, into a large empty space, and pirouetted there, absently."[4] As a
student, too, Plath frequently feels handicapped by what she perceives as
an insufficient memory: "All I have ever read thins and vanishes: I do not
amass, remember" (*J* 405). In her poetic writing, Plath speaks of insuffi-
cient memory as if it were a physical defect or a personal flaw. In "Little
Fugue," she has her speaker state bluntly, "I am lame in the memory"
(*CP* 188). Plath leaves it open whether this is experienced as troublesome
or rather as convenient, as the playful and ironic title "Little Fugue" may
suggest. For this is the reverse side of memory: while on one hand, some
memories are desired, others are quite readily and comfortably forgotten.
In "Full Fathom Five," the blame the speaker attributes to the sea for her
unstable and vague memory may be her projection. Her inability to visu-
alize the "old man" fully may be generated by her unconscious resistance
to memory: after all, she fears she might "collide" with an "iceberg."
Lamenting the difficulty of personal memory, the speaker in "Full Fath-
om Five" is also protected and relieved by her amnesia.

The practice of personal memory in "Full Fathom Five" is further
complicated by its representation in poetry. Although presented as a
highly subjective and introspective poem, there is hardly an element in
"Full Fathom Five" that is *not* borrowed from the poetic tradition. Plath
borrows the idea to depict the waves of the sea through the line lengths
from concrete poetry. The sea is a conventional trope in American litera-
ture. In the founding days of America, westward expansion began with
the hazards of having to cross the Atlantic Ocean. Later on, the sea be-
came a trope of "a utopian counter-space to the increasing rigidity and
social divisiveness of modern capitalist society."[5] John Peck claims that
"because the sea was central to their identity Americans turned to the sea
to understand themselves."[6] The sea is also a frequent metaphor when it
comes to representing processes of memory. The sea evokes feelings of
temporal distance and depth that are at the heart of memory, the French
philosopher Paul Ricoeur believes.[7] Both being New Englanders, the sea
is personally as meaningful to Plath as it was to Emily Dickinson.[8] By
reiterating the sea metaphor, Plath echoes, for example, Dickinson's
poem "She Rose to His Requirement":

> She rose to His Requirement—dropt
> The Playthings of Her Life
> To take the honorable Work
> Of Woman, and of Wife—

> If ought She missed in Her new Day,
> Of Amplitude, or Awe—
> Or first Prospective—Or the Gold
> In using, wear away,
>
> It lay unmentioned—as the Sea
> Develop Pearl, and Weed,
> But only to Himself—be known
> The Fathoms they abide— [9]

The sea hides and protects "pearl" and "weed" as metaphors for the dislocated parts of the female self after the woman has adapted to "His Requirement." In association with Dickinson's poem, the sea in "Full Fathom Five" is not an image representing loss but dislocation of memories that may possibly be retrieved. "Pearl" and "weed" are metaphors of poetic memory and represent the true, yet sunken aspects of the self. But in Plath, this core of the self is conflated with the dead "father," and instead of pearl, the bottom of her sea only hides "knuckles, shinbones, / Skulls." Plath's attempt at overcoming inner division, at uniting land and sea, puts the speaker at risk: it threatens to overthrow the order the land maintains at the cost of being cut off from the sea.

"Full Fathom Five" echoes two other literary landmarks concerned with processes of memory: Shakespeare's *Tempest* and Marcel Proust's *Swann's Way*. Plath's mode of imagining and expressing the emergence of memories is strikingly similar to how the narrator in Proust's novel describes remembering: "I feel something start within me, something that leaves its resting-place and attempts to rise, something that has been embedded like an anchor at a great depth; I do not yet know what it is, but I can feel it mounting slowly; I can measure the resistance, I can hear the echo of great spaces traversed." [10] Both Plath and Proust resort to images of the sea, to images of rising or surfacing from great depth, crossing distances and disappearing again into the darkness of the ocean. In Proust, however, mnemonic labor, even if it does not yield results right away, is eventually crowned with the retrieval of most vivid and intimate memories: "Ten times over I must essay the task, must lean down over the abyss. . . . And suddenly the memory revealed itself." [11] The whole world of Combray, instigated by so little as the fragrance of a cup of tea and the taste of a madeleine, is recovered: "so in that moment all the flowers in our garden and in M. Swann's park, and the water-lilies on the

Vivonne and the good folk of the village and their little dwellings and the parish church and the whole of Combray and its surroundings, taking shape and solidity, sprang into being, town and gardens alike, from my cup of tea."[12] In "Full Fathom Five," however, the speaker's struggle for memory remains futile. Instead of recovering a solid landscape, she remains caught up in the ever-fluctuating seascape.

"Full Fathom Five" borrows its title from the song of Ariel, the "airy spirit," in *The Tempest*. Prospero orders Ariel to lead the shipwrecked Ferdinand to him. Ferdinand is the son of Alonso, king of Naples, who helped Antonio unseat his brother Prospero, the former duke of Milan. Ariel sings him a song to gain his attention and guide him:

> Full fathom five thy father lies,
>   Of his bones are coral made;
> Those are pearls that were his eyes;
>   Nothing of him that doth fade,
> But doth suffer a sea-change
> Into something rich and strange.
> Sea-nymphs hourly ring his knell:
> (*Burden*): Ding-dong.
>   Hark! Now I hear them—Ding-dong bell.
>   (I.2, 397–407)[13]

Ariel soothes Ferdinand, who lost sight of his father in the shipwreck that Prospero caused, so he could capture his enemies. Ferdinand's father not only turns out to be alive by the end of the play, but also, as Ariel insinuates, will have undergone a transformation, a "sea-change," and repent his plotting. This change in reality is prepared by the improved image of the father in Ferdinand's imagination and memory, which are metaphorized as the bottom of the sea. Instead of undergoing a metamorphosis into coral and pearl, the remembered father in Plath's poem is all "knuckles, shinbones, / Skulls." The speaker imitates Ferdinand's example, imagining that the father is still alive; but instead of being soothed by the memory, she is left "dry" and "exiled." In Shakespeare, the rhythmic precision of the alliterated line "full fathom five" points to a very precise place where the "father's memory" is to be found. Plath, however, ironizes such certainty by contrasting the almost hammered title with the wavelike shape of her terza rima stanzas composed in syllabic verse, which simulate the crest and trough of sea waves and contrast with the smooth surface and clear water one associates with Ariel's entrancing song.

Miranda, whom her father Prospero will betroth to Ferdinand, is also granted her early memory and the truth about her origins by her father:

> Miranda: You have often
>   Begun to tell me what I am, but stopped,
>   And left me to a bootless inquisition,
>   Concluding, "Stay: not yet."
>
> Prospero: The hour's now come.
>   The very minute bids thee ope thine ear.
>   Obey and be attentive.
>   (I.2, 33–38)

Plath's speaker never gets an answer to her "bootless inquisition." Plath stresses the speaker's marginality and solitude during the process of re-membering. Paralleling the island as the setting of Shakespeare's drama, the speaker in Plath's poem is also situated in a place bordering on the sea. She finds herself all alone, though, and the potential "narrator" is absent. He has officially been buried, but the speaker still suspects that he roams the bottom of the sea from where he "defies" her questions and lets her "walk dry" on his "kingdom's border."

In "Full Fathom Five," the poetic speaker tries both methods of memory suggested by Proust and Shakespeare: images and narrative. She seeks to decipher the images rising from the ocean's depth and, like Miranda, she questions the "old man" on the bottom of the sea. Neither mode of remembering works: no images are produced by *mémoire involontaire*, and there is no possibility of memory being transmitted via narration. The invocation of the literary tradition enriches the mnemonic resources of Plath's poems, but it also reveals the discrepancy between Plath's lyrical speakers and their literary predecessors. Even if, as Christina Britzolakis suggests, Plath makes "literary allusions [to] seek to authorize writing with reference to a line of paternal succession"[14] and looks for literary father substitutes in Proust and Shakespeare, among other authors, the references are also forced and stem from her dependence and lack of choice. If her speaker aims at retrieving personal memory, both the father she calls out to in the poem as well as the two literary forefathers she turns to prove useless. While "Plath is a highly self-conscious student of tradition, who reflects upon her own insertion into literary history,"[15] she also ironizes her very attempts at insertion. Poetically searching the sea for memories and thus reapplying a literary topos does not render a lost world, coral or shiny pearl, but bestows intimations of an uncanny other roaming on the bottom of the sea and the desire for death.

Unlike her models, the subject in "Full Fathom Five" is not able to construe a sense of self through memory. Memory does not function, because what the subject desires to remember has become other. The discursive positions in a poem, in contrast to the novel (*Swann's Way*) or the drama (*The Tempest*), may designate distinct fractions of subjectivity rather than separate characters. What is both other to and part of the speaker's self is her forgotten past. Trying to resurrect the "old man," "father," or "you" is a form of practicing poetic memory. The "You," projected as distant and indifferent, has a haunting quality, for it can neither be resurrected nor forgotten. Plath exceeds the literary models by dramatizing the speaker's conviction that there is a memory that keeps evading her, one that she cannot resuscitate by following poetic convention. In this sense, personal memory is not represented, but *affirmed* by the speaker's excessive, unsatisfiable desire, her ambivalently entreating and withholding attitude, her begging and scorn, and the silence that the "You" persists in.

This conflict between personal and literary memory in "Full Fathom Five" is, I argue, a variant of the relation between personal and collective memory as put forward by the French sociologist Maurice Halbwachs. In his study *Les Cadres sociaux de la mémoire* (1925), Halbwachs points out the delusion of memory being private property: "One is rather astonished when reading psychological treatises that deal with memory to find that people are considered there as isolated beings. These make it appear that to understand our mental operations, we need to stick to individuals and first of all, to divide all the bonds which attach individuals to the society of their fellows. Yet it is in society that people normally acquire their memories. It is also in society that they recall, recognize, and localize their memories."[16] Halbwachs believes that memory is fundamentally a social phenomenon and is acquired by the individual through social and cultural interaction. He goes as far as to doubt the existence of personal memory altogether because, he argues, memory is inherently dependent on reinforcement by the group. Over time, memories cannot be sustained apart from the collective. The individual will mostly remember what the social group he belongs to remembers and repeats to him:

> Most of the time, when I remember, it is others who spur me on; their memory comes to the aid of mine and mine relies on theirs. There is nothing mysterious about recall of memories in these cases at least. There is no point in seeking where they are preserved in my brain or in some nook of my mind to which I alone have access: for they are recalled to me externally, and the groups of which I am a part at any time give me the means to reconstruct them, upon condition, to be sure, that I turn toward them and adopt, at least for the moment, their way of thinking. . . . It is in this sense that there exists a collective memory and social frameworks of memory; it is to the degree that our individual thought places itself in these frameworks and participates in this memory that it is capable of the act of recollection. [17]

The French philosopher Gaston Bachelard complements in interesting ways Halbwachs's thesis of the dependence of personal memory on its maintenance by collective memory. The self, Bachelard holds, is the product of "our history as told by the others" or, in Halbwachsian terminology, our socially reinforced self. "When, all alone and dreaming on rather at length, we go far from the present to relive the times of the first life, several child faces come to meet us. We were several in the trial life (*la vie essayée*), in our primitive life. Only through the accounts of others have we come to know of our unity. On the thread of our history as told by the others, year by year, we end up resembling ourselves. We gather all our beings around the unity of our name." [18] Bachelard suggests a different hierarchy of subjectivity and narrative: instead of adapting the narrative to the experience that leads to a sense of subjectivity, subjectivity is adapted to the story others tell us about ourselves. He concludes that many of our selves are lost in the course of our actual life because they were not included in our story made up by the people around us. This is where Bachelard interestingly joins Halbwachs's argument, which insists that all of our memory is embedded in socially transmitted systems of time, space, and language. Of course, the group has, strictly speaking, no memory but needs the individual rememberer. Halbwachs and Bachelard do not negate the existence of personal memory per se, but insist on the importance of narrative when it comes to preserving personal memory. Narrative is the path on which the collective encroaches on the personal. Personal memory is, above all, that which is retained and confirmed by narrative as a constitutive dimension of collective memory. While in theory personal and collective memory can be differentiated, they are inextricably linked in poetic practice.

"Full Fathom Five" enacts the conflict between personal and collective memory, as elaborated above, not only on the literary level (literary memory dominates the poet's personal memory) but also on the social level, which Halbwachs and Bachelard have in mind. Plath's speaker resists collective memory and asserts the possibility of poetic memory when she remains strangely skeptical of what she has been told by others and dismisses their affirmation of the "old man's" death as mere "rumors": "The muddy rumors // Of your burial move me / To half-believe: your reappearance / Proves rumors shallow." Poetic *memory* challenges collective *knowledge*: instead of accepting the collectively approved fact of his death, the speaker stubbornly affirms the "old man's" aliveness. Within the logic of the analogy between Plath's speaker and Shakespeare's Ferdinand, her suspicions are justified, because Ferdinand's father Alonso turns out to have survived the shipwreck. The speaker seeks support in the literary tradition against collective social memory. She struggles to assert poetic over historic memory, to preserve psychic over objective truth. Yet the discrepancy between subjective and collective memory leads to the unsettlement of the socially transmitted grids of language, space, and time and thus to the upheaval of the way in which reality is structured. Language, that is, the "rumors," is not believed anymore. The sea is a representation of timelessness (or eternity) and spacelessness (an eternally floating, unstable surface). The haunting presence of the "You" has the effect of "whirlpools" that upset all dimensional order and "make away with the ground— / Work of the earth and the sky's ridgepole." The spatial dimensions are turned upside down, as linear time is replaced by the repetitive eternity of the tides. The speaker's memory is linguistically, temporally, and spatially unanchorable, and thus destined to remain blank.[19]

As literary memory exemplifies, collective thoughts enter the individual mind via the medium of language:

> To be sure, everyone has a capacity for memory [mémoire] that is unlike that of anyone else, given the variety of temperaments and life circumstances. But individual memory is nevertheless a part or an aspect of group memory, since each impression and each fact, even if it apparently concerns a particular person exclusively, leaves a lasting memory only to the extent that one has thought it over—to the extent

that it is connected with the thoughts that come to us from the social milieu. One cannot in fact think about the events of one's past without discoursing upon them. But to discourse upon something means to connect within a single system of ideas our opinions as well as those of our circle.[20]

Expressing thoughts in language is a way to make them conscious and consciously memorable. Verbalizing thoughts entails their assimilation to "social frameworks of memory," as which Halbwachs identifies "time, space, and the order of physical and social events as they are established and recognized by the members of our groups."[21] In this definition, language figures implicitly as the medium in which the "order of . . . events" can be "established" and "recognized." When thinking about individual impressions, Halbwachs writes, one links them to "thoughts from the social milieu." This process of memory formation can also be understood as the genesis of historic memory. Literary memory develops in like manner, and individual acts of reading or writing are linked to our literary foreknowledge, often based on the literary canon. In using language as readers or writers, we "connect within a single system of ideas," and this system is not only that of social but also of literary experience. Writers write and readers read within a literary tradition.

REASSEMBLING THE SHARDS OF MEMORY

Whereas in "Full Fathom Five" literary memory is only implicitly identified as a hindrance to personal memory, this critique is explicit in "The Colossus" (*CP* 129–30), a poem that lends Plath's first published book of poetry its title and is representative of her poetics. While "Full Fathom Five" practically tries the mnemonic methods suggested by other works of literature, the following poem reflects on memory on a metalevel. In "The Colossus," the "work of memory" is performed by a speaker who compares herself to an ant in a landscape of ruins, puzzling the pieces and bones of the "father" together:

> I shall never get you put together entirely,
> Pieced, glued, and properly jointed.
> Mule-bray, pig-grunt and bawdy cackles
> Proceed from your great lips.
> It's worse than a barnyard.

Perhaps you consider yourself an oracle,
Mouthpiece of the dead, or of some god or other.
Thirty years now I have labored
To dredge the silt from your throat.
I am none the wiser.

The speaker takes a stance of resignation toward her impossible task. As in "Full Fathom Five," the speaker has not been able to communicate with her addressee. Although she has been "dredge[ing] the silt from . . . [his] throat" for thirty years, the other's message has remained unintelligible. Contrary to the "father" in "Full Fathom Five," the "colossus" does not remain silent, but, worse, ridicules and demeans the speaker with obscene animal noises ("Mule-bray, pig-grunt and bawdy cackles"). In return, she mocks his authority as an "oracle" or "mouthpiece of the dead" when caricaturing his utterances as barnyard cackles. She is growing impatient and disillusioned with her attempt at interpreting the voices from the past. Still, with an ant's tenacity and discipline, she tries to reconstruct him physically:

Scaling little ladders with gluepots and pails of Lysol
I crawl like an ant in mourning
Over the weedy acres of your brow
To mend the immense skull-plates and clear
The bald, white tumuli of your eyes.

The ant-speaker's is a work of mourning, tending the "father's" remains. The task is performed not only devotedly, but also mechanically and slavishly by a subject whose existence is reduced to that of a genetically programmed insect.

Only by leaving the confines of the immediate "construction zone" and by overseeing it from a "hill of black cypress" can the speaker admit the colossus's grandeur:

A blue sky out of the Oresteia
Arches above us. O father, all by yourself
You are pithy and historical as the Roman Forum.
I open my lunch on a hill of black cypress.
Your fluted bones and acanthine hair are littered

In their old anarchy to the horizon-line.
It would take more than a lightning-stroke
To create such a ruin.

Plath abandons the register of menial, agricultural labor to endow the colossus's remains with a mythohistorical aura. What before were "the weedy acres of your brow" now become the "ruin" of "Your fluted bones and acanthine hair." The sky above this wasteland is called the "blue sky out of the Oresteia" and links the broken colossus of the poem to Agamemnon, another "ruined" father in Greek mythology. This analogy would turn the speaker into Electra, Agamemnon's devoted and mournful daughter. Besides Greek myths, Plath also draws her images from the collective memory of ancient Rome. The father is "pithy and historical as the Roman Forum." The speaker is situated "on a hill of black cypress," possibly one of the seven hills of Rome, and the metaphors found to describe the scattered remains are derived from ancient architecture. The bones are "fluted," his hair is "acanthine" like the plant whose shape served the decoration of ancient pillars, his tongue resembles a "pillar," and his left ear is compared to a cornucopia. In the poem, the cornucopia, which in Greek mythology was the horn of the goat that suckled Zeus and would fill with whatever its owner desired, indicates the speaker's need and desire to be equally nourished. The mythohistorical diction in the middle of the poem stands in stark contrast to the barnyard register in the beginning. The classical beauty of the colossus's remains does not fit his animal utterances. This seemingly contradictory attitude to the colossus may be due to the speaker's altered perspective. Resignation and frustration dominate when the speaker depicts herself within the remains; the shattered body is awe-inspiring, however, when one looks at it from afar. This shift of perspective reflects the situation of the writer who, Plath suggests, when having to write from within literary memory, is driven into a state of exasperation, and who, when looking at literary memory from outside, is able to admire it and acknowledge its "greatness."

To take her lunch, the speaker may withdraw to the nearby "hill of black cypress," but to do her work, she has to immerse herself in the field of ruins, which lie "littered . . . to the horizon-line." Ironically, the speaker is unable to escape his remains even if he is nothing but a heap of old bones. She is both his reconstructor and his lonely victim:

> Nights, I squat in the cornucopia
> Of your left ear, out of the wind,
>
> Counting the red stars and those of plum-color.

> The sun rises under the pillar of your tongue.
> My hours are married to shadow.
> No longer do I listen for the scrape of a keel
> On the blank stones of the landing.

Her experience of the world remains determined by her position within the colossus's skull. From here, she contemplates the stars and the sunrise. The final two lines of the poem indicate the speaker's submission to the broken "colossus" of cultural and historical memory and her dissipating hope for escape. Whereas in "Full Fathom Five," the speaker is caught in between the realms of land and sea, begging the latter for an *ex machina* recovery of the father, the speaker in "The Colossus" has accepted her existence on the land amidst the ruins of the past.

"The Colossus" is another allegory about processes of memory, but the model Plath devises for memory differs greatly from that in "Full Fathom Five." Most notably, the speaker in "Full Fathom Five" hopes to retrieve memory as an entity, whereas the leading image of the mnemonic model in "The Colossus" is that of an unfinishable puzzle. Writing as a mnemonic activity, Plath implies, *is* reassembling or *re*-membering the pieces of literary and cultural memory. The "personal" or "subjective" finds expression not in the quality of the shards, but in the mode of their *re*-arrangement into the poem. Writing has a dimension of mourning because reassembling the shards amounts to tending and curating the remains of the past and endowing death with "shape" and meaning. The speaker's realization that she must remember and write within a historical context finally enables her to abandon the sea as a miraculous source of subjective memory and ingenious inspiration. Accordingly, the poem ends on the note: "No longer do I listen for the scrape of a keel / On the blank stones of the landing."

While acknowledging the poet's dependence on the cultural legacy, Plath implicitly argues that writing is impossible if all the poet has to write from are the remains of a disaster. Despite its "colossal significance," the mnemonic context does not offer an adequate structure in which to embed personal memory. Plath rhetorically blames the fragmentation of personal memory on this lack, which includes the absence of a suitable literary memory as well as the degenerate state of history and culture at large. Like Halbwachs's collective memory, the mnemonic resources in the poem are both imperative and inhibiting.

In "The Colossus," Plath negotiates her relationship to the Modernists. Plath engages with Eliot's poetry through the lens of his criticism, and she perceives Eliot's criticism through the lens of the New Criticism, which had established Eliot as an icon of neoclassical ideals of tradition. She positions herself as a female poet inheriting Eliot's *The Waste Land* and as a daughter in bondage to the fallen father. Her poem can be read as a parody of Eliot's essay "Tradition and the Individual Talent." There, he suggests that "tradition" implies "some pleasing archeological reconstruction," the very task the ant, although anything but "pleased" by it, commits herself to. He gives further instruction as to how the poet may acquire a tradition:

> Tradition is a matter of much wider significance. It cannot be inherited, and if you want it you must obtain it by great labour. It involves, in the first place, the historical sense, which we may call nearly indispensable to any one who would continue to be a poet beyond his twenty-fifth year; and the historical sense involves a perception, not only of the pastness of the past, but of its presence; the historical sense compels a man to write not merely with his own generation in his bones, but with a feeling that the whole of the literature of Europe from Homer and within it the whole of the literature of his own country has a simultaneous existence and composes a simultaneous order.[22]

In "The Colossus," Plath, who certainly knew Eliot's essay, expresses her awareness that tradition will not be a matter of facile inheritance. She makes the speaker compare herself to an animal as insignificant as an ant and puts the ant to "great labour," thus ironizing the task of "sweating" for a tradition from the start. Being twenty-seven years old when she wrote "The Colossus" and thus qualifying as a poet who sticks to her literary call "beyond . . . [her] twenty-fifth year," Plath—eminently subversive in her obedience—lives up to her role as a disciple of the great male poets and mockingly follows Eliot's recommendation to labor for a "historical sense" and a sense of the past's presence. She imagines her poetic speaker in the very center of a field overloaded with history so that the "presence" of the colossus must indeed appear overwhelming. Physically lacking the "bones" to carry "her own generation," the poetic speaker as "ant" lives in the bones of "the whole of the literature of Europe." The bones lie "simultaneously" scattered rather than "ordered" on the field.

Plath further complicates the discipleship Eliot asks for by introducing the idea of a gendered memory and tradition. The speaker's work of memory is impeded by the characteristics of the fragments she is meant to reassemble, for the ruins are the "father's" bones and the remains of "an overwhelmingly male tradition."[23] As Britzolakis points out, "the speaker's classicism is seen as perverse; she is in love with a paternal law invested in the petrified *membra disjecta* of tradition, 'littered / In their old anarchy to the horizon-line'. Her endless work of impossible restitution and repair has become merely fetishistic, an obsessive dwelling upon the ornamental or academic detail ('your fluted bones and acanthine hair')."[24] The space inside male history and tradition is alienating and, worse, mocks and demeans her with "bawdy cackles." The mnemonic labor is ridiculed by an obscene cacophony of voices. The efforts undertaken to hear "the dead" or "some god" have no interpretable result. So the narrative components of memory remain unintelligible just as the visual elements, the ruins, cannot be reconstructed. The oppressive nature of the other's voice is emphasized again in the final stanza: "The sun rises under the pillar of your tongue. / My hours are married to shadow." The "pillar" is a phallic metaphor invoking a patriarchal form of oppression. Because the male other still has the authority of voice weighing on the speaker like a pillar she cannot cast off, she has to remain silent and in shadow. Visual and narrative memory fail because the cultural tradition is designated as "male."

Plath's ironization of the cultural legacies of patriarchy[25] raises the question of her relationship to a female writing tradition. Plath's journal entries provide more direct insight into her attitude toward female writers than her poems. Generally speaking, a female writing tradition would have been available, but Plath's attitude toward female writers who would qualify as literary predecessors is ambiguous. Although she frequently acknowledges her indebtedness to some female authors—about Virginia Woolf she writes that "her novels make mine possible" (J 289)— she also chooses a self-consciously competitive tone when comparing herself with them: "Arrogant, I think I have written lines which qualify me to be The Poetess of America. . . . Who rivals? Well, in history— Sappho, Elizabeth Barrett Browning, Christina Rossetti, Amy Lowell, Emily Dickinson, Edna St. Vincent Millay—all dead. Now: Edith Sitwell & Marianne Moore, the ageing giantesses & poetic godmothers. Phyllis McGinley is out—light verse: she's sold herself. Rather: May Swenson,

Isabella Gardner, & most close, Adrienne Cecile Rich—who will soon be eclipsed by these eight poems" (*J* 360). Plath is aware of female writers, but since they had not yet been canonized, she does not conceive of them as a tradition in which she could position herself. Her seeming dismissal of them reflects the condescending attitude of the male writing tradition toward "women writers," for Plath unabashedly categorizes them as "dead," "ageing," or "soon to be eclipsed." She passes this judgment in an ambivalent gesture of theatrically anticipating and ironizing her own claims to greatness. In another journal passage, Plath expresses her long-ing for female model writers: "Why did Virginia Woolf commit suicide? Or Sara Teasdale—or the other brilliant women—neurotic? Was their writing sublimation (oh horrible word) of deep, basic desires? If only I knew. If only I knew how high I could set my goals, my requirements for my life! I am in the position of a blind girl playing with a slide-ruler of values" (*J* 151). Plath's use of the word *requirement* calls to mind again Emily Dickinson's poem "She Rose to His Requirement." Contrary to the patriarchal "requirement" to which the subject in Dickinson's poem adapts, Plath, like the female writers she names, wants to set her own requirement. But defining the stakes of her ambition or "requirement" independently leads her on treacherous grounds that have proved peri-lous for women of literature.

Although she declares her need for a form of mentorship, Plath lacks Virginia Woolf's theorized awareness of the importance of a female writ-ing tradition that Woolf elaborates in *A Room of One's Own* in 1929. As-sessing the quality of writing by women, Woolf argues that the greatest difficulty they faced was "that they had no tradition behind them, or one so short and partial that it was of little help. For we think back through our mothers if we are women. It is useless to go to the great men writers for help, however much one may go to them for pleasure."[26] Woolf de-sires a specifically female literary memory. To Woolf, the lack of a tradi-tion amounts to a lack of "help," that is, a pragmatic repertoire of meth-ods handed down to younger female writers. Woolf's concept of a "tradi-tion" relates to the concept of "collective memory" insofar as it would provide a set of *practices* sustaining the body of collective memory. Col-lective memory is a more comprehensive concept than tradition, because beside the practice of memory, it also comprises its theorization.

Plath, in need of literary models to overcome the "provinciality" of her "jumping-off place" (*J* 45), mainly went to the literary canon for help.

At the time, the canon consisted almost exclusively of male writers. Consequently, Steven Gould Axelrod has no difficulty demonstrating Plath's focus on canonized male writers in her academic papers at Cambridge, in the courses she taught at Smith College from 1957 to 1958, and in her personal library.[27] Still, Plath's use of female mythological figures and her knowledge of female writers demonstrate her need for ample, that is, male *and* female models and influence. Her eagerness to learn from the Modernist poets was only the beginning of her sustained efforts to write herself out of the Modernist tradition.

Relating a poet's sense of history to his studiousness, Eliot distinguishes between those aspiring young poets who "can absorb knowledge" as easily as Shakespeare, who "acquired more essential history from Plutarch than most men could from the whole British Museum," and the "more tardy," who "must sweat for it."[28] Plath does not count herself among either of the two groups. Although she certainly does not consider herself to lack "individual talent," knowledge does not seem to be easily absorbable, and the speaker's precarious position in the historical ruins of the colossus manifests this. Plath rather, as pointed out before, was haunted by the fear of forgetting: "All I have ever read thins and vanishes: I do not amass, remember" (*J* 405).[29] While sometimes lamenting her mnemonic inaptitude, Plath rebels against any form of educational patronization in other places. In some journal entries, Plath grows suspicious of her own studiousness and refuses to be counted among "the more tardy [who] must sweat" for knowledge and a tradition. In a mode of self-detachment and self-objectification Plath contemplates herself and the other tireless female student assimilating the masses of history:

> —God, who am I? I sit in the library tonight, the lights glaring overhead, the fan whirring loudly. Girls, girls everywhere, reading books. Intent faces, flesh pink, white, yellow. And I sit here without identity: faceless. My head aches. There is history to read—centuries to comprehend before I sleep, millions of lives to assimilate before breakfast tomorrow. . . . I'm lost. Huxley would have laughed. What a conditioning center this is! Hundreds of faces, bending over books, fans whirring, beating time along the edge of thought. It is a nightmare. There is no sun. There is only continual motion. If I rest, if I think inward, I go mad. There is so much, and I am torn in different directions, pulled thin, taut against horizons too distant for me to reach. To stop with the German tribes and rest awhile: But no! On, on, on. Through ages of empires, of

decline and fall. Swift, ceaseless pace. Will I never rest in sunlight again—slow, languid & golden with peace? (*J* 26–27)

Like Eliot, Plath equates her relationship to history with her knowledge of history that must be acquired through study. She is aware and critical of the larger cultural and social implications of her studies and mourns her loss of innocence as a side effect of education. She participates in a conditioning center and repeats history—the run of the German tribes, "through ages of empires, decline and fall"—even if only in her imagination. She voices her reluctance to have her memory manipulated by a history and tradition not her own in another journal passage: "God, I scream for time to let go, to write, to think. But no. I have to exercise my memory in little feats just so I can stay in this damn wonderful place which I love and hate with all my heart" (*J* 33). Her education, as enabling as it is, is an external influence that she, to remain herself, simultaneously needs to resist. These scholastic exercises of memory are experienced by her as a threat to her capacity for poetic memory, for a memory of the self beyond the parameters of its collective definition.

In the quotation above, Plath detaches herself from Eliot's advice and draws closer to the position held by Emerson, Eliot's counter-model concerning questions of tradition and the past. In "The American Scholar," Emerson writes:

> Books are written by thinkers, not by Man Thinking; by men of talent, that is, who start wrong, who set out from accepted dogmas, not from their own sight of principle. Meek young men grow up in libraries, believing it their duty to accept the views which Cicero, which Locke, which Bacon, have given; forgetful that Cicero, Locke, and Bacon were only young men in libraries when they wrote these books. Hence, instead of Man Thinking, we have the bookworm. Hence, the book-learned class, who value books, as such; not as related to nature and the human constitution, but as making a sort of Third Estate with the world and the soul.[30]

Although Emerson and other nineteenth-century American thinkers had made their mark on Eliot, the self-consciously Europeanized attitude toward history and tradition he presents in his essays makes a dramatic contrast with Emerson's adamant Americanism. Plath demonstrates awareness of the differences between historical self-conceptions in Europe and the United States when she remarks that she had to learn "dates" when she moved to Europe. Mimicking a classical teacher-student relationship, Plath relates to her mother how helpful Ted Hughes is in introducing her to a "European" approach to the past: "He is so helpful and understanding about my studies and has made a huge chart of the English writers and their dates (dating and knowing style is necessary here and I had nothing of that, unfortunately, at home) and stuck it up all over one wall of the bedroom where I can learn it."[31] The "huge chart" puns on the "Hughes" chart. "Dating and knowing style" form the antithesis of Emerson's setting out from one's "own sight of principle," and the various passages from Plath's writing reveal her shifting views—also depending on what kind of text she is writing and to whom she addresses it—about the necessity of acquiring a tradition.

Plath's remark on the student's obligation to assimilate thousands of lives in history and to follow the run of the Germanic tribes is reminiscent of Virginia Woolf's idea of the artist's capacity for assimilating "foreign matter": "the mind of an artist, in order to achieve the prodigious effort of freeing whole and entire the work that is in him, must be incandescent, like Shakespeare's mind, I conjectured, looking at the book which lay open at Antony and Cleopatra. There must be no obstacle in it, no foreign matter unconsumed."[32] However, if the material the writer needs to assimilate is alien—and here Plath's awareness of a gendered memory comes in again—the process may not go untroubled. The female writer is obligated to digest the material collective memory makes available to her. But having to process material for which her digestive system may be partly unfit complicates the process of consumption. Instead of a place of healthy digestion, Plath refers to her mind as a dump for separately rotting items: "My mind is, to use a disgustingly obvious simile, like a wastebasket full of waste paper; bits of hair, and rotting apple cores" (*J* 33). The self needs to be affirmed constantly if it is to survive internalizing the chunks of a tradition that both sustains and corrupts. The incompatibility between the system that wishes to assimilate and the material it receives for assimilation is described by Woolf as a periodical detachment of female consciousness from the world around and from places symbolizing state or patriarchal authority: "Again if one is a woman one is often surprised by a sudden splitting off of consciousness, say in walking down Whitehall, when from being the natural inheritor of that civilisation, she becomes, on the contrary, outside of it, alien and critical."[33]

Plath's position in a field of historical and cultural ruins also bears the seeds for the construction of something new on top of the old—seeds potentially fertilized by an American enthusiasm for the creation of the new. As Emerson puts it in "Circles," "the Greek sculpture is all melted away," and Plath's broken colossus pays tribute to this declaration. Emerson continues: "For the genius that created it creates now somewhat else. The Greek letters last a little longer, but are already passing under the same sentence, and tumbling into the inevitable pit which the creation of new thought opens for all that is old. The new continents are built out of the ruins of an old planet; the new races fed out of the decomposition of the foregoing."[34] Compared to this passage, which needs to be read as part of Emerson's pantheistic view of the world in which everything transforms and no element is lost, Plath's vision of the cultural tradition significantly differs. The construction of the new strongly depends on the old and is simultaneously enabled and obstructed by it. Contrary to Emerson's idea of organic transformation, Plath views struggle and resistance as inevitable elements of change. She thinks of cultural change not in terms of a transformative process but rather as a process of integrating the fragments of the old into the new. Here, she might draw closer again to Eliot's conception of change as expressed in *The Waste Land*. Reading "The Colossus" as referencing *The Waste Land*, the broken colossus is also that which will fertilize the growth of the new, for Eliot writes, alluding to Chaucer: "April is the cruellest month, breeding / Lilacs out of the dead land, mixing / Memory and desire, stirring / Dull roots with spring rain."[35] Memory and desire are the ingredients that enable the "dull roots," as a metaphor of the old, to bring forth "Lilacs." The old is endowed with new vitality and generates the new while simultaneously becoming a part of it.

Plath's relationship to the Modernists is marked by need and resistance, and the speaker's stance toward the colossus in the poem is emblematic of it. As elaborated above, the speaker's attitude changes with the position she chooses in relation to that tradition. A resigned and abiding attitude dominates when she depicts herself as somebody at the center of the remains of the tradition who, Sisyphus-like, labors to form the pieces into a new whole. But when she looks at it from the top of a hill, she admits the classical beauty of the colossus, which can still be recognized from its fragments. To translate the poem into Plath's relationship to the Modernists: she is willing to grant them their importance, since without their legacy there would not be any "leftover" material to work with.

Finding her way within that tradition, however, is projected as alienating, degrading, and often fruitless.

DADDY'S DEMISE

In "Full Fathom Five," poetic memory and subjectivity become manifest in the gap that Plath constructs between the faithful reiteration of literary motifs and their mnemonic failure. In "The Colossus," the speaker's self-reflective mode frees her from mere mnemonic repetition. "Daddy" (*CP* 222–24) is the elegy of a daughter who is tormented by the lingering presence of her deceased father, a presence vivid enough to haunt her but too elusive to come to terms with.[36] The poem can also be read as a commentary on memory: it dramatizes the process by which personal memory is gradually swallowed and replaced by collective modes of memory. By exposing the subtle interventions of collective memory, Plath uncovers how subjective or poetic memory tends to be thwarted. The more personal historic memory fails, the further collective memory penetrates the speaker's mind. Because the poem represents the development of her mnemonic struggles, my reading will follow the stanzas in consecutive order.

Imitating the tone and motifs of nursery rhymes, the speaker proclaims she has lived life meekly, as if trapped in a "black shoe":

> You do not do, you do not do
> Any more, black shoe
> In which I have lived like a foot
> For thirty years, poor and white,
> Barely daring to breathe or Achoo.

This oppressed existence is over, she declares, and instead of "Barely daring to breathe or Achoo," she finally speaks out. Accordingly, the tone drastically changes in the next stanza: "Daddy, I have had to kill you. / You died before I had time—." The innocent tone of the playfully and simplistically rhyming first stanza ("you," "do," "shoe," "Achoo") is dramatically contrasted with the statement of an already accomplished murder. The speaker does not threaten to kill "daddy"; she informs him that the killing has already occurred. The paradox of speaking to somebody dead is resolved when "killing daddy" is read as killing her memory of him. In a reminiscing tone, the speaker proceeds to recapitulate past events, possibly the events leading to the "killing." Rhetorically, the poem becomes a confession and, indirectly, an apology.

The line "You died before I had time—" is semantically incomplete. Plath does not say what the speaker wanted more time for. She may have lacked time to know "Daddy" or to consolidate her memory of him. Literally, he may have died before she could psychologically and historically anchor her life in time. The father registered in her memory as a quasimythical, timeless figure, a "Ghastly statue with one gray toe / Big as a Frisco seal // And a head in the freakish Atlantic."

The speaker has undertaken considerable efforts to remember "daddy": "I used to pray to recover you." Plath puns on "recover," a verb that can also mean to "cover up again." This secondary meaning is reinforced by the "head in the freakish Atlantic," which the sea threatens to submerge any moment. The speaker insinuates that she tries to forget the father as much as she desires to remember him. This reading is supported by a similar image in the poem "Words," where the infliction of pain on the psyche is compared to a lake whose surface is broken by a rock that the water tries to close again:

> Water striving
> To re-establish its mirror
> Over the rock
>
> That drops and turns,
> A white skull,
> Eaten by weedy greens.
> (CP 270)

In this poem, the equivalent of the "head" in "Daddy" is the "rock," which at second sight turns out to be a head in decay, a "white skull, / Eaten by weedy greens." Regardless of whether the speaker in "Daddy" wants to "retrieve" or "cover" the head, remember or forget him, both fail, and she is haunted by almost-memories or half-amnesias.

Collective memory, instead of helping her to remember the father, only distorts the speaker's ideas of him further.

> In the German tongue, in the Polish town
> Scraped flat by the roller
> Of wars, wars, wars.
> But the name of the town is common.
> My Polack friend

> Says there are a dozen or two.
> So I never could tell where you
> Put your foot, your root,
> I never could talk to you.
> The tongue stuck in my jaw.

The war disfigured the German language, which was the father's mother tongue, and disqualifies it as a possible access to him. We should note in this context Plath's incessant efforts to learn German.[37] Plath enumerates the terms that are associated with National Socialism and that contaminated the language: "barb wire snare," "Dachau, Auschwitz, Belsen," "Luftwaffe," "Aryan eye, bright blue," "Panzer-man," "swastika," and "Fascist." Trying to speak "daddy's" language makes the poet's "tongue" stick in the "jaw," a word onomatopoetically sounding the tone of muffled speech. The war also deprived places of their distinctiveness, and the name of the "Polish town," which is the father's home town, is "too common." The speaker cannot reconstruct the father's past: "So I could never tell where you / Put your foot, your root." Ironically, collective memory erased the memory of the father instead of, as it had always claimed, preserving it.

In a space and language flattened out, homogenized by collective memory, it is difficult to assert subjectivity: "Ich, ich, ich, ich, / I could hardly speak." The speaker's subjectivity put at risk, her memory too becomes precarious, and she starts filling the lacunae with commonplaces and overgeneralizations: "I thought every German was you." As the father is turned into a cliché, the speaker's subjectivity too becomes increasingly unstable and stereotypical:

> An engine, an engine
> Chuffing me off like a Jew.
> A Jew to Dachau, Auschwitz, Belsen.
> I began to talk like a Jew.
> I think I may well be a Jew.

She becomes the Nazi's counterpart, a Jew who, Derrida writes, "is the other who has no essence, who has nothing of his own or whose essence is not to have one."[38] The speaker's subjectivity depends on the father's, her memory needs his. Deprived of both, she disfigures him and herself by projecting stereotypes from the stocks of popular collective memory.

A photograph triggers memories of the father as a teacher:

> You stand at the blackboard, daddy,
> In the picture I have of you,
> A cleft in your chin instead of your foot
> But no less a devil for that, no not
> Any less the black man who
> Bit my pretty red heart in two.

Strikingly, the father's picture does not produce any personal memories of him. He continues to be projected as a person in a role and in an office. He is also a figure overdetermined by myth, fairy tales, and gothic fiction. The furious daughter vilifies him as the "devil," the "black man," and as a cannibal hungry for her heart. On one hand, "daddy" is the victim of the daughter's assault, but on the other hand, he, as a teacher, was responsible for the dissemination of collective memory in the first place. Killing "daddy" by distorting his memory through a grotesque assortment of stereotypes, the speaker defeats him by means of his own teaching.

First, the speaker relates, she turned her difficulty remembering into suicidal aggression against herself: "I was ten when they buried you. / At twenty I tried to die / and get back, back, back to you. / I thought even the bones would do." The poem references the "bone" motif, emblematic of the mnemonic strategies pursued in "Full Fathom Five" and "The Colossus." Eventually, she started to attack him who can be neither remembered nor forgotten:

> But they pulled me out of the sack,
> And they stuck me together with glue.
> And then I knew what to do.
> I made a model of you,
> A man in black with a Meinkampf look
>
> And a love of the rack and the screw.

What could be interpreted as the subject's defeat—after all, her memories of the father are horrible now—is staged as her triumph:

> So daddy, I'm finally through.
> The black telephone's off at the root,
> The voices just can't worm through.
>
> If I've killed one man, I've killed two—
> The vampire who said he was you
> And drank my blood for a year,

Seven years, if you want to know.
Daddy, you can lie back now.

There's a stake in your fat black heart
And the villagers never liked you.
They are dancing and stamping on you.
They always *knew* it was you.
Daddy, daddy, you bastard, I'm through.

The speaker seizes the most horrific elements of popular collective memory to smash the remaining fragments of her personal memory. She implies that the loss of memory can be both: the defeat of the subject, but also her only survival strategy. Projecting the father as a Nazi and life-sucking vampire keeps his otherwise haunting and overpowering mnemonic force at a distance. Exaggerating the intrusions of collective memory allows the speaker both to protest their assaultive nature and to detach from a past that eludes her. Outdoing the horrors of collective memory is a way of undoing them and asserting poetic memory.

The speaker prefers horrible memories to vague memories, and the substitution is legitimated by the community. This means adjusting her feelings to those of the "villagers," who "never liked . . . [him]." A passage from the *Journals* in which Plath outlines her story "The Shadow" parallels the pressure "the villagers" exercise on the speaker's memory. Stronger than the daughter's relation to the father, in this story, is the community's influence on her. The father is scapegoated by the daughter in response to the scapegoating he suffers from the community: "My present theme seems to be the awareness of a complicated guilt system whereby Germans in a Jewish and Catholic community are made to feel, in scapegoat fashion, the pain, psychically, the Jews are made to feel in Germany by Germans without religion. The child can't understand the larger framework. How does her father come into this? How is she guilty for her father's deportation to a detention camp?" (*J* 453). Having participated in the collective "guilt system" by rejecting the father, the speaker is finally allowed to forget: "So daddy, I'm finally through. / The black telephone's off at the root. / The voices just can't worm through." By allowing her personal memory to be swallowed by the collective and by transforming it into something hateful and appalling, she is provided the excuse for killing it: "There's a stake in your fat black heart." "Daddy" is a Nazi, devil, vampire all at once, and everybody would applaud, not punish, the one who "killed" him.

"Daddy" enacts the process of "working through," a Freudian concept of psychological healing that Plath perhaps alludes to in the lines "So daddy, I'm finally through" and "The cries just can't worm through." In psychoanalytic theory, trauma can only be overcome if, through narration, the victim exposes herself once again to the events that caused the trauma. This is arguably the case in "Daddy" where the speaker kills the father in narrative after his actual death had occurred a long time ago. The paradox, however, is how to live through or work through traumatic experiences again if trauma, by definition, is that which escapes memory and representation. Accordingly, Plath's speaker in "Daddy" cannot successfully reproduce the trauma because it occurred before the speaker "had time." Memory, as Halbwachs would agree, requires time as a collective framework to secure it. Mourning too is impeded by the absence of memories. Plath seems to mock the possibility of healing: making "a model" of "daddy" and creating a narrative do not allow the speaker to make peace with the past; rather, "daddy" is projected as evil and then rejected as other.

As in "The Colossus," Plath also parodies Modernist poetics in "Daddy." Eliot describes the poet's mind as "a receptacle for seizing and storing up numberless feelings, phrases, images, which remain there until all the particles which can unite to form a new compound are present together."[39] Posing as a studious disciple of the Modernists, the speaker does indeed form the memory of "daddy" as a "new compound" from "numberless feelings, phrases, images" taken from different registers of literary, historical, and popular memory. Applying Eliot's theory of poetic creation with sardonic devotion in "Daddy," Plath pushes this principle of Modernist aesthetics to gruesome extremes.

RAISING THE PHOENIX

In "Lady Lazarus," Plath brazenly uses the performative mode to claim space for the personal and the subjective. All concern for the father's memory has vanished, and the speaker engages in deliberate, theatrical self-fashioning. "Lady Lazarus" is the star of a one-woman show. At the heart of her performance, she exaggerates, exceeds, outdoes, and thereby attempts to master the predetermination of the self through the invasive influence of collective varieties of memory. She has the beaming lights of a stage shine on the practice of poetic memory. Her art, as that of her biblical name-giver, is to rise from death:

> I have done it again.
> One year in every ten
> I manage it—
>
> A sort of walking miracle, my skin
> Bright as a Nazi lampshade,
> My right foot
>
> A paperweight,
> My face a featureless, fine
> Jew linen.
>
> Peel off the napkin
> O my enemy.
> Do I terrify?—
>
> The nose, the eye pits, the full set of teeth?
> The sour breath
> Will vanish in a day.
>
> Soon, soon the flesh
> The grave cave ate will be
> At home on me
>
> And I a smiling woman.
> I am only thirty.
> And like the cat I have nine times to die.
>
> This is Number Three.
> What a trash
> To annihilate each decade.

The speaker addresses us in the immediate aftermath of her rebirth; she has "done it again." Her tone is proud and assertive: after all, she is a "walking miracle." Her resuscitation is so fresh, her features still bear the traces of death, represented by Holocaust images: her color of skin is "Bright as a Nazi lampshade," her "right foot" a "paperweight," and her "face" a "featureless, fine / Jew linen." As if this were a magician's show in which the magician pulls off the cloth to reveal the magic he performed, the speaker commands her "enemy" to "Peel off the napkin."

The victim is in charge, and the perpetrator is her auxiliary. Her success is too horrible to be spelled out, and it is represented by the dashes following the rhetorical question: "Do I terrify? —." What the napkin, once removed, reveals is "The nose, the eye pits, the full set of teeth." She sardonically soothes her, she hopes, horror-struck "enemy" by pointing out that "Soon, soon the flesh" that "The grave cave ate will be / At home on me." The first act of the show is over, and she stands as "a smiling woman," "only thirty." Despite her proud and imperious manner, the speaker is also aware that her show has a price: "What a trash / to annihilate each decade."

The violent intimacy between the speaker and "her enemy" is interrupted by the audience's admission to the show. Once the "peanut-crunching crowd" has "shoved in," her "hand and foot" are "unwrapped." The act of "peeling off the napkin" becomes a "big strip tease," and the setting changes from a "magic" Nazi laboratory into a peep show for the masses. The speaker is now magician and assistant in one person and proclaims:

> Gentlemen, ladies
>
> These are my hands
> My knees.
> I may be skin and bone,
>
> Nevertheless, I am the same identical woman.

Although visibly marked by the strenuous art of dying and coming back to life, she asserts she is the same self. Peeling off layers of identity does not change who she is.

Posing as an expert in dying, the speaker, from stanza 15 on, gives an account of her *ars moriendi* — however, not in philosophical terms but in advertising style. As if the poem were her personal marketing slogan, she uses excessive anaphoras and rhymes in short, syntactically identical sentences:

> Dying
> Is an art, like everything else.
> I do it exceptionally well.
>
> I do it so it feels like hell.
> I do it so it feels real.

I guess you could say I've a call.

It's easy enough to do it in a cell.
It's easy enough to do it and stay put.
It's the theatrical

Comeback in broad day
To the same place, the same face, the same brute
Amused shout:

'A miracle!'
That knocks me out.

Dying is not something to be invented; it is something to be repeated. The speaker does not lay claims to originality but distinguishes herself by doing dying "exceptionally well." Due to her experience and expertise, her "art" is good enough to put up in a show.

Plath confuses the binarism of authenticity versus acting by depicting the speaker both as a specimen from a Nazi laboratory and as a stripper performing for a crowd. The reader grows uncertain whether to interpret her account as sincere—after all, the comparison to a Nazi victim holds a moral imperative—or as rhetorical.[40] Plath jokes about the way the sacred is made profane or traumatic experience is trivialized. The speaker insists on being real: "These are my hands / My knees. I may be skin and bone, // Nevertheless, I am the same, identical woman." She also has scars and a heart that "really goes." Although she undergoes a dramatic transformation, dies and is reborn, she comes back to a scene that has remained completely unaffected. It is "the same place, the same face, the same brute / Amused shout: // 'A miracle!' / That knocks me out" (*CP* 246). The crowd reacts in conventional ways and calls Lady Lazarus, in analogy to biblical Lazarus, a "miracle." They take the speaker's "reality show" for an act. Promoted by a culture of mass entertainment, Lady Lazarus's painfully real art of dying must be perceived as a showpiece. But the speaker refuses the audience their comfortable disbelief and will make them pay for their voyeuristic pleasure. As if her body were a souvenir stand vending items from the show, she demands a "large charge" for "the eyeing of . . . [her] scars," "for the hearing of . . . [her] heart," for "a word or a touch / Or a bit of blood // Or a piece of . . . [her] hair or . . . [her] clothes."

Lady Lazarus is both harmed and sustained by her audience's mis-interpretation of her art as a show. She hopes the public will redeem her *ars moriendi* by acknowledging its "reality" value. Yet to justify her contempt for the crowd and remain the only heroine, she needs them to demonstrate their vulgar appetites. Presenting herself as startled by the crowd's incomprehension ("'A miracle!' / That knocks me out."), the speaker mocks her desire to exhibit herself and receive the audience's recognition and sympathy. Unlike Lazarus, she does not count on a male god to help her come alive and must rely on her own resources to effectuate her rebirth.

Having dismissed her ignorant audience, the speaker, in the third part of the poem, turns back to "Herr Enemy." He is "concerned" for his "opus," his "valuable," his "pure gold baby," whom he can expose and sell to the world. The speaker plots her revenge:

> So, so, Herr Doktor.
> So, Herr Enemy.
>
> I am your opus,
> I am your valuable,
> The pure gold baby
>
> That melts to a shriek.
> I turn and burn.
> Do not think I underestimate your great concern.
>
> Ash, ash—
> You poke and stir.
> Flesh, bone, there is nothing there—
>
> A cake of soap,
> A wedding ring,
> A gold filling.
>
> Herr God, Herr Lucifer
> Beware
> Beware.
>
> Out of the ash
> I rise with my red hair
> And I eat men like air.

She will disappear under an outrageous combination of cliché images drawn from the Holocaust ("ash," "cake of soap," "wedding ring," "gold filling"), gothic fiction (the "pure gold baby" uncannily transforms into a "shriek" and burns to "ash"), and the gender-oppressive soap operas ("cake of soap") typical of postwar American commercial culture. She will stop being Herr Doktor's "opus" and, by becoming something else, destroy him. She projects herself as the Phoenix rising from his own ashes. Her "red hair" evokes the colorful bird but also endows her with witchlike traits, and the witch's magic will turn "Herr God" and "Herr Lucifer" into nothingness, into "air," which can be obliterated in a breath.

Plath strikes the registers of historical, popular, and cultural memory to meld images of the Holocaust, theater, eroticism, gothic fiction, consumer and mass culture, the Bible, and classical mythology into a ghastly self-projection. Lady Lazarus, Harriet L. Parmet points out, takes on many partial identities suited to what the audience desires:

> Lady Lazarus is a different person for each of her audiences, and yet none of her identities is bearable for her. For the Nazi Doktor, she is a Jew, whose body must be burned; for the "peanut-crunching crowd," she is a stripteaser; for the medical audience, she is a wonder, whose scars and heartbeat are astonishing; for the religious audience, she is a miraculous figure, whose hair and clothes are as valuable as saints' relics. And when she turns to her audience in the middle of the poem to describe her career in suicide, she becomes a self-conscious performer.[41]

The various guises the speaker adopts are all traditionally female roles: actress, victim, stripper, object of sexual desire, victim of physical abuse.[42] The woman in the poem is a male construction. Instead of creating social and historical contexts to exteriorize Lady Lazarus's inner struggles, as Parmet suggests,[43] Plath enacts Lady Lazarus's appropriation by different strands of collective memory. The poem unmasks contemporary subjectivity as the gruesome "opus" of postwar American culture. The repetition of the speaker's death—she claims she is dying nine times—demonstrates her failure to acquire a sense of self. The absence of subjectivity, which is a taboo in a culture fetishizing the individual, is pulled into the beaming lights of a stage. Yet the stage also has the power to transform the "opus" or object into an agent and a subject. The speaker's fragmentation through the projection of many partial identities becomes a strategy for survival[44]: if one "self" dies, there are others to take its place. In "Lady Lazarus," the speaker turns the malleability of her selfhood, induced and then exploited by Herr Doktor and Herr Enemy, against her creators; she translates her vulnerability to being shaped into many selves into an "art of dying"—which is also an art of resurrection: "Out of the ash" she will "rise with . . . [her] red hair / And . . . eat men like air." It is through performance, through the act of staging multiple identities, stripping some off and taking others on, that the speaker is at all able to acquire a self.

Plath exceeds the confines of collective memory through parody and achieves this parodic effect by means of what Judith Butler calls the "subversive repetition of . . . style."[45] Butler's argument depends on three assertions that are also relevant for Plath's practice of poetic memory. First, gender identity is a repetition of acts, and can therefore be changed when the acts are changed. "If the ground of gender identity is the stylized repetition of acts through time, and not a seemingly seamless identity," Butler writes, "then the possibilities of gender transformation are to be found in the arbitrary relation between such acts, in the possibility of a different sort of repeating, in the breaking or subversive repetition of that style."[46] Second, these acts of gender constitution are not devised by the individual, but have a history and are collectively recognized. In Butler's words, "The act that gender is, the act that embodied agents are inasmuch as they dramatically and actively embody and, indeed *wear* certain cultural significations, is clearly no one's act alone."[47] Third, the meaning of these acts depends on the sociopolitical context of their enactment and on whether they are perceived as part of a show or as part of reality. A transvestite, which Butler offers as an example, will not be minded on a stage but may shock some of us on a bus.[48]

There are several instances of conjunction between poetic subjectivity and Butler's ideas about gender constitution. Butler suggests that the acts by which a person constructs her or his gender are not her or his invention, but are acts that have existed before and that are performed by many others. In "Daddy" and "Lady Lazarus," the speaker's subjectivity does not depend on personal memory but on the clichés of collective memory. Gender acts cannot be abolished or reinvented, but they can be subverted through "a different sort of repeating." A different repetition is realized by *decontextualizing* these acts and by putting them into an *arbitrary relation* to each other. Plath decontextualizes by transplanting popular registers and the "cruder" idioms of public discourses into poetry. In

the place of the benignly musing persona of poetic convention, she sub-
stitutes a subject who risks her own disintegration when exposing the
contrary influences that lay claims on her subjectivity. The voice of the
raging "I" in both "Daddy" and "Lady Lazarus" is unheard of in "wom-
en's poetry." "Daddy" overthrows the conventions of the elegy by com-
memorating the father as a Nazi and a vampire.[49] Butler's "performative
acts" figure literally in "Lady Lazarus" who really is a performer and
whose performance is the topic of the poem. Lady Lazarus's act is decon-
textualized because she performs on stage what ethically and convention-
ally does not belong there: actual dying. Performative acts are put into
arbitrary relation—the second mode of achieving a "different sort of re-
peating"—when Plath's speaker in "Daddy" draws eclectically on collec-
tive memory to reconstruct the memory of the father and when in "Lady
Lazarus" she assumes antagonistic identities, such as the dying martyr
and the resurrected Phoenix, the victim and the avenger, Herr Doktor's
"opus" and the self-generative "red hair." Butler claims that decontextu-
alized and arbitrarily related performances aim at subverting gender. I
suggest that Plath also employs performance to unmask the constant
interference of collective memory with the expression of subjectivity. Her
concern is not only with how people become men and women, but also
with whether they can constitute themselves as subjects. Not by means of
what they say but of *how* they say, the poems hint at the possibility of
personal memory and subjectivity. They commemorate their speakers'
performative resistance to collective memory and store the memory of its
impaired authority.

RELEASING THE WORDS

"Words" (*CP* 270) presents the reader with a remarkably less combative
speaker. The preceding poems laid open the conflictual process by which
collective memory, by means of worded images, becomes constitutive of
the speaker's subjectivity; the "I" in "Words" is a mere facilitator, only an
observer of the flow of words.[50] The poem is imagistic: in short, free verse
lines, avoiding abstraction and generalization, it presents a flux of com-
pelling imagery. By the very act of being submerged in the flow of
worded images, the speaker manifests her greater detachment from
them.

Words

Axes
After whose stroke the wood rings,
And the echoes!
Echoes traveling
Off from the center like horses.

The sap
Wells like tears, like the
Water striving
To re-establish its mirror
Over the rock

That drops and turns,
A white skull,
Eaten by weedy greens.
Years later I
Encounter them on the road—

Words dry and riderless,
The indefatigable hoof-taps.
While
From the bottom of the pool, fixed stars
Govern a life.

The imagistic sequence of the poem begins with a tree struck by axes, thereby emitting sounds, or more precisely "echoes," reminiscent of horses "traveling / Off." The wound of the tree bark produces "sap" or resin, which is compared to tears. As a tree covers its wounds with "sap" and the psyche its wounds with "tears," a lake tries to "re-establish" its mirror surface after being struck not by an axe but by a rock. The speaker imagines how the rock "drops"—probably to the bottom of the lake—and "turns." The subject disappears or drowns and, at second sight, the "rock" turns out to be a decaying "white skull." The speaker uses "I" for the first time when reencountering the "echoes" and "horses" she described in the first stanza "years later." The concepts of words and horses remain mended in the images: they are "encountered" on "the road," they are "dry and riderless," but still move in the form of "indefatigable hoof-taps." From the perspective of the "bottom of the pool," the speaker's restlessness gives way to calm and serenity when observing that "fixed stars / Govern a life."

The speaker is strikingly independent from her words. The poem is framed by the speaker's literalized encounters with language, compared to "horses" that, at the beginning, "travel off from the center" and that "years later" are encountered again, "dry and riderless." No subject sends them out on their travels, no subject intends to capture them "on the road." Whereas in the poems discussed previously the speaker took highly emotional stances toward having to speak in a language not her own, this speaker almost indifferently, even serenely, lets go of any attempt to direct or control the words. Words and worded images move, merge, and morph on their own behalf, possibly "governed" only by "fixed stars."

Language, Plath implies, has its origin in a wound inflicted by an axe stroke. The metaphor of the axe stroke can be interpreted as a traumatic blow after which the "wood rings" and sends forth "echoes." Plath puns on "wood rings," which can be read as a noun plus verb signifying the sound wood gives off on being struck, or it can form a nominal group and refer to tree rings as symbols of memory accumulated by the tree over the years. Thus, she associates the origin of words with memory. The stroke not only makes the wood ring, but also memory itself. Interestingly, Plath does not speak of "words" traveling off, but of "echoes." The echoes are the result of the wound; they merely echo the stroke. Words, too, then are only echoes, sounds that remember their first enunciation. Words are traces, they are poetic memories, not the thing itself. This reading is supported by associating the term *echo* with Greek mythology: Echo is a nymph who loved Narcissus but was shunned by him and pined away until nothing but her voice remained. An echo is the remaining trace of unrequited love. Echoes and words are what is left after the fateful blow. Being characterized as "indefatigable hoof-taps" in the final stanza, the words last and will be reencountered as the remains and the reminders of the initial wound.

The words "travel off," drawn associatively toward literary memory, and again, the speaker finds herself remembering and borrowing from other texts. "Words" echoes Plath's earlier poem "Full Fathom Five," H.D.'s "Oread," and a passage from Shakespeare's *King Lear*. The skull on the bottom of the lake is reminiscent of the "father's bones" on the bottom of the sea in "Full Fathom Five," an image, as elaborated before, parodying the "coral and pearl" in Shakespeare's *Tempest*. From H.D.'s

Imagist poem "Oread,"[51] Plath borrows the figurative "skeleton" of her poem, that is, the motifs of tree, sea, and rock.

Oread

Whirl up, sea —
whirl your pointed pines,
splash your great pines
on our rocks,
hurl your green over us,
cover us with your pools of fir.

Similar images are connoted differently in the two poems. While H.D. invokes the violent, primordial force of the sea, Plath attributes to water a healing and protective function: it attempts to cover the breach in the tree bark and reestablish the surface of the lake over the rock. Interestingly, H.D. incorporates the "pine" or "fir" into the image of the sea. The tree-related projection of the sea could emphasize the grandeur and pointed-ness of the waves, or the word *pine* could relate to Echo's "pining away"; it is phonetically close to *pain*. *Fir* only misses the letter *e* to make *fire*. Consequently, and contrary to the water in "Words," the sea in H.D.'s poem would be the element bringing about emotional intensity. In Plath's poem, the pool is, like the well, rather an image for the psyche. It hides a skull on its bottom, which may be a symbol of *memento mori*, a reminder of the inevitability of death, an event both remembered and anticipated.

Alluding to Shakespeare's *King Lear*, Plath concludes the poem with an image of serene though inscrutable order: "From the bottom of the pool, fixed stars / Govern a life." This line rephrases a passage from the drama in which Kent says: "It is the stars, / The stars above us govern our conditions" (4.3.33–34). Kent's is one of three positions that Shakespeare presents when he has his characters struggle with the tragedy of human life caused by lack of judgment, immaturity, and the passions, and when debating the greater question of the relationship between humans and gods. Contrary to Kent, whose position Plath embraces, Gloucester believes that humans are simply the gods' toys ("As flies to wanton boys are we to the gods, / They kill us for their sport," 4.1.38–39), and Edmund holds that man is the only master of his fate ("An admirable evasion of / Whoremaster man, to lay his goatish disposition on the / charge of a star," 1.2.126–28). Echoing Kent, Plath chooses the most optimistic of the three, adopting neither the view of man being at the mercy of irresponsible gods nor of his utter aloneness, but putting forward her confidence in the existence of a godly principle that, to humans, remains unintelligible.[52]

The poem concludes on an optimistic note. The strike that both the tree and the pond suffer and that first only lays bare a rotting skull, finally also permits a glimpse of the well's hidden treasure. If the psyche has previously been compared to a lake broken up by pain and disclosing a skull, it is now filled with "stars." The words' ride contrasts with the fixity of the stars, but it is the speaker's skill with words that allows her to fathom and represent the stars in the end. The fixed stars of the psyche may be a reflection of the stars in the sky and purport a connection between the self and the universe.

"Words" is a meditation on language as the carrier of literary but also of poetic memory. It investigates the origin of words and characterizes them as "echoes" sounding from a wound in memory. Although intimately connected to the subject's past, they "travel off" "riderless," as if the subject had temporarily forgotten their significance. She has no control over their effect in the world. Other modes of language or memory insert themselves, here in the form of Plath's allusions to H.D. and Shakespeare. However, instead of contending with such imposition as in "Daddy" or "Lady Lazarus," the speaker is reconciled by her belief in an inscrutable order. The subject emerges through language but realizes her distinctiveness from it. Collective memory intervenes, but by recognizing such intervention, the poetic subject can possess and control it rather than be possessed and controlled by it.

Many writers well into the twentieth century would have subscribed to Augustine's formulation of the relationship between memory and subjectivity in his *Confessions*: "In my memory I meet myself."[53] Plath would have to rewrite that phrase as "In my memory, I meet an other." Memory is a faculty that is never one's own, that is both immanent and detached, subjective and collective. Halbwachs evaluates the predominance of the collective elements in a person's memory in neutral terms. Plath, however, dramatizes the impingement of collective on personal elements in memory, and this is a version of the conflicting tendencies of poetic and historic memory.

Strikingly, personal memory remains precarious in a poetry often reduced to its biographical appeal. If anything is *not* remembered in the poems, it is the purely subjective. Subjectivity cannot escape the always already existing mnemonic fusion of personal and collective elements. Subjectivity does not emanate from the invention of "styles" but from their rearrangement and their "subversive repetition," in Butler's sense. Plath asserts poetic memory, the intimations of a self truer than the historically transmitted and verbally accessible self, through the exaggerated parodic performance of collective memory. Historic memory is led ad absurdum by revealing its collaboration with by collective memory. If the poems do not primarily feed on personal memory, their categorization as "confessional" becomes questionable. The poems are "personal" only insofar as they depict a subject's confrontation with her inner otherness.

Plath not only problematizes the possibility of representing subjectivity as such, she also challenges the *poem*'s capacity to do so. If collective memory predetermines subjectivity, literary memory predetermines the poem. Poems reference the tropes, diction, and poetic form of other poems, and we read poems in the convention of the genre. Plath unsettles our literary expectations when, for example, confronting us excessively with a persona very different from the lyrical "I" of romantic poetry, which speaks to us in sincere and contemplative ways. Her poems not only reiterate but change and expand the body of literary memory. The poem and memory condition one another in their genesis: the poem draws on memory to come into existence, and memory draws on the poem to be altered and extended.

Although both have their roots in Modernism, Sylvia Plath and Susan Howe have been classified by literary critics as belonging to essentially different strands of American poetry writing—"confessional" versus "objectivist," "formalist" versus "experimentalist." But once the personal element in Plath's poetry is devalued and recognized as much less prominent than the history of her reception makes one believe, the picture changes. If Plath reveals the continuous interference of collective memory in her poems, Howe will make it a deliberate and invaluable part of her poetics. Howe is not concerned with adapting other voices into her own writing but lets them stand for themselves. The experimental poet who throws the formal norms of poetry overboard will also dramatically alter the guises of memory in poetry.

NOTES

1. Plath scholarship of the past forty years has roughly revolved around three main positions: considering her poems as autobiographical; reading the texts independently from biography, although biography may serve as the point of poetic departure; or, particularly in recent studies, focusing on sociopolitical and historical influences. In the same order, these positions have been argued, among others, by A. Alvarez, Jacqueline Rose, and Tracy Brain. Such arguments often failed to account for the dialectics between the individual and the greater cultural context, which the concepts of personal and collective memory will help to elucidate.

2. Maurice Halbwachs, *On Collective Memory*, ed. and trans. Lewis A. Coser (Chicago: University of Chicago Press, 1992). The book was first published as *Les cadres sociaux de la mémoire* (Paris: Librairie Alcan, 1925).

3. Sylvia Plath, *The Bell Jar*, 1963 (New York: Harper and Row, 1971), 165.

4. Ibid., 145.

5. Klaus Benesch, Jon-K. Adams, and Kerstin Schmidt, eds., *The Sea and the American Imagination* (Tübingen, Germany: Stauffenburg Verlag, 2004), 11.

6. John Peck, *Maritime Fiction: Sailors and the Sea in British and American Novels, 1719–1917* (Houndmills, UK: Palgrave, 2001), 94.

7. Paul Ricoeur, *La Mémoire, l'histoire, l'oubli* (Paris: Editions du Seuil, 2000), 140. "Or, c'est lui finalement le vrai souvenir, si, comme je le crois, l'expérience temporelle fondamentale est celle de la distance et celle de la profondeur temporelle." (So this is finally the true memory if, as I believe, the fundamental experience of time is that of distance and of temporal depth [my translation].)

8. Sabine Sielke, "'Rowing in Eden' and Related Waterway Adventures: Seaward Visions in American Women's Writing," in *Sea and the American Imagination*, 111–34.

9. Emily Dickinson, *The Complete Poems*, ed. Thomas H. Johnson (New York: Little, Brown, 1960), 359.

10. Marcel Proust, *Remembrance of Things Past. Vol. 1. Swann's Way*, trans. C. K. Scott Moncrieff and Terence Kilmartin (New York: Random House, 1981), 49.

11. Ibid., 50.

12. Ibid., 51.

13. William Shakespeare, *The Tempest* (London: Penguin, 1968), 78.

14. Christina Britzolakis, *Sylvia Plath and the Theatre of Mourning* (Oxford: Oxford University Press, 1999), 48.

15. Ibid., 41.

16. Halbwachs, 38.

17. Ibid.

18. Gaston Bachelard, *The Poetics of Reverie: Childhood, Language, and the Cosmos*, trans. Daniel Russell (Boston: Beacon Press, 1969), 99.

19. Although the conflict between personal and collective memory also comes to bear on a sociological level in the poem, it exists predominantly between the poet's memory and literary memory. Extrapolating from Halbwachs, who claims that the memory of the individual is dependent on the memory of the group, the poet's memory would be dependent on literary memory. *Literary memory* is a term that I suggest to designate specifically the literary portion of collective memory. Memory researchers have begun to differentiate the broad concept of *collective memory*, which may evoke inappropriate associations of totalization and comprehensiveness and which is mis-

leading by suggesting that memory is carried by groups rather than by individuals. Aleida Assmann suggests that we distinguish between social, political, and cultural memory and thereby demarcate a sense of the smaller and greater collectivities that share memories. Social memory refers to the memory of families and circles of friends and the memory of a specific generation. Political memory is not dependent on the remembering individual but is already transformed into materialized symbolic representation and therefore has greater longevity. As a mode of *top-down* memory investigated and initiated by political institutions, it differs from the *bottom-up* mode of social memory. Cultural memory transcends the temporal scope of the other memory formats and, as Assmann writes, "disconnect[s] them from individuals, groups and institutions that were once its carriers and reconnects them with an open community of readers." Aleida Assmann, "Four Formats of Memory: From Individual to Collective Constructions of the Past" (paper presented at Yale University, April 16, 2003). This paper has also been published in German: "Vier Formen des Gedächtnisses," *Erwägen, Wissen, Ethik* 13, no. 2 (2002): 183–90.

20. Halbwachs, 53.

21. Ibid., 172.

22. T. S. Eliot, "Tradition and the Individual Talent," in *Selected Essays* (New York: Harcourt, Brace and World, 1960), 3–4.

23. Pamela J. Annas, *A Disturbance in Mirrors: The Poetry of Sylvia Plath* (New York: Greenwood Press, 1988), 33.

24. Britzolakis, 64.

25. Steven Gould Axelrod reads the image of the colossus as "a monumental image of patriarchal poetry." Steven Gould Axelrod, *Sylvia Plath: The Wound and the Cure of Words* (Baltimore: Johns Hopkins University Press, 1990), 47–50.

26. Virginia Woolf, *A Room of One's Own* (New York: Harcourt, 1929), 76.

27. Axelrod, 35–40.

28. Eliot, "Tradition and the Individual Talent," 6.

29. In her struggle to improve her knowledge and memory of the (male) literary canon, Plath projects Hughes as her link to it. She writes to her mother that "Ted has me memorizing a poem a day, which is very good for me." Sylvia Plath, *Letters Home: Correspondence 1950–1963*, ed. Aurelia Schober Plath (New York: Harper Collins, 1975), 289.

30. Ralph Waldo Emerson, "The American Scholar," in *Emerson's Prose and Poetry*, Norton Critical Edition, ed. Joel Porte and Saundra Morris (New York: Norton, 2001), 59.

31. Plath, *Letters Home*, 293.

32. Woolf, 56.

33. Ibid., 97.

34. Ralph Waldo Emerson, "Circles," in *Emerson's Prose and Poetry*, 174–75.

35. Eliot, *Complete Poems and Plays*, 37.

36. My reading of "Daddy" as a memory poem offers an alternative to earlier biographical interpretations that raised the question of how the poet's assault on her father as a Nazi could be justified, if Otto Plath had nothing to do with National Socialism and left Europe well before its rise. A. Alvarez and M. L. Rosenthal accused Plath of using disproportionate means for the representation of (merely) personal anguish. These critics were opposed by feminists who felt that the Nazi imagery was an appropriate means of representing patriarchal oppression. See A. Alvarez, "Sylvia Plath," *Beyond All This Fiddle: Essays 1955–1967* (London: Allen Lane, 1968), 46–57; M.

L. Rosenthal, *The New Poets: American and British Poetry Since World War II* (London and New York: Oxford University Press, 1967). For an overview of the poem's reception and a third, nonbiographical point of view, see Jacqueline Rose, *The Haunting of Sylvia Plath* (London: Virago, 1991).

37. Numerous passages in Plath's *Journals* give evidence of her wish and constant efforts to learn German: "I am enjoying myself with a great lessening of worry: the dregs of dissatisfaction with myself: not writing enough, not working hard, not reading hard, studying German—are things I can do if I want & will do. It is the hate, the paralyzing fear, that gets in my way and stops me. Once that is worked clear of, I will flow" (*J* 441). "My projects falter. I will go from now on to the library and read for four hours every afternoon: no phone, no visitors. That will give me peace. Will study German. This is a main wish and concern" (*J* 464). "It is as if I have been pushing myself so hard for so many years, I am slack once the outer demand is gone, resting only, I hope. Then to work on German and French" (*J* 470). As a high school student, Plath maintained a four- to five-year correspondence with a German pen pal named Hans-Joachim Neuport. Copies of the letters are at the Plath archive at Smith College. See also Langdon Hammer, "Plath's German" (paper presented at the Sylvia Plath 75th Year Symposium at Oxford University, Oxford, October 28, 2007).

38. Rose, *Haunting of Sylvia Plath*, 217. Rose refers to Jacques Derrida's essay on Paul Celan to argue that the comparison of the lyrical *I* with a Jew does not imply the same suffering, but a similar lack of identity. Derrida writes, "The Jew is also the other, myself and the other; I am Jewish in saying: the Jew is the other who has no essence, who has nothing of his own or whose essence is not to have one."

39. Eliot, "Tradition and the Individual Talent," 8.

40. Mutlu Konuk Blasing comments on Plath's confusion of acting and authenticity when calling Plath's "concept of her own voice . . . problematic. . . . In one sense, she sounds from the beginning a distinctive voice and articulates a distinctive set of preoccupations; in another sense, however, her voice is always already distanced, and her changes are changes only in the masks she assumes in exile. In her earlier work, these masks tend to be the voices of other poets; in the later work, they tend to be the voices of the poetic mechanism itself. Indeed, Plath appears to think of her own voice in rather literal terms—as literally a voice that internalizes and speaks the masking process." Mutlu Konuk Blasing, *American Poetry: The Rhetoric of Its Form* (New Haven, CT: Yale University Press, 1987), 61. Susan B. Rosenbaum discusses Plath's "Lady Lazarus" as a poem in which "the ritualized death of the poetess . . . [becomes] necessary to a 'transcendent,' 'authentic' work of art." Yet "the sincere ideal is simply another feminine costume." She concludes, "Plath suggests that the female elegy as embodiment of a sincere ideal is also a commercial transaction that feeds the basest desire for a voyeuristic experience of death." Susan B. Rosenbaum, *Professing Sincerity: Modern Lyric Poetry, Commercial Culture, and the Crisis in Reading* (Charlottesville: University of Virginia Press, 2007), 146–47.

41. Harriet L. Parmet, *The Terror of Our Days: Four American Poets Respond to the Holocaust* (Bethlehem, PA: Lehigh University Press, 2001), 72.

42. Susan Van Dyne, *Revising Life: Sylvia Plath's Ariel Poems* (Chapel Hill: University of North Carolina Press, 1993), 55. Van Dyne points out that in "Lady Lazarus," the female role is complementary and subjected to the male: "In the worksheets, the ire of this poem is directed not at the monolithic brute of "Daddy" but at multiple forms of male authority; many more are named in the drafts than in the finished poem: enemy, professor, executioner, priest, torturer, doctor, God, Lucifer. What Lady Lazarus suf-

fers is not male brutality but the gendered asymmetry of her relationship to power in which her role is always defined as dependent and defective: to male professor she is student, to executioner, criminal; to priest, sinner; to doctor, patient."

43. Parmet, 73.

44. Van Dyne, *Revising Life*, 57.

45. Judith Butler, "Performative Acts and Gender Constitution: An Essay in Phenomenology and Feminist Theory," in *Performing Feminisms: Feminist Critical Theory and Theatre*, ed. Sue-Ellen Case (Baltimore: Johns Hopkins University Press, 1990), 271.

46. Ibid.

47. Ibid., 276.

48. Butler elaborates this thought: "In a theatre, one can say, 'this is just an act,' and de-realize the act, make acting into something quite distinct from what is real. Because of these distinctions, one can maintain one's sense of reality in the face of this temporary challenge to our existing ontological assumptions about gender arrangements. . . . On the street or in the bus, the act becomes dangerous, if it does, precisely because there are not theatrical conventions to delimit the purely imaginary character of the act, indeed, on the street or in the bus, there is no presumption that the act is distinct from a reality; the disquieting effect of the act is that there are no conventions that facilitate making this separation" (278).

49. For an in-depth study of Plath's development of the modern elegy see Jahan Ramazani, "'Daddy, I Have Had to Kill You': Plath, Rage, and the Modern Elegy," *PMLA* 108, no. 5 (1993): 1142–56.

50. Also see Anne Mounic, *Poésie et mythe: Edwin Muir, Robert Graves, Ted Hughes, Sylvia Plath, Ruth Fainlight* (Paris: L'Harmattan, 2000–2001), 185: "Le poème 'Words' (Mots) se présente comme poème du deuil, deuil des mots eux-mêmes." (The poem "Words" presents itself as a poem of mourning, of the words mourning themselves [my translation].) In her book *"Kein Sterbenswort, Ihr Worte!" Ingeborg Bachmann und Sylvia Plath: Acting the Poem* (Tübingen, Germany: Francke, 2000), Annette Burkart reads "Words" as "Gedicht, das ausschließlich auf Ebene der Sprache agiert" (239), (a poem that acts exclusively on the level of language [my translation]). About the lyrical *I* she writes, "Agens ist es . . . nicht, sondern nur machtloser Beobachter und zufällig kurzfristiger Weggefährte der Worte" (240). (It is not the agent, but only the powerless observer of the words and their accidental, short-term companion [my translation].)

51. H. D. (Hilda Doolittle), *Collected Poems 1912–1944*, ed. Louis L. Martz (New York: New Directions, 1983), 55.

52. William Shakespeare, *King Lear*, Arden Shakespeare, ed. R. A. Foakes (Walton-on-Thames, UK: Thomas Nelson, 1997).

53. Augustine, *Confessions*, ed. F. J. Sheed (Indianapolis, IN: Hackett, 1993), 179.

TWO

Susan Howe's Nonconformist Memorials

How does one remember a nonconformist? That is the question implied by the title of Susan Howe's collection of poetry *The Nonconformist's Memorial*. The nonconformists Howe commemorates have fallen almost into oblivion: Mary Magdalene, who in St. Peter's noncanonical gospel is "nameless" (*NM* 6); the unknown author of *The Eikon Basilike, The Pourtraicture of His Sacred Majestie in his Solitude and Sufferings*, a book dedicated to the memory of the English King Charles I; and the Irish poet James Clarence Mangan, whom Howe identifies as an important influence on Herman Melville. Whereas, as Howe argues, Mary Magdalene is threatened by cancellation from the record as one of many women in history, the author of *The Eikon Basilike* and James Clarence Mangan self-consciously initiated their oblivion by not conforming to the rules of writing and authorship. The title *The Nonconformist's Memorial* implies that remembering nonconformists differs from conventional or historic memory. This chapter will investigate the modes of memory practiced in these poems as well as their deviation from the mnemonic strategies of those texts toward which Howe takes a critical stance. Howe certainly would not argue for a "right" and a "wrong" way to remember, but she is very much aware of the power structures involved in the production, publication, and circulation of literature. She also would not claim that all nonconformists are condemned to oblivion, but that in textual memory certain mechanisms standardize the memory of a person and adapt his memory to "ideological necessity." Experimenting with "nonconformist"

71

textual strategies of commemoration, Howe's book simultaneously ir-
onizes her claim of being able to do so for she calls it a "memorial" and
thus associates it with the massiveness of commemorative monuments
that would not suit the memory of somebody who planned, or at least
did not do anything against, his oblivion.

Although I will occasionally draw on other poems from *The Noncon-
formist's Memorial* and Howe's other volumes of poetry and criticism, the
long poem "Melville's Marginalia," which is the last poem in the book
and the best model of Howe's mnemonics, will be at the center of this
chapter. My reading of this poem counters the predominant classification
of her poetics as "disjunctive,"[1] a characterization referring to her collage
technique, the experiments with printing and line arrangements, and her
transcendence of grammatical convention. My reading of "Melville's
Marginalia" as a memory poem highlights its *conjunctive* characteristics.
Above all, the poem is a memorial of James Clarence Mangan, the figure
linking the poem's many divergent elements. The poem is the result of a
reading process, and this genealogy of readers and writers, as con-
structed by the poet, forms another conjunctive device. Quotation is an
important poetic technique associating the pastiche of texts that form the
second part of the poem. Howe's practice of poetic memory not only
aims at representing memory but also at representing forgetting. Seem-
ingly disjunctive elements in the poem—such as her use of typographical
disjunction, the disrupted word, the marginal, and the blank—will be
reinterpreted as devices of poetic memory. Howe's mode of remember-
ing nonconformists is influenced by the postmodern discourses of her
time, and when occasioned by the poem, I will point out how she nego-
tiates questions of poststructuralist theory, such as the nature of author-
ship, the "origin" of texts, or the limitations of the symbolic system.
Howe's "nonconformist" mnemonics radically questions the possibility,
or even desirability, of fixing memory and consolidating the self. Hinting
at the self via its encounters with cherished figures from literature and
history, via associative marginal scribbling, and via stutters and silences,
Howe is deep in poetic memory.

Howe writes her "memorials" on the basis of other textual sources. In
"The Nonconformist's Memorial," she relies on the Gospel according to
St. John; in "Eikon Basilike," she draws on Edward Almack's *Bibliography
of the King's Book*; and in "Melville's Marginalia," she takes the marginal
annotations Melville wrote in the books he read as her starting point.

Why does Howe invest herself in Melville's marginalia rather than seek-ing inspiration from his writings that became cornerstones of the literary canon? In "Melville's Marginalia," Howe transfers her interest "in the dark side of history"[2] and in the margins of history[3] to the visual layout of a text by taking the metaphorical expression "margins of history" liter-ally and by looking at the margins of texts. The underlying assumption is that the material dimension of writing—paper, print, visual layout of texts—amounts to a form of geohistorical mapping. Moreover, Howe believes that reading marginalia leads to a most intimate encounter with their writer. "Marks in the margins," Howe explains, "are immediate reflections" (*BM* 15) and "Margins speak of fringes of consciousness or marginal associations" (*MM* 91). Howe quotes Edgar Allan Poe who shares her preference for marginalia: "In the *marginalia* . . . we talk only to ourselves; we therefore talk freshly—boldly—originally—with *abandon-ment*—without conceit—" (*BM* 7). Poe implies that marginalia have great-er immediacy for their writer because they have been jotted down with-out his habitual self-consciousness. Howe holds that the immediacy of marginalia is also due to the lack of editorial interference: analogous to marginal historical people who are not considered important to the his-torical master narrative, "Marginal notes are not works" (*BM* 15). There-fore, editorial control neglects or rather spares, as Howe might put it, marginalia. Melville's marginalia are also significant from a scholarly point of view. They date from the period after "the critical and public failure of *Moby-Dick* and then *Pierre* in 1851–53," when Melville increas-ingly withdrew from his social entourage and invested himself in solitary reading and writing. The marginalia thus trace a period in his life that his "works" do not.

"Melville's Marginalia" can be subdivided into three parts. The first consists of an epigraph that is simultaneously an epitaph ("March 20, 1639–40— / buried Philip Massinger / <u>a stranger</u>"); the "Brief Chronology of James Clarence Mangan," titled "Parenthesis"; and the "Preface," in which Howe unfolds the genesis of the poem. The first part presents three historical figures: Philip Massinger, James Clarence Mangan, and Herman Melville, whose relationship, at this point, still remains obscure. Howe only hints at Mangan's literary influence on Melville:

> **1849**   Dies [Mangan; my insertion] in the Meath Hospital, Dublin, June 20, probably from starvation.

1853   At sunrise on November 8, 1853, there appears, suddenly as
Manco Capac at the lake Titicaca, a figure, pallidly neat, pitiably re-
spectable, incurably forlorn, in *Putnam's Monthly Magazine* in New
York City. It is Bartleby. (*MM* 87)

Howe does not end Mangan's biography on the note of his death but
with his literary "resurrection." The relationship Melville formed to Man-
gan by reading him and by thus maintaining a "conversation" (*MM* 89)
with him grew so intense, Howe implies, that he resurrected the de-
ceased writer in the form of a literary character: Bartleby, the Scrivener.
Melville himself was a marginal figure until his rediscovery in the 1920s.
His concern with Mangan parallels Hart Crane's "resuscitation" of Mel-
ville in his poem "At Melville's Tomb" written in 1926. Howe parodies
the textual format of a "chronological biography" by concluding it with a
new beginning, a resuscitation. Her disrespect for biographical chronolo-
gies, which purport to capture a poet's life in a few lines and dates, is also
reflected by the title of this section, "Parenthesis," that is, something that
might be left out without harming the sense of the whole.[4]

The relationship between Mangan and Melville is elaborated in the
second part of "Melville's Marginalia" (*MM* 93–110). In this section,
Howe's own passages alternate with about twenty text fragments from
writing not her own, and the quotations are taken from a large variety of
textual genres: editorial comments, footnotes, prefaces, passages from
autobiography, quotes and literary criticism, bibliographical references to
published articles, and parts of public lectures. Between these quotations
or "found texts," Howe situates about ten poems, usually poems with
unconventional line arrangement. Toward the end of this second part,
Howe inserts another meta-poetic passage explaining her method and
how Mangan comes into the poem: "I began to write Melville's Marginal-
ia by pulling a phrase, sometimes just a word or a name, at random from
Cowen's alphabetically arranged *Melville's Marginalia* and letting that
lead me by free association to each separate poem in the series" (*MM*
105). She points out two main reasons for her great interest in Mangan.
The first is biographical, for Mangan reminded Howe of her Irish roots:
"Why was I drawn to Mangan? / Only that I remembered the song called
'Roisin Dubh' from childhood and my great-aunt's garden one summer
years ago beside Killiney Bay near Dublin" (*MM* 105).[5] The second is the
desire of the poet as literary critic to expound the strong influence Man-
gan, the marginal Irish writer, must have had on Melville, the literary

giant of the American Renaissance. Melville "heavily scored" Mitchel's introduction to Mangan's poems, and Howe takes this as an indication of Melville's identification with Mangan. Howe seeks to remedy the lack of recognition by asserting Mangan's importance for Melville. In this meta-poetic passage, Howe also points out that her intuitive guessing of that relationship by means of "poetry telepathy" (*MM* 106) came first, followed by a problem of "chronology" (*MM* 106). For how should one convincingly argue that Mangan "is the progenitor of fictional Bartleby," if Melville acquired his copy of *Poems by James Clarence Mangan* in 1862, nine years after having written "Bartleby, the Scrivener"? The solution to this is, Howe argues, that Melville must have known about Mangan much earlier, for example, from the October 1851 issue of the *United States Magazine and Literary Review*, which carried the title "Some Irish Poets" and was "entirely devoted to Mangan." So, "by the time Melville acquired Mitchel's edition of Mangan's poems in 1862, he was already familiar with the poet's life and work" (*MM* 107).

Part three of "Melville's Marginalia" (*MM* 111–50) encompasses forty pages with one poem per page. These poems, free-associated from Melville's marginalia, are, in contrast to the ones in the second part, all centered on the page and written in mostly conventionally arranged lines. Prose poems written in syntactically complete sentences vary with poems devoid of syntactical order and consisting of words torn apart or typed on top of each other. They frequently pick up topics relating to Mangan and focus on, for example, Mangan the reader (*MM* 111), the rebel against English rule (*MM* 112), the veiled writer (*MM* 113), the receiver of "whispered information" (*MM* 125), the librarian (*MM* 126), the "polyglot" (*MM* 128), and the sorrowful (*MM* 131), and they also mention or allude to other writers, such as Dryden, Melville, Percy Bysshe Shelley, Mary Shelley, Marianne Moore, Joyce, Byron, and Shakespeare.

The structure of "Melville's Marginalia" simulates the process of memory acquisition. The poem not only remembers Melville and Mangan, but also self-reflexively enacts the stages of memory formation. Howe starts out gathering information (or food for memory) on Mangan and begins the poem with a "Brief Chronology of James Clarence Mangan" (*MM* 85–87). This newly acquired information is then gradually appropriated and assimilated to her own mnemonic apparatus. She highlights specific passages from writings by Mangan's critics by quoting them in the second part of the poem (*MM* 93–109). Reworking these with her own associations results in the poems that alternate with the quotes. These associations are "immediate reflections" and still unsuitable for the "tidier" format of standard literary texts. At this stage, the experimental layout of Howe's poems still contrasts with the standard printing format of the quotations. Their "unfinished" form emphasizes their contiguity to the lines that inspired them. Like marginalia, they belong both to the writer who wrote the lines they are based on as well as to the writer who "continued" them. In the third part (*MM* 110–50), Howe writes poems of greater "formal finish," displaying their increased distance from the texts that she "continues." The past, formerly other, has become part of the poet's subjectivity. This process of making something other or outside "inner," and of thus interweaving it with one's subjectivity, results in the sequence of poems of the third part of "Melville's Marginalia."

While the structure of the poem imitates the process of memory acquisition, its collage character diffuses memory formation. The collage elements comprise quoted or explanatory paragraphs, a line, or just a word, and these fragments lack the textual glue usually provided by narrative transition and context. The ensuing effect of fragmentation is still augmented by the inclusion of many different voices, many different genres, and Howe's experimental use of the space of the page. Yet the pastiche character of "Melville's Marginalia" is also a crucial means of devising "nonconformist memory." It initiates a mode of memory different from that of the linear, coherent, and complete account of the past. Fragmentation slows down, halts, and redirects the reading process. Fragments alone, however, do not suffice for memory constitution. They are linked by narrative conjunctions that become visible when the long poem is read as "one piece."[6] These conjunctions comprise the figure of James Clarence Mangan, who is the gravitational center for the collage of quotations in the second part of the poem, the genealogy of readers and writers presented in the poem, and the "genealogy" or history of the usage of words explored in the poem. The demanding task of adding these conjunctions is assigned to the reader, who is invited to perform consciously what goes mostly unnoticed in the work of memory.

REMEMBERING JAMES CLARENCE MANGAN

Howe takes interest not in Melville's canonized writings but in his marginalia, and among the books he annotated in the margins, she is less interested in his reading of the "great ones" such as "Homer, Dante, Shakespeare, Milton, Marvell, Balzac, Byron, Goethe, Emerson, Hawthorne, Schopenhauer" (*MM* 105) but in his reading of Mangan, "the man with the name so remarkably like *margin*" who "has been all but forgotten by serious literary criticism" (*MM* 105). Mangan fits into the line of "nonconformists" to whom the book is dedicated because his resistance to literary, editorial, and other social authority prepared his cancellation from the literary records. In the second part of "Melville's Marginalia," the quotations from Mangan's and from his critics' writings seem unrelated, yet, at second sight, testify to his "nonconformist" qualities. As quotations in the context of the poem, the reproduced passages acquire a sense of irony they did not have in their original form. Quotation is not identical with reproduction of meaning, and most of the quotations criticize the power structures interfering with the production, publication, and circulation of literature. Quoting these passages, Howe questions conventional notions of authorship and of the genesis of texts. Thus, "Melville's Marginalia" comes to deal with theoretical questions of poststructuralism that Howe asks explicitly in "Eikon Basilike," the poem preceding "Melville's Marginalia": "Can we ever really discover the original text? Was there ever an original poem? What is a pure text invented by an author? Is such a conception possible?" (*EB* 50). The quotations by and on Mangan are not only a critique launched at the grasp ideology has on cultural production, but also a means of ironizing conventional notions of memory acquisition. Summarizing Mangan's "nonconformist" qualities in the subsequent section, I will examine how the poet parodies "conformist" assumptions as to the nature of our literary memory.

From the catalog of Mangan's "oddities," Howe chooses his looks as point of departure. His contemporaries describe Mangan's outward appearance as a potpourri of "fashion" styles, and his editor C. P. Meehan depicts him as follows:

> And the dress of this spectral-looking man was singularly remarkable, taken down at haphazard from some peg in an old clothes shop—a baggy pantaloon that was intended for him, a short coat closely buttoned, a blue cloth cloak still shorter, and tucked so tightly to his person that no one could see there even the faintest shadow of those lines called by painters and sculptors drapery. The hat was in keeping with this habiliment, broad-leafed and steeple-shaped, the model of which he must have found in some picture of Hudibras. Occasionally he substituted for his head-gear, a soldier's fatigue cap, and never appeared

abroad in sunshine or storm without a large malformed umbrella, which, when partly covered by the cloak, might easily be mistaken for a Scotch bagpipe. (*MM* 99)

If one considered Mangan's eccentric clothing a text, it would be characterized as transgeneric, eclectic, fragmented. And as if there were a relationship between clothing and writing, Mangan respects the norms of fashion as little as he satisfies standards of writing. As early as in the nineteenth century, he refused to adhere to the generic requirement of "truthfulness" in autobiography, and his memoirs, significantly entitled "Fragment of an Unfinished Autobiography," are anything but the precise and "true" account of his life. Mangan relates, for example, that he entered school in 1820 when he was eleven years old. However, his editor Meehan points out an error and insists that Mangan was born in 1803 and must have started going to school before 1820 (*MM* 93). In the same work, Mangan describes his family's living and housing circumstances as desolate and then freely admits to Meehan that this had only been a dream (*MM* 97). Instead of insisting, like his editor Meehan, on the satisfaction of generic expectations Howe applauds Mangan's deliberate distortions and celebrates them as the poet's entitlement to "verbal / association / in a strange // order," for unlike the historian, "A / poet / does not relate / real / events" (*MM* 94). Ventriloquizing through Mangan, Howe mocks our generic expectations of autobiography. Why should not a poet favor fiction over facts, she asks implicitly, if fiction is more suitable to the account as a whole? Poets interested in subjective truth favor poetic over historic memory.

Mangan not only "distorted" his own writing, he also "falsified" texts of other writers. As much as he disregarded the conventions of autobiographical writing, Mangan disobeyed the rules of translation. Howe quotes the titles of some of his "translations" in the second part of the poem, for example, the "SAYING OF NEDSCHATI. / OB. 1508. / (FROM THE OTTOMAN.)" (*MM* 101) or "'Lamii's Apology for his Nonsense, (From the Ottoman.)'" (*MM* 109), by which Mangan may self-ironically refer to his own doings. In the third part of "Melville's Marginalia," Howe sheds some light on Mangan's mysterious "translations":

Mangan was not the polyglot

he pretended to be

Translations were the rage

of the moment

and he turned them out

as regularly and as competently

as he had turned out

acrostics some years before

From 1837 onwards

Mangan deluged

the *Dublin University Magazine*

with "translations"

from the Turkish Arabic Persian

Welsh Coptic Danish French German

Russian Spanish Swedish Frisian

Bohemian

(*MM* 128)

Mangan not only invented the languages he supposedly translated into English, such as "Coptic," "Frisian" (which is a German dialect), and "Bohemian," he also must have made up the "originals." Howe ironizes our belief in the possibility of translation, that is, the accurate transmission of literature into another language. But Mangan's "method" has still deeper significance, because his "translations" provide Howe with an occasion to make certain claims about the nature of writing: Mangan called texts he invented "translations," thereby questioning "originality" as a paradigmatic requirement for art and the artist. The poet as translator, Howe claims with Mangan, reworks already existing material. The poet is one who transforms into another medium and creates an approximation of his model text or experience.

Howe not only ironizes translation from one into another language but also undermines our confidence in the authentic transmission of literature from the past to the present. More concretely, she mocks claims for the "authenticity" of the literary canon through Mangan. He insists, for example, that Antony in Shakespeare's *Julius Caesar* does not ask Romans to "lend me your ears" but "to lend me your cars" — which to Mangan is the logical announcement of Antony's departure to prepare for Caesar's funeral: "Julius was killed near a car-stand, and Antony wanted to provide a decent funeral. What could be more absurd than to ask for a loan of their ears?" (*MM* 95). Even if the reading "lend me your cars" is at least as absurd as the "original" passage, Mangan's comment underlines the arbitrary element in the genesis and in the history of reception even of "high" literature.

Howe is not only skeptical of the concept of the "original text," she also doubts our idea of the "author." She subscribes to Mangan's depiction of the writer as an "eternal wanderer":

> Your surprise, Reader, is, doubtless, excited—ah! you know not what a vagabond I am! Perhaps I may communicate my history to the Irish people, and if I should have no hesitation in assuring them that they will pronounce it without a parallel in the Annals of the Marvellous and Mournful. Only see the result!—for me there is no stopping place in city or country. An unrelenting doom condemns me to the incessant exercise of my pedestrian capabilities. It is an awful thing to behold me at each completion of my term scampering off like Van Woedenblock of the Magic Leg—galloping along roads—clearing ditches—dispersing the affrighted poultry in farm yards as effectually as a forty-eight pounder could. Other men sojourn for life in the country of their choice; there is a prospect of ultimate repose for most things; even the March of Intellect must one day halt; already we see that pens, ink, and paper are—stationary.
>
> James Clarence Mangan, "My Bugle, and How I Blow It." *Prose Writings of James Clarence Mangan*, ed. D. J. O'Donoghue, 1904. (*MM* 104)

The writer in this humorous and ironic self-portrait is a "vagabond" whose illustrious lifestyle deserves an entry in the "Annals of the Marvellous and Mournful," a mocking term for the records of history. The writer is "doomed" to the "incessant exercise of . . . [his] pedestrian capabilities," and only writing, the materialization of his thought on "stationary," makes him halt temporarily. But "at each completion of . . . [his] term" he finds himself again "scampering off like Van Woedenblock of the Magic Leg." The "prospect for ultimate repose" is Mangan's euphemistic definition of death, and the writer's necessary recourse to "stationary" is a way of risking death. As soon as his "term" is finished, he walks off again and will sit down to his next piece as somebody altered. Writing may be a record of the moment, at most. At the moment of expressing himself in writing, Mangan undergoes new transformation and remains unrepresented by his text. To translate this into the characteristics of poetic and historic memory, Mangan would claim that historic memory must intrinsically miss the self it seeks to create. The self eludes its fixation through language. Howe finds a mode to represent Mangan in terms of poetic memory: she introduces this passage very slowly, very carefully, which is suggested by the space left between the two parts of the first sentence, "If you step forward to meet him,   he" (*MM* 104). The attempt to approach Mangan is then bashfully countered and escaped by Mangan's galloping, turbulent lines. Howe concludes: "Secret footsteps cannot bring him." The line is simultaneously overwritten with "M e l v i l l e ' s M a r g i n a l i a." Howe frames the passage with lines advocating poetic memory, a form of memory that respects Mangan's elusiveness at a moment when he cannot assure it for himself anymore. "If you step forward to meet him,   he" will suddenly withdraw from you, could be the short completion of the sentence. Even the "secret footsteps" in the form of careful and tentative marginalia "cannot bring him." Howe reminds us that if we think we can remember a writer through his texts, we are mistaken.

Living up to his self-fashioning as the eternal wanderer, Mangan prepared his cancellation from the literary records by adopting different names "at each completion of . . . [a] term": "The eleventh edition of the *Encyclopaedia Britannica* (1911) says his fame has been deferred by the inequality and mass of work, much of it lying buried in inaccessible newspaper files under so many pseudonyms" (*MM* 109). Obviously, Mangan had anticipated that the abundance of pseudonyms would complicate the identification and compilation of his "works." To Howe, Mangan's many pseudonyms represent a trope for her notion of the "author" who is somebody writing from a multitude of influences and who therefore may justifiably take on many names. The author as "translator," to refer to a preceding passage, writes as many.

Besides Mangan's opposition to standard notions of "the author" and "his texts," his stance also held important political implications. His commentator Mitchel attributes the lack of recognition of Mangan's work to his rebellion against British rule:

> The comparative unacquaintance, also, of Americans with these poems may be readily accounted for, when we remember how completely British criticism gives the law throughout the literary domain of that semi-barbarous tongue in which I have the honor to indite. For this Mangan was not only an Irishman, —not only an Irish papist, —not only an Irish papist rebel;—but throughout his whole literary life of twenty

years, he never deigned to attorn to English criticism, never published
a line in any English periodical, or through any English bookseller,
never seemed to be aware that there was a British Public to please. He
was a rebel politically, and a rebel intellectually and spiritually,—a
rebel with his whole heart and soul against the British spirit of the age.
The consequence was sure, and not unexpected. Hardly anybody in
England knew the name of such a person; (*MM* 106-7)

Mitchel unabashedly declares that Mangan's rebelliousness against Brit-
ish patronization constitutes the reason for his disappearance into obliv-
ion, although officially, as put forward in the 1911 *Encyclopaedia Britanni-
ca*, Mangan's "inequality and mass of work" and the "many pseudo-
nyms" are responsible for his marginal status. To Howe, it is no coinci-
dence that academic authorities "restrict" access to a writer who resists
them in burlesque ways. Howe cites the case of a critic who is not granted
access to Mangan materials supposedly because the British Museum is
taking (too) good care of them and momentarily "re-binding" (*MM* 95).
Access is denied under the pretext of preserving, ordering, and standard-
izing the materials.

Mangan's many nonconformist practices determined his memorial or
rather non-memorial. To Howe, a passage from James Joyce's lecture on
Mangan is emblematic of the mode of nonconformist memory Mangan
initiated for himself. The following excerpt can also be read as a commen-
tary on Mangan's ironic self-depiction. Joyce appears, indeed, as the an-
nalist of a "Marvellous and Mournful":

"Giacomo Clarenzio Mangan"

All his poetry records injustice and tribulation, and the aspiration of
one who is moved to great deeds and rending cries when he sees in his
mind the hour of his grief. This is the theme of a large part of Irish
poetry, but no other poems are as full, as are those of Mangan, of
misfortune nobly suffered, of vastation of soul so irreparable. . . . [I]s it
not perhaps a profound sense of sorrow and bitterness that explains in
Mangan all the names and titles that he gives himself, and the fury of
translation in which he tried to hide himself? For he did not find in
himself the faith of the solitary . . . and he waits his hour, the hour that
will end his sad days of penance. Weaker than Leopardi, for he has not
the courage of his own despair, but forgets every ill and forgoes all
scorn when someone shows him a little kindness, he has, perhaps for
this reason, the memorial that he wished, a

[*one page missing*]

James Joyce, from "Giacomo Clarenzio Mangan," one of three public lectures in Italian at the Università Popolare in Trieste. 1904. Editorial note in brackets. (*MM* 108–9)

Joyce has his own interpretation of Mangan's reasons for using a variety of pseudonyms and for his many "translations." To Joyce, the cause lies in Mangan's "sorrow and bitterness" and his attempt to "hide himself" in the translations. As elaborated before, Howe assigns Mangan's nonconformist writerly practices different motives. She quotes this excerpt as part of her "nonconformist" mode of remembering Mangan. Just when Joyce wants to detail "the memorial that he wished," the document breaks off. Mangan wants a memorial that is none, Howe implies. He wants to be remembered in nonrepresentation. If ever he found entry into the "annals," he would want to be remembered as a missing page.

As suggested before, the structure of "Melville's Marginalia" simulates the process of memory acquisition, but the collage technique necessitates a self-conscious form of memory practice on the reader's part and thus introduces a self-reflective dimension to the poem. On the semantic level, Mangan, it was my argument, constitutes a link alleviating the effect of fragmentation and enhancing the formation of conjunctive memory. Howe grants his memorial an appearance of objectivity and makes her reader confide in this newly acquired knowledge: the list of Mangan's biographical data and the many quotations function as pieces of evidence. However, at second sight it becomes obvious that the poem undermines the reader's hope of acquiring his/story. We cannot trust its "objective appearance" but we must rather question the preconceptions of our memory. First of all, the objectivity of the quoted passages is undermined by the poet's partial selection. Howe has a case, and this case is to prove Mangan's nonconformism, a nonconformism resulting from him being ahead of his time. Second, the quotations unsettle our literary predispositions: they confuse our expectations of literary genres, our assumptions of original texts created independently by authors, and our wish to identify the writer behind the text. The quotations even destroy our confidence in quotation: they do not reproduce meaning, but they add layers of meaning when contextualized differently by the poet. Third, we as readers must be aware that memory depends on the rememberer. Memory cannot be objectively ordained but consists of that which is personally meaningful to the rememberer in the present—here, Howe's commitment to Mangan's nonconformist qualities.

READING

"Melville's Marginalia" is the product of a reading process, and reading is a form of practicing memory. This reading process not only encompasses Howe's reading but also the readings of all the writers mentioned in the poem. Therefore, I suggest, the poem traces a genealogy of readers and writers, a genealogy that is not based on blood but on words. This genealogy is made most explicit in the second part and then extended by Howe's poems in the third part. The writers Howe reads to become acquainted with Mangan are all readers and critics of his work. They comprise, of course, Herman Melville, who admired and marginally annotated Mangan's poetry; Father James Meehan, who was Mangan's friend and editor; Brendan Clifford who edited Mangan's "The Thug's Ditty"; Louise I. Guiney, who published a study on Mangan in 1897; John Desmond Sheridan, the author of a biography of Mangan (1937); D. J. O'Donoghue, who edited the *Prose Writings of James Clarence Mangan* (1904); John Mitchel, who wrote the biographical introduction to *Poems by James Clarence Mangan* (1859); Francis J. Thompson, who published the article "Mangan in America: 1850–1860" in *Dublin Magazine* in 1952 (*MM* 94–107); and, as the only recent study, David Lloyd's *Nationalism and Minor Literature: James Clarence Mangan and the Emergence of Cultural Nationalism* (*MM* 105). Ironically, it is Mangan's propensity for dispersion and escape that links the many quotes from a variety of writers and genres. Most of the quotations have the same tenor: they testify to Mangan's unconventionality. They remark on inconsistencies and improbabilities in Mangan's writing (Meehan, Clifford); they mention the unavailability of Mangan's texts due to the "care" the archives take of them (Clifford); they notice the young Mangan's resemblance to Shelley when he was a boy (Guiney); they relate anecdotes of Mangan's "strangeness" (Guiney) and his "odd" or, to put it positively, unclassifiable appearance (Meehan); they describe Mangan's opposition against British rule (Mitchel); and they study Mangan's influence on New York writers such as Herman Melville (Thompson).

One important element—in fact, the origin of this chain of readers and writers—has so far remained unmentioned: Philip Massinger. What seems to be his epitaph forms the poem's epigraph: "March 20, 1639–40— / buried Philip Massinger / <u>a stranger</u>" (*MM* 83). Howe found these lines among Melville's marginalia. How is Massinger related to Mangan and Melville? In the "Brief Chronology of James Clarence Mangan," Howe explains that Mangan opened his "Fragments of an Unfinished Autobiography" with a quote from Massinger: "a heavy shadow lay / On that boy's spirit: he was not of his fathers" (*MM* 87). It turns out that Mangan read Massinger, which makes Massinger the starting point of the genealogy of readers researched and presented in the poem. Grounding the poem on Massinger's "epitaph" not only makes him Mangan's poetic forefather but also the "ancestor" of all the writers mentioned in the poem, while, at the same time, they are the keepers of *his* memory. Mangan chose the quote from Massinger as the introduction to an "autobiographical" piece because he may have felt the same "shadow" on his "spirit." By quoting Massinger, Mangan suggests that both men belong to each other rather than to their fathers. Howe implies that, just as Mangan was resurrected as Melville's Bartleby, Massinger continued his being in Mangan's texts. Howe also uses Massinger for *her* epigraph as an introduction to her mnemonics. Melville's marginalium on Massinger takes the form of an epitaph,[7] and an epitaph can be interpreted as a trope for a memorial aphorism dedicated to a deceased person. Melville probably meant to express the idea that, although Massinger's writings have been handed down to posterity, nothing is known about his life circumstances. By quoting these lines, Howe assigns them additional meaning. Introducing a "nonconformist's memorial" with an analogy to someone who "died a stranger" advocates a kind of memory that grants the dead their strangeness.

The argument that the writers Howe quotes form a community of readers is emphasized by her favorite authors' indefatigable passion for reading. Howe calls Melville and also Hawthorne "library cormorants" (*BM* 5). After the failure of *Moby-Dick* and *Pierre*, Howe writes, Melville's life was taking place more and more in the form of conversation with his preferred writers through books. The epigraph Howe chooses for the "Preface" of "Melville's Marginalia" is taken from *Moby-Dick* and testifies to Melville's fervent exploration of the world—or rather, the sea, to anticipate his metaphor—of books: "But I have swam through libraries" (*MM*

89). Reproducing this line from *Moby-Dick* simultaneously makes it Howe's own. Both writers swim through libraries, produce or study marginalia, and are thus engaged in "a conversation with the dead" (*MM* 89).

In Howe's poems, memory is projected as a mysterious, powerful, and excitable faculty capable of overcoming the division between past and present, allowing the rememberer to participate in the past and granting the dead an active role in the present. Howe's practice of reading contributes to understanding her frequent conflation of past and present; she comments on her enchantment with the past: "I feel that I am alive, that I am present in the past."[8] The poet feels present in the past and the presence of the past. Instead of looking at the past retrospectively from the point of view of the present, she asserts she dwells *in* the past. Contrary to common sense, Howe thus conceives of the past not as an imaginary construct transmitted to us through various modes of representation, but as an actuality. Howe admits that she works for her "sense of the past" and confesses to be an ardent student of history, devouring any material she can find once she gets "obsessed" by a person or an event in history.[9] Howe's claim for an entirely unmediated "experience" of the past must therefore be relativized, and she admits, "Of course I can't *really* bring back a particular time. That's true. Or it's true if you think of time as moving in a particular direction—forward you say. But what if then *is* now" (*K* 4). "Then" becomes "now" precisely in reading, and the mnemonic implications of reading are key to understanding Howe's experience of the past as presence. Reading, understood as mnemonic practice, makes texts present and can endow the past with presence.

In the case of Melville's marginalia, Howe practices a mode of reading that still amplifies the experience of immersion into the past. She writes that she not only aims at knowing *what* Melville read and *what* he paid sufficient attention to in order to comment on it, but also at catching a glimpse of *how* he read: "I thought one way to write about a loved author would be to follow what trails he follows through words of others" (*MM* 92). "If there are things Melville went looking for in books so too there were things I looked for in Melville's looking" (*MM* 105). Howe is less interested in the marginalia as the *products* of Melville's reading, but in his reading *process*, that is, "Melville's looking." Strictly speaking, the way Howe reads the marginalia does not generate a conversation between her and Melville; she joins an already ongoing conversation be-

tween Melville and Mangan. She eavesdrops on a dialogue as she ima-
gines it to have been maintained in the past. She remembers Melville
remembering Mangan. Looking for "things in Melville's looking" is
aimed at deciphering thought processes before they attain the scripted
level of marginalia. Her memory thus attempts to reach back to thoughts
when they were conceived in the past and before they were materialized
into the signifier. Such mnemonic immersion into the past or, more con-
cretely, into Melville's thought processes, becomes the source for her
poems.

The epitome of memory, Howe projects, lies in instances of reciprocity
between the past and the present. Remembering the dead may, at one
point, stop being a one-directional activity but be equally initiated by the
one who is read or remembered. Then the dead actively "walk in . . . [her]
imagination" (*BM* 4). Only as a reciprocal process can reading truly be-
come "a conversation with the dead" (*MM* 89). The "conversation" with
Melville, of which the poem is the result, began at the moment his margi-
nalia "found" *her*: "One day while searching through Melville criticism at
the Temple University Library I noticed two maroon dictionary-size vol-
umes, lying haphazardly, out of reach, almost out of sight on the topmost
shelf. That's how I found *Melville's Marginalia* or *Melville's Marginalia*
found me" (*MM* 89). She claims to have been "found" by the marginalia a
second time in the poem: "what if these penciled single double and triple
scorings arrows short phrases angry outbursts crosses cryptic ciphers
sudden enthusiasms mysterious erasures have come to find you too,
here, again, now" (*MM* 92). Being "found" by the marginalia is like re-
ceiving a calling, instigating the poet "to follow what trails he [Melville;
my insertion] follows through words of others" (*MM* 92). In the passage
immediately following the episode in Temple University Library, Howe
gives an example of what such a reciprocal "conversation" might look
like. If Melville speaks to "Susan," he does not only speak to one specific
Susan: "I built a cottage for Susan and myself and made a gateway in the
form of a Gothic Arch, by setting up a whale's jaw bones" (MM *90*). He
speaks to every Susan (or reader) who feels spoken to. So the present
Susan's love for Melville does not remain unrequited. Surprisingly, the
sentence is not only Melville's but also Hawthorne's, and it appears in
Melville's *Moby-Dick* "Extracts" and *Melville's Marginalia* but also in
Hawthorne's *Twice-Told Tales*. Having been "told" more than "twice," [10]
this sentence links Howe's technique of quotation to her literary models.

The quote can be interpreted as Melville's and Hawthorne's invitation to "Susan" to enter into a book, for it metaphorically refers back to the epigraph: "But I have swam through libraries." In accordance with the image, the library is a sea of books, and a book is a fish. The whale's jawbones that are set up archlike as an entrance to the house simulate an entry into the whale's belly or absorption into a book. Although swimming through libraries does not yet imply the reader's absorption into a book, trespassing into the interior of a whale would amount to the symbiosis with a story. Literally, "an author takes the reader in. Enchantment of the other" (*BM* 15). The invitation into the book is implicitly compared to a wedding ritual: Herman and Nathaniel put up an arch for Susan to stride through it together. Howe implies that she does not impose herself on Melville and Hawthorne, but that Melville and Hawthorne entice her into the book. Therefore, the literary genealogy in "Melville's Marginalia" is not only poetic artifice put together in an idiosyncratic way, but it also is triggered by the present force of the past.

To Howe, a poet is inhabited by the voices of other writers. To follow her poetic calling is to uncover this largely unconscious lineage. Howe's poems make reader and writer aware of their ties with the past and the profoundly mnemonic character of reading and writing. Howe's relationship to the (literary) past stands in stark contrast with that expressed by Plath. Whereas Plath, if one thinks back to "The Colossus" or "Daddy," is also aware of being inhabited by the literary tradition and experiences this as an inhibiting burden, Howe creates for herself a position in a literary lineage. The fragments of Western civilization that constitute the massive and inescapable surroundings of Plath's speaker in "The Colossus" are assembled, in a specific selection, in Howe's poem. Howe browses the textual traces of her favorite writers and succeeds in reconstructing the literary remains that cause Plath's speakers despair. In this manner, Howe's collage poems can be read as a commentary on Plath. Their diverging attitudes are also a result of writing at different moments in the postwar era. Whereas Plath still negotiates her relationship to the canon, Howe deliberately ignores the canonical in "Melville's Marginalia." Plath could only position herself as a serious writer, if her poems in some way paid homage to the "masters," while Howe as a poet of the avant-garde of American poetry never had to plead for such approbation. Therefore, Howe is to be clearly distinguished from writers beset by an "anxiety of influence."[11] As Fiona Green remarks, Howe does not identify with this oedipal pattern in literary relationships and wrote in her sketchbook from 1974, a year after Harold Bloom's study had been published: "I think the crucial theme running through my life and I am sorry for it has been the search *for* not away from (or to slay) the father."[12] Howe is avant-garde, paradoxically, in the way she reexplores the past and its texture. Intertextuality is not only a necessary evil that obstructs the writer's ingenuity, it also is a tool always at work whose importance Howe's method lays bare. Howe asks rhetorically, "What is writing but continuing."[13]

QUOTING

Howe's abundant use of quotation has at least a twofold mnemonic purpose: it is a most intimate form of remembering the nonconformists she quotes, and it aims at the memory of the word itself. Quotation is intimate when past words express the thoughts of the present poet so perfectly that she feels incited to quote. If subjectivity is constituted in language, quotation signifies an almost symbiotic relationship with the one from whom one quotes. Moreover, quotation is a suitable practice of memory when remembering nonconformists: instead of assimilating the other to one's memory of him, he is remembered in the words that he chose himself.

If the word itself becomes the object of memory, what is its mnemonic value? Any use of words and any thinking about words are necessarily connected to the past and an act of memory. Words are containers of the past because their formal and semantic modifications reflect the changes of history.[14] In her "critical" as well as in her "poetic" writing, Howe explores the semantic scope of a word by following its different meanings through the history of its (literary) use. Making the word itself the object of memory through quotation is not only typical of a language poet but also expresses Howe's poetics of finding ideas for words instead of finding words for ideas. She assembles as many of the word's historical significations as possible and thus writes its semantic history. Her favorite tool for investigating prior meanings and semantic nuances of a word is the 1852 edition of Noah Webster's *American Dictionary of the English Language*. Howe exercises such semantic archaeology, for example, on the term *library cormorant*. She finds the expression in Coleridge, who refers to himself as a "library cormorant," that is, as somebody "*deep* in all out of the way books" (*SM* 26). Coleridge's understanding of the term is complemented by a dictionary-like depiction of the actual bird in, however, almost poetic images: "They are underwater swimmers who feed on fish; they are voracious." "Swimming under clear water, they seem to be flying." "Cormorants are strand birds; they occupy cliffs by the ocean, where they perch upright upon rocks, often motionless for long periods of time, with wings extended" (*SM* 26). Howe also mentions Milton's depiction of Satan as a cormorant, relates Chinese and Japanese superstitions regarding the cormorant, and quotes a passage from a study by Berthold Laufer on *The Domestication of the Cormorant in China and Japan*. By scrutinizing, or remembering, the origin and use of a term, Howe extends its (metaphorical) signification. Having fathomed its semantic depth, Howe makes it her own and refers to Melville (*BM* 5) and other ardent readers with the ability of immersing themselves into books as "library cormorants." Writing the semantic history of the word also reveals the lineage of those who used it. To Howe, language constitutes a joint between people even if historically they lived centuries apart. The word that is used similarly by different persons manifests an affinity between them. If a word speaks to somebody in particular, it is meant to teach him about himself, and it simultaneously aligns him with the person who said it before. Having re-membered or traced the semantic layers of a word, Howe quotes it to send it on. Words are "the articulation of sound-forms in time," as the title of another poem by Howe reads, and want to be received, repeated, and then sent on to travel across time and space. Quotation acknowledges and does homage to this destiny of the word.

A special case of quotation is the repetition of names. Howe is not only interested in the semantic dimension of a word, but also in its phonetic characteristics. She frequently declares that the acoustic is the guiding principle of her work, as her reference to words as "sound-forms in time" shows. Contrary to other forms of quotation, names are primarily important for the way they sound. Arguably, Howe introduces her poem with Massinger's epitaph because she was attracted by Massinger's name, which combines the words *messenger* and *Mangan*. To Howe, the almost-homonym that "Massinger" forms with "messenger" implies that Mangan not only read Massinger, but that Massinger also had a message for Mangan and wanted to be read by him. She remarks on the "coincidence" that the name of a marginal writer like Mangan should phonetically be so close to the word *margin*. Not only Mangan's reading of Massinger, but also their names bind those two linguistically, who are historically separated by a period of two hundred years. Howe prefers to believe names rather than historical fact. When Melville writes "I built a cottage for Susan and myself" (*MM* 90), he not only addresses the historical Susan, but the authority of the name also allows the Susan who is presently reading Melville to feel addressed by it. The same principle applies to Emily Dickinson's letters to her sister-in-law Susan. Reading a letter addressed to Susan, Howe reproduces a line which, due to the "tie" between her and Dickinson, she feels, was also intended for her: "The tie between us is very fine, but a Hair never dissolves (*L* 1024)" (*BM* 29). Names indicate affinities between people from different centuries. If Melville, Hawthorne, and Dickinson say "Susan," they also address Susan Howe. If Massinger, Mangan, Meehan, and Melville are related intellectually and artistically, the bonds between them seem to be prescribed by the likeness of their names. Howe makes her suspicion of the metaphysical quality of names explicit in a comment on her poem "Eikon Basilike": "The coincidence of the name Charles (then I pulled Charles Dickens into it—) was one of those accidentals that make you feel the thing was planned in advance" (*TI* 175). The sameness of their first names also indicates an affinity between the king and Dickens. The significance Howe finds in the first name has, in most cultures, been an implicit assumption of the name all along: the custom to adopt one's parents' names is based on the logic of a likeness of members from the same family. Howe reverses this principle: instead of considering family ties first and then deriving the sameness of the name from this similarity, she gives the name priority and derives a relationship between the carriers of the same name.

Because words hint at the affinities between a person in the present and her namesakes in the past, they are carriers and constituents of subjectivity. The name resonates with the echoes from the many people who were given it in the past and, in this sense, forms a "multiplicity." The "multiplicity" that Howe associates with names is also embraced by Gilles Deleuze and Félix Guattari whom she quotes in *Singularities*: "The proper name *(nom propre)* does not designate an individual: it is on the contrary when the individual opens up to the multiplicities pervading him or her, at the outcome of the most severe operation of depersonalization, that he or she acquires his or her true proper name. The proper name is the instantaneous apprehension of a multiplicity. The proper name is the subject of a pure infinitive comprehended as such in a field of intensity."[15] Deleuze and Guattari argue the opposite of common notions of the first name as the marker of an individual. Howe translates this idea into the lines "Pronoun *I* or the name / utter immensities whisper" (*NM* 20).

Howe's texts exceed both what Michel Foucault calls the traditional "author-function" and poststructuralist notions of the "writing subject" who is not an author anymore. At first sight, her use of names and quotation seems to support the Foucaultian notion of "the effacement of the writing subject's individual characteristics."[16] Also, critics have frequently remarked on Howe's "absenteeism" and "authorial distance."[17] Before the deconstruction of the "author-function" by poststructuralist criticism, Foucault argues, the coherence of a written text had been considered as emanating from the unity of the writing subject. The author-function used to be

> the principle of a certain unity of writing—all differences, having to be resolved, at least in part, by the principles of evolution, maturation, or influence. The author also serves to neutralize the contradictions that may emerge in a series of texts: there must be—at a certain level of his thought or desire, of his consciousness or unconscious—a point where contradictions are resolved, where incompatible elements are at last tied together or organized around a fundamental or originating contradiction. Finally, the author is a particular source of expression that, in more or less completed forms, is manifested equally well, and with similar validity, in works, sketches, letters, fragments, and so on.[18]

In other words, the "author" was a concept invented to secure both the idea of the rational human being, here as writer, and the ideological conformism of his work. Accordingly, Foucault designates this traditional "author-function" as the creation of "the juridical and institutional system that encompasses, determines, and articulates the universe of discourses."[19] Howe, too, is acutely aware of the structural power surrounding the production of texts: "I am drawn toward the disciplines of history and literary criticism but in the dawning distance a dark wall of rule supports the structure of every letter, record, transcript: every proof of authority and power. I know records are compiled by winners, and scholarship is in collusion with Civil Government. I know this and go on searching for some trace of love's infolding through all the paper in all

the libraries I come to" (*BM* 4). The grip of authority on texts is so reso-
lute because, Howe believes, writing is often, to say it with Thoreau, a
form of "civil disobedience." Howe would agree with Foucault on the
authoritarian implications of the term *author* and on the critique of the
ideological control exercised through the "author-function."

Howe's unconventional practice of authorship emanates particularly
from the poetic function she assigns quotation. Through quotation she
adopts a stance of authorial reticence deviating from the traditionally
imposing "author-function." Howe ventriloquizes through the writers
she cites and makes other voices put forward her argument. She rhetori-
cally achieves Mangan's characterization as a "nonconformist," for exam-
ple, by selecting and arranging quotations. No word in this argument is
her own. In a gesture of understatement, Howe characterizes speaking in
her "own" voice as "following" (*MM* 92) and declares being "indebted to
everyone" (*SM* 39). She views herself in a tradition of authorial reticence
shared by the other writers in the poem. Neither Melville nor Mangan,
Howe believes, draws attention to the singularity of their personalities to
assist the memory of later generations. Both rather point out that it will
be impossible to pin them down in memory. Mangan's self-stylization as
a "restless wanderer" has already been elaborated. Melville, in a letter to
Hawthorne, ponders the inescapable flow of time and the imposition of
change that make it impossible for a correspondent to write back to the
person who just sent a letter:

> This is a long letter, but you are not at all bound to answer it. Possibly,
> if you do answer it, and direct it to Herman Melville, you will missend
> it—for the very fingers that now guide this pen are not precisely the
> same that just took it up and put it on this paper. Lord, when shall we
> be done changing? Ah! It's a long stage, and no inn in sight, and night
> coming, and the body cold. But with you for a passenger, I am content
> and can be happy. I shall leave the world, I feel, with more satisfaction
> for having come to know you. Knowing you persuades me more than
> the Bible of our immortality. (*MM* 91–92)

By quoting this passage, Howe complicates its meaning. It supports
Howe's notion of the ungraspable author who changes in the process of
writing and who has already partly disappeared once the text is finished.
Accordingly, Melville explains that Hawthorne will not be able to answer
the very person whose letter he received. In a sense, the only way to
answer the person who wrote the letter is to repeat the letter. Subjectivity

is text-bound and the subject can only be addressed via the text in which he becomes manifest. Howe also quotes the letter as an echo of Mangan's self-depiction as "Van Woedenblock of the Magic Leg." Both writers speak of life in terms of a journey on which, for Mangan, there is "no stopping place" and for Melville, there is "no inn in sight." Melville evokes Mangan's idea of "stationary," for the pen that his hand holds is the only stable element while "the fingers that now guide this pen" are continuously changing. Both ponder mortality, which to Mangan is the "ultimate repose," and for Melville more gloomily "the night coming, and the body cold," which, however, is warmed and given hope by having come to know kindred spirits like Hawthorne.

Howe's use of quotation contains an implicit critique of what she considers the straitjacketing of voices in other texts. She lets a voice speak for itself without "rectifying" it in any way. In *My Emily Dickinson*, she studies Dickinson's use of space and of alternative words that get standardized or erased in the published editions of her poems. In her essay on the captivity narrative of Mary Rowlandson, she points out instances of "ideological corrections" whenever Rowlandson's narrative threatens to undermine the Puritan/Savage binarism. In her poem on the biblical empty grave scene, also titled "The Nonconformist's Memorial," she criticizes the evangelists' "formulae of striking force" (*NM* 13), which effectuate Mary Magdalene's erasure from the story, at least in St. Peter's gospel: "In Peter she is nameless" (*NM* 6). His "act of Uniformity ejected her" (*NM* 5). Howe is astonished by the evangelists' urge to separate the story from the storyteller: "Mary, the disciple, the first one who witnesses the resurrection, the one whose story we go by, gets dropped away almost at once" (*K* 11). Whereas the encounter with Jesus puts Mary into a state of ecstatic joy, the disciples approach her testimony with intellectual sobriety. They attempt to master Mary's testimony through "Intellectual grasp" (*NM* 15). In her interview with Lynn Keller, Howe explains that the term *grasp* carries sexual connotations and implies the simultaneity of the violation of the transgressive experience by the narrative's "striking force" and of the violation and erasure of the female witness by the male usurpers of the story.[20] Howe contrasts the disciples' violating "grasp" with Mary's loving submission to Jesus's demand *not* to cling to him or to her desire for intellectual penetration of the experience.[21]

Although Howe's poetics partly embraces Foucault's author critique, she would vehemently refute his idea of the diminished importance of meaning in texts or the reduced "mark of the writer." Foucault holds that "we can say that today's writing has freed itself from the dimension of expression. Referring only to itself, but without being restricted to the confines of its interiority, writing is identified with its own unfolded exteriority. This means that it is an interplay of signs arranged less according to its signified content than according to the very nature of the signifier."[22] Although in "Melville's Marginalia" Howe emphasizes the importance of the signifier, the goal is still to signify content. Howe produces meaning precisely because she arranges her texts according "to the very nature of the signifier." Analogous to his idea of the freedom from expression in contemporary writing, Foucault advocates the idea of the writing subject's freedom from his "particular individuality": "Using all the contrivances that he sets up between himself and what he writes, the writing subject cancels out the signs of his particular individuality. As a result, the mark of the writer is reduced to nothing more than the singularity of his absence; he must assume the role of the dead man in the game of writing."[23] Howe resolutely contests his conclusion: "My voice," she writes in *My Emily Dickinson*, "formed from my life belongs to no one else."[24] If Howe quotes other voices, these augment and authenticate her self rather than diminish and relativize it. Howe's practice and Foucault's theory of authorship start out from different assumptions. Foucault questions terms such as *author* and *work* as the ideological remains of nineteenth-century bourgeois society. Howe questions these terms as a poet and not as a theorist. Her ideological critique is embedded in her personal design and experience of authorship. She does not want to deconstruct the author-subject, she wants to redefine it.

Even if Howe's poems are marked by the poet's absence, they are highly expressive of subjectivity; subjectivity only figures in unconventional ways. Instead of deriving subjectivity from the subject as a separate entity, subjectivity to Howe is a set of characteristics particular individuals throughout the centuries share. Subjectivity lies in the transcendence of difference between the subject and the other. Subjectivity is the result of a reading process and depends on the ability of memory to recognize affinities with figures from the past. Voices from the past are integrated into Howe's poems precisely because they speak what she would have spoken. Only writers such as "antinomians" or "library cormorants," toward whom she feels an intimate relation, are eligible. Formerly unconscious or unexpressed parts of subjectivity rise to consciousness, are remembered, when she discovers them in voices from the past. Expressing subjectivity through words of others or using their words as points of departure for her own poems, Howe redefines subjectivity. Subjectivity finds expression in the textual practice of "writing as continuing," with its variants of elaborating, or taking prior texts as starting points for her own; filling, or going into the gaps and silences of texts and reimagining the past they represent; and repeating, or quoting particularly resonant text passages and individual words. Instead of criticizing "Melville's Marginalia" and the other poems in *The Nonconformist's Memorial* for authorial opacity, I suggest that the poet is intensely present through different means. Subjectivity in Howe's poetry is mnemonic subjectivity, because the "I" is recognized in the other and remembered by means of a detour to the other.

TYPOGRAPHICAL DISJUNCTION

The poems in the second part of "Melville's Marginalia" strike the reader with their unconventional line arrangements that "interrupt" the quotations by and on Mangan and whose form increases the impression of fragmentation. Analyzing the functions of the line arrangement, which Howe says is "subconscious" (*K* 8), is to find the narrative conjunctions that produce meaning and make the poem memorable. In the case of the poem starting with "THE MANNER OF LIVING" (*MM* 95), for example, the regularly, sometimes slightly diagonally written lines read: "THE MANNER OF LIVING / WITH / GREAT MEN / Led I used not to see / Whose life was spent / in going from one house / to another / Those who have been wronged / now in literature." The upside-down lines from bottom to top are: "Magnanimity cannot / naturally / Life deceives us / x what delicate irony / take it to be their privilege / and birthright to insult me." The fragmented nature of this poem allows for many readings, but I will present only a few interpretations that can be derived from the context and the text's placement in the poem as a whole. The "great men" are contrasted with "those who have been wronged" and who supposedly are "now in literature." The lines that are written regularly and in capital letters ("THE MANNER OF LIVING / WITH / GREAT MEN") imitate an official voice or "The bark of parchment," the line by which the second version of the poem is introduced (*MM* 96). The "bark" refers to the materiality of parchment or paper but also puns on the verb "to bark" and invokes the commanding violence of the paper inscribed by "great men." The lines following the ones in capital letters emanate from "living with great men": the speaker is being "led" and does not "see." She does not see "Whose life was spent / in going from one house / to another" and that she was "wronged." Compared to the regularly typed lines that can still be read successively and that are tentatively contextualized within this succession, the reversely typed lines stand more independently: "Magnanimity cannot," "naturally," "Life deceives us," "x what delicate irony" (*MM* 95). Strikingly, the only more elaborate, syntactically complete, and semantically intelligible sentence is typed upside down and placed in between the capitalized line "THE MANNER OF LIVING / WITH / GREAT MEN": "Take it to be their privilege / and birthright to insult me" (*MM* 95). Arguably, these two lines, which exemplify the "delicate irony" mentioned in the preceding line, are formally the most solid and stable lines, as opposed to the authorial and capitalized, typographically inflated voice of the "great men."

Particularly when the lines are not read in two groups—first the regular and then the reversed ones—but in the order in which they appear on the page, upside-down lines can be interpreted as demonstrating visually that "voices from the past constantly interfere" (*K* 13). Thus, the reversed lines function as the interruption of narrative and as the intrusion of "some other thought going in some other direction" (*K* 9). Their frag-

THE MANNER OF LIVING
WITH
and birthright to insult me *(upside down)*
GREAT MEN
Led I used not to see
take it to be their privilege *(upside down)*

what delicate irony x *(upside down)*

Life deceives us *(upside down)*
Whose life was spent
naturally *(upside down)*
in going from one house
Magnanimity cannot *(upside down)*
to another
Those who have been wronged
now in literature wronged

Figure 2.1. (*MM* 95)

mented state could be explained as their reemergence from repression, nonrecognition, or marginalization. Howe attributes this function to the reversed lines when she presents her poems in poetry readings and meticulously elaborates in which order, pitch, and speed to read the lines. "If I read the poem aloud," she explains, "I whisper all the upside-down words, and that way they sound like another voice—the hissing return of the repressed" (K 11). Because these lines signify the "return of repressed" voices, they simultaneously represent the voices' prior erasure. So the reversed lines also remember the silences of the historical accounts in which they were obliterated. Possibly, the voices of the "repressed" in "Melville's Marginalia" represent those that "have been wronged" by "living with great men." Because they are "now in literature," the voices could refer to *any* marginal writer. Therefore, Susan Schultz's feminist interpretation of the reversed lines as "the woman's voice, upside-down as it is," which "does appear, and shows up (quite literally) the masculine voice, for all its typographical certainty about itself," must be received with reservation. [25]

Howe's experimental poems can also be read as visual constructs depicting voices on a stage. As if directing a theater performance, Howe chooses the position of the lines on the page according to acoustic criteria: "The getting it right has to do with how it's structured on the page as well as how it sounds—this is the meaning" (K 19). The poet's elaboration on how she prepares for a reading reveals her emphasis on the acoustic, a preference she frequently declares: "I think sound is *the* element in poetry" (K 8). She explains that her interest in voice is possibly a consequence of being the "product of radio days" and has also been stirred by her experiences as an actress. Together with the acoustic, the element of space, which is constitutive of her poetics and remains to be elaborated, enters the poem when Howe imagines voices not abstractly but in the context of a theater: "Sometimes I think what I'm doing on the page is moving people around on stage." Howe designates "Eikon Basilike," for example, as a dramatic poem with voices moving on the stage of the page. In "Eikon Basilike," the typography is meant to express visually the violence of King Charles I's death as well as the theatrical aspects of his execution:

> In the "Eikon Basilike," the sections that are all vertically jagged are
> based around the violence of the execution of Charles I, the violence of
> history, the violence of that particular event, and also then the stage

drama of it. It was a trial, but the scene of his execution was also a performance; he acted his own death. There's no way to express that in just words in ordinary fashion on the page. So I would try to match that chaos and violence visually with words. But a lot of what determines the arrangement is subconscious, in that I would start with the lines I wanted to use (which might change somewhat) and I would just arrange them on the page until they satisfied me. (*K* 8)

Howe's arrangement of voices on the page is also inspired by her training as a painter. As she explains the origin of her poetic form in the interview with Lynn Keller, she started out plastering words on walls and developing an eye for their material form. Howe eventually began writing books after a friend of hers suggested that she transform these collages on walls into collages on the page (*K* 6). Charles Olson's "open field" poetics finds its most literal implementation in Howe's poems. Her pages look indeed as if people had walked and jumped across a field and left imprints—not in the shape of feet, but in the shape of words.

In the interview with Edward Foster, Howe explains the relationship between form and subject matter in the poem "Eikon Basilike." The material and formal aspects of the poem are intended to reflect Edward Almack's impossible bibliographical project to trace the King's Book back to origins that, from the beginning of its circulation, had been obscure: "So I wanted to write something filled with gaps and words tossed, and words touching, words crowding each other, letters mixing and falling away from each other, commands and dreams, verticals and circles. If it was impossible to print, that didn't matter. Because it's about impossibility anyway. About the impossibility of putting in print what the mind really sees and the impossibility of finding the original in a bibliography" (*TI* 175). Howe's attempt to represent Almack's unfeasible bibliographical project typographically also succeeds by inducing a perplexing reading process. Lines and voices interfere, cannot be brought into coherent succession, and perturb conclusions as to "meaning," "authorial intention," and "authorial identity." Confronting "the impossibility of putting in print what the mind really sees," Howe generates "not seeing" rather than "seeing" and infinitely prolongs the reading process by never allowing a final "vision."

The poem "THE MANNER OF LIVING / WITH / GREAT MEN" offers another typographical solution to the "impossibility of putting in print what the mind really sees." Instead of imitating the futility of searching for authorial coherence, this poem represents the various layers and facets of thought suppressed but still present in "THE MANNER OF LIVING / WITH / GREAT MEN." These capitalized, inflated, and encrusted lines suppress the lines below representing the perspective of "those who have been wronged." But the "great men's" reign is threatened: the regular lines following the capitalized ones are derived from the "oppression" by "great men" and express a state of resignation. The reversed lines, however, climb back up to the top and squeeze in between the capitalized lines. Only seemingly do they *underline* them; above all, they *undermine* them. Print, in its most powerful, capitalized form, is reserved for the discourse of "great men," while excluded and marginalized voices constitute an "impossibility of putting in print." However, by printing unconventionally that which is not allowed in print, that is, in unlinked, diagonal, or reversed fashion, the poet finds means to represent poetic memory or, here, the "repressed" portions of the past.

The adjacent poems provide "THE MANNER OF LIVING" with a context and constitute another technique of narrative conjunction. Howe frequently writes two poems from the same lines, leaving the lines mostly unchanged and only changing their arrangement. The poem "THE MANNER OF LIVING / WITH / GREAT MEN" has a second version on the following page. The lines that before were printed in standard typography are now written upside down, while the previously reversed lines can now be read regularly, as if the poet wanted to rule out any possibility of ignoring them. The regular lines now are: "Magnanimity cannot / naturally / Life deceives us / x what delicate irony / take it to be their privilege / and birthright to insult me." The upside-down lines read: "The bark of parchment / THE MANNER OF LIVING / WITH / GREAT MEN / Led I used not to see / Whose life was spent / in going from one house" (*MM* 96). The difference between versions one and two of the poem can be interpreted as the overthrow of the former hierarchy by "Those who have been wronged / now in literature." The omission of these lines in the second version of the poem implies that the formerly "wronged" are now speaking. Accordingly, the line added in the second version and now printed in reverse on the very bottom of the poem, "The bark of parchment," was the voice speaking in the first version. The two versions of the poem fathom and represent voices almost extinguished by the "bark of parchment." They redeem these voices by granting them priority over those of "great men."

On the page preceding "THE MANNER OF LIVING," Howe prepares for the reign of the "great men" as the protagonists of history when she compares the poet's task with the historian's: "A / poet / does not relate / real / events / 2. For then / she would clash / with the histo- / rian connect- ing / them / by a verbal / association / in a strange / order" (*MM* 94). The binary opposition Howe establishes between poet and historian can be viewed as a commentary on the poem. What distinguishes poet and his- torian, according to Howe, is the "order" into which they put events. The two versions of the poem "THE MANNER OF LIVING" consist of the same fragments but in alternating arrangement. Howe argues that no matter whether arranged by the poet or the historian, assembling the pieces of the past is always a work of memory and merely the criteria for the assemblage vary.

Having contrasted the poet's with the historian's work, Howe quotes from Mangan to attenuate this binarism: ". . . A song supposed to be sung by a migratory gang of Thugs from India, lies before us. Fortunately it is of questionable authenticity . . ." (*MM* 94). This quotation gains greatest complexity when considered as a "definition" of historiography: history is a "song" and thus generically conflated with literature. Mangan speaks not of the "great men" of history but pejoratively calls them a "migratory gang of Thugs from India," also referring to the migratory movements of those tribes that generated the fall of the Roman Empire and that later on would be called "Europeans." In this profoundly ironic tone, Mangan continues: "Fortunately it is of questionable authenticity" (*MM* 94). Con-

The bark of parchment
THE MANNER OF LIVING
WITH
and birthright to insult me
GREAT MEN
Led I used not to see
take it to be their privilege
what delicate irony $_x$

Life deceives us

Whose life was spent
naturally

in going from one house
Magnanimity cannot

Figure 2.2. (*MM* 96)

tending with claims of objectivity and truthfulness, Mangan asserts this "song" is not trustworthy at all, and "fortunately" so because history is not the story of "great men" but of "thugs." Mangan uses the language of literature to make a radical claim about history of which, due to the register he chooses, he cannot be accused.

Mangan pursues the opposite strategy, that is, speaking like a historical investigator about a piece of literature, in a passage directly following "THE MANNER OF LIVING / WITH / GREAT MEN." Mangan discusses Antony's oration over Caesar's corpse and argues that it is much more plausible to read the line "lend me your ears" as "lend me your cars" (*MM* 95). After all, he maintains, Antony needed a car to organize Caesar's funeral. Mangan plays the truth- and fact-loving historian who subjects literary artifice to logical inquiry without, however, finding an explanation that would in any way be less absurd. He mocks "logical" approaches to the past while simultaneously playing with his listeners and their "obligation" as rational beings to yield to such argumentative cogency.

Intratextual reference and doubleness are conjunctive techniques that, as in the case of the two versions of "THE MANNER OF LIVING / WITH / GREAT MEN" and the two passages blurring the tasks of poet and historian, serve to relativize the formerly "said," even though the formerly "said" may already allow for many different readings itself. The reader is challenged with a second version that does not allow him the safety of his initial understanding. Howe deconstructs the binarisms she sets up between "great men" and "those . . . wronged," between historians and poets.

THE DISRUPTED WORD

Howe writes poetry not only of syntactical fragments but also of fragmented words, and in poems experimenting with the materiality of the signifier, the margins and the blank space on the page become more prevalent elements. Howe's poetry is energized by the tension between the represented and the unrepresentable, between the text and the nontext. In Peter Quartermain's words, there is tension "between Howe's enchanted fascination with and desperate possession by history and with language, and her intense desire to be free of them; between her desire for the secure, the stable, and the defined, and her apprehension of them as essentially false; between her impassioned attraction to, and sheer terror of, the wilderness."[26] Howe's experiments with the materiality of the signifier are conditioned by her ambivalent attitude toward words as both hindering and enabling our memory. On the one hand, "words are used as buoys, and if they start to break up . . . [. . .] Then everything goes because words connect us to life" (*TI* 178). The metaphor of the "buoys" implies that words offer orientation in a shifting, changing, and unfathomable reality. Accordingly, "Words are the only clues we have" (*TI* 178). They are clues that trigger thinking, for words are also "a wood for thought" (*SWS* 39). On the other hand, Howe remarks, the thinking process that they inspire may be insubstantial, and then "Words are an illusion / are vibrations of air / Fabricating senselessness" (*SWS* 38). In their fixity, they also form an "impediment" (*MM* 149) to memory. Like the densely inscribed pages of a history book that not only transmit memory but also form a wall between the historical narrative and the past that the narrative leaves out, the word, too, both enhances and debilitates our memory of the past. In the process of "immersing herself in the past," Howe says she reads everything she can find on her selected topic; yet she questions the credibility of the texts. To her, skepticism toward texts as carriers of history is a symptom of "memory mutinies."[27]

In "Melville's Marginalia," Howe experiments with the material shape of the word on the page. The typographical or orthographic play with the signifier reveals much more meaning than its regular form in print. This is the case, for example, in the poem that revolves around the line "coffin the sea," in which Howe imagines the sea as a coffin.[28] While the noun *coffin* keeps its shape throughout the poem, the word *sea* constantly changes. To play on the pun that also entered Sylvia Plath's "Full Fathom Five" via intertextual reference to *The Tempest*, not only the sea changes, but the seeing too. The line could be read as "coffins see," almost a homonym for "coffin the sea." But Howe does not exactly write *sea* either; the letter *e* is rather printed on top of the syllable *sa*. Such printing changes the tense of "coffins see" into "coffins saw" and suggests the simultaneity of present and past. If one reads the two vowels separately, as the typography suggests, the word *seer* appears, which would also be the pronunciation of the second line where *sea* is printed as *se a*. In slurry speech, the line reads "coffin's here." Similarly, the third line "Coffin th s woorD" (the *r* is written into the capital *D*) suggests "coffin's wood" or "coffin the wood." Printed with the small *r* within the space of the capital *D*, the word *wood* is combined with the word *word*, whence probably Howe's aphorism "Language a wood for thought" (*NM* 39). Then again, *thought* can be read as a variant of *sought*, and words would thus become a material, that is, wood, that is sought or must be searched for. Phonetically, "wooD" is the past tense and the past participle of the verb *to woo*: coffins woo the speaker or are wooed by her. The verb *woo* is very close to *woe*, as if courting somebody was related to mourning somebody. Reading "woorD" with the preceding *s*, the word *sword* emerges and transforms the line into "coffin the sword."

"Coffin the sea" is an elegy. As an object, the coffin holds somebody who is wooed and woed. It functions as a "sword" cutting the dead off from the living. As a word, its meaning is as ungraspable as the shifting signifier "sea." At the end of Melville's *Moby-Dick*, a coffin ironically bobs to the surface of the sea after the *Pequod* has been shipwrecked, and Ishmael, the narrator, uses it as a raft to save his life. The meaning of the coffin is indeterminate; it constitutes "wood for thought." The poet's experiments with fragmented words epitomize her ambivalent attitude toward language, both hopeful and despairing.

Disruption, as displayed in the poem "coffin the sea," is a mode of poetic memory and has several mnemonic implications. First, by playing with the signifier, Howe experiments with the search for the origins of language and sound. Second, if the poem is concerned with death, one way of representing death would be to hint at the disintegration of lan-

Coffin th &a

Coffin th se a

Coffin th s   wooD

ŕ e wr t ebly quell

in pencil s c atte

but poetry

Coffin th se ʍ

Coffin th se w

Coffin th se wooD

Figure 2.3. (*MM* 123)

guage and sound. Simulating a process in which language gradually dissolves may correspond to the attempt to follow the deceased person as far as the living subject can before her own death in language. Third, diffusing the signifier may not only be an attempt to approximate death but, in psychoanalytic terms, also to approximate the period *before* the "advent of the Symbolic."

Although my reading of the poem shows how words are "impediments" and how, when "torn to pieces," a greater variety of meaning surfaces, it is not clear how all this is the deed of memory. Equally enigmatic as the line "the impediment of words torn to pieces by memory" (*MM* 149) is Howe's characterization of words as an "infinite chain leading us underground" (*TI* 178). To start with the latter, the term *underground* suggests that Howe conceives of the signifier as a surface structure covering a space beneath it. Arguably, the exploration of the grounds beneath the signifier *crust* is a mnemonic enterprise, because it follows the signifier back into its past and to its formative stages. Dissolving the materiality of the signifier, Howe seeks to approximate language's "place of origin." This place of "primeval Consent"[29] is the origin of individual sounds that over time came to form increasingly complex sound patterns or "sound-forms in time," the term Howe prefers in reference to words. The poet assumes that words, almost like the universe, are in constant expansion. Howe poetically inverts the formative processes of language by dissolving sentences into fragments, words into letters and smallest sound units, and typography into the blank of the page. Reversing the evolution of language also implies going back to a world less dissected, analyzed, and categorized by language than the increasing verbalization of culture has entailed over time. At the same time, it must not be forgotten that the grid of language cast on the world is meant to capture it for the purpose of its "preservation" and that the dissolution of the grid entails the loss of what it preserved. Tracing their phonetic and semantic evolution back and searching for a moment and place where things took the turn of which the present situation is the momentary result amounts to the mnemonics of the word. Whereas Howe would subscribe to the idea that language is only an approximation of what it represents, she would not agree with poststructuralist notions of two disconnected, sliding but never touching levels of the signifier and the signified. Howe does not conceive of language as a closed, abstract system cut off from the world but rather approaches language as a sensual experience. Language, to the poet, has a physical dimension, and its material and acoustic qualities make it root in the world.

Howe's dispersion of the signifier points not only to death, but also to what psychoanalysts call the presymbolic phase before the advent of language. In particular, Howe's mnemonics of the word evokes Julia Kristeva's concept of the semiotic element in language. Kristeva has worked on the avant-garde poetics of Mallarmé and Lautréamont, and she has elaborated the concept of the semiotic to account for the relationship between disrupted (poetic) text forms and the text as an expression of subjectivity. Complementing the symbolic and strictly "logical" dimension of language ("logical" in both senses of logos and coherence), Kristeva defines the semiotic as the "psychosomatic modality of the signifying process"[30] or as "drives and their articulations."[31] Whereas, to Lacan, the Symbolic imposes the structures on the psyche subsumed under the concept of the "Law-of-the-Father," such as logic, order, and cognition, and dismisses the body from language, the concept of the semiotic allows Kristeva to have the body reenter language.

By undermining the symbolic order in her texts, Howe's poetics energizes the semiotic dimension. Kristeva claims that poetic language reactivates the semiotic dimension of language most radically. "When poetic language—especially modern poetic language—transgresses grammatical rules," Kristeva writes, "the *positing* of the symbolic . . . finds itself subverted, not only in its possibilities of *"Bedeutung"* or denotation . . . , but also as a possessor of *meaning* (which is always grammatical, indeed more precisely, syntactic)."[32] Differentiating between *"Bedeutung"* and "meaning," Kristeva distinguishes between the generation of meaning on the level of the signifier (*"Bedeutung"*) and on the level of its position in a syntactical construct ("meaning"). The deconstruction of meaning represents the more systematic and therefore thorough unsettlement of the symbolic structure.[33] Howe subverts the symbolic order on both signifying levels of language, on the levels of *"Bedeutung"* and "meaning." The typographical and orthographic deconstruction of the signifier invites the reading of many signifiers within the one: *sea* also means *see, saw,* and *seer; s woorD* could be *wood, word, sword, wooed,* and *woed.* Sometimes, the dissolution of the signifier alone already entails the upheaval of the grammatical structure: both *wooed* and *woed* could be the *active* simple past forms of the infinitive *woo* and *woe* or the *passive* past participles. This raises the question of who is wooed or woed by whom. Howe's

syntactical fragments often do not allow for the anticipation of a gram-
matical structure as the frame for meaning. In both "coffin the sea" and
"coffin the s word" the predicate is omitted. But the predicate negotiates
the relationship between subject and object or between the subject and
the world.[34] Its deletion shakes the very grounds on which the constitu-
tion of subjectivity has taken place. In Howe's poem, the reader tends to
recreate the relationship between the two nouns—*coffin* and *sea*, *coffin* and
sword—by reading the object (*sea* and *sword*) as verb (*see* and *woo*/*woe*).
This predication of the object signifies the subject's rebirth into the world
through wooing and woeing. Having been put at risk by its approxima-
tion to death, subjectivity is reconstructed in the reading process.

Howe's play with the signifier also highlights the material and acous-
tic dimension of language and could therefore be ascribed a semiotic
effect by allowing the "body" back into language. Howe's disrupted texts
accentuate the pre-symbolic blank space of the page and allude to what
has been canceled out by language. Reminiscent of Howe's emphasis on
the page as uninscribed space, Kristeva designates the semiotic as a
"space" underlying the symbolic side of language by which it is simulta-
neously restrained: "Indifferent to language, enigmatic and feminine, this
space underlying the written is rhythmic, unfettered, irreducible to its
intelligible verbal translation; it is musical, anterior to judgment, but re-
strained by a single guarantee: syntax."[35]

Although Howe's experience of the physicality of language seems to
bring her closer to Kristeva's semiotic notion of language, the poet's texts
exceed that theory. Whereas, to Kristeva, the semiotic is the dimension of
language that produces *jouissance*, Howe's emphatically "semiotic" poem
"coffin the sea" seems to enact anything but *jouissance*. The disruption of
the symbolic order here rather reflects an experience of death ("coffin the
sea") and traumatic loss ("coffin the sword"). This interpretation of the
tone of the poem is also supported by the intertextual reference it makes
to Marianne Moore's poem "A Grave."[36] As in Howe's poem, in Moore's
poem the sea is compared to a grave: "the sea has nothing to give but a
well excavated grave." The sea is connoted with loss—"the sea is a collec-
tor, quick to return a rapacious look"—and a sense of forgetting and
decay: "There are others besides you who have worn that look— / whose
expression is no longer a protest; the fish no longer investigate them /
for their bones have not lasted." Also, Kristeva tries her theory on fin de
siècle *male* poets, such as Mallarmé and Lautréamont. Looking at the

presence of the semiotic in texts by female poets, however, Kristeva does not credit it with the antinomian quality and success of their male counterparts, but views Virginia Woolf's, Marina Tsvetayeva's, and Sylvia Plath's play on the verge of language as following "the call of the mother" and as a step on their path to suicide. If a woman immerses herself into the preoedipal realm of the mother and allows language, the symbolic order of the father, to be "torn apart by rhythm," Kristeva believes, "the moorings of the ego begin to slip, life itself can't hang on."[37] Disregarding Kristeva's pessimism, Howe draws successfully on the semiotic dimension of language. She can risk the unsettlement of the symbolic order because the self remains anchored in the way it resonates with voices from the past. These carefully selected voices of kindred spirits occupy a transitional space between the absence of the symbolic order and its normative imposition. The poet recognizes her self in a past that exceeds her historic memory. She encounters her self by practicing poetic memory through the texts she finds or is found by.

THE MARGINAL

When examining disjunctive poetry, one can either focus on the disrupted words and texts or on what they are disrupted by: the margins and the blank of the page. Relating typography to memory, print would correspond to the remembered, the margin to the risk of forgetting, and the blank to the forgotten. Only that which finds expression and materialization in language can be remembered. The rest disappears into oblivion. In Howe's poetry, the white space plays a much more important and active role than that of space which has simply not been inscribed. An "economically" structured page consists of a lot of print and narrow margins. The opposite proportion between print and blank on Howe's pages shows her preoccupation with those dimensions of the past not contained by our (textually mediated) memory of it.

If the page represents degrees of remembering and forgetting, typography functions as a means of historical cartography. This analogy between a page of poetry and a map is supported, for example, by the spatial, botanical, and bibliographic meanings of the term *margin*: "A margin is a border, edge, brink or verge of land. In botany a margin is the edge of a leaf. In books the margin is the edge of a page, left blank or to be filled in with notes" (*SM* 28). It is implied that the analogy between geography and the book is not constructed by the poet but required by the semantics of the word *margin*, which stands for edges in many different contexts, and in Howe's use, generally signifies a position "close to the limit" (*MM* 92). More precisely, the page, to Howe, is a trope for a map of American space and history. "What interested me in both Olson and Robert Smithson,"[38] Howe writes, explaining the relationship between writing and mapping, "was their interest in archaeology and mapping. Space. North American space—how it's connected to memory, war, and history. I suppose that's the point at which it began to dawn on me that I needed to do more than just list words. I was scared to begin writing sentences" (*K* 5). Writing sentences, to Howe, means leaving marks on history and writing history at the same time. She compares her poetry to "Historiography of open fields" (*EB* 58). By "open field" she refers to all those characteristics of her poetry that distinguish her writing from "closed texts." While "historiography of open fields" is a way to describe poetic memory, "closed texts" refer to historic memory.

Most explicitly, Howe explores the relationship between North American space and history in "Thorow," a poem composed in memory of Henry David Thoreau on the shores of Lake George in the Adirondacks. Here, the poet is situated at the borders of American civilization, which she equates with the limits of history: "I thought I stood on the shores of a history of the world where forms of wildness brought up by memory become desire and multiply."[39] This pivotal line in "Thorow" qualifies as a poetic manifesto: Howe imagines the lakeshore as the shore of history, and geographical topography becomes historical cartography. The American "wilderness" is paired with the "dark side of history."[40] Howe is thrilled by the marginal position on the brink of the western settlements and on the verge of history because it bestows intimations of wildness on her. She conceives of memory as poetic memory, and she designates memory as the mediating faculty between the wilderness and civilization.

Howe also identifies with the margins of historical narratives because she is a woman. The margins are more likely to render the poet a past she can accept as hers: "If you are a woman, archives hold perpetual ironies. Because the gaps and silences are where you find yourself" (*TI* 158). Seeking a home in history, Howe searches "the dark side of history" for marginalized and straitjacketed voices, for the voices of "antinomians" and "nonconformists." Consequently, many of Howe's essays are peopled with figures—Anne Hutchinson, Dorothy Talbye, Mrs. Hopkins, Mary Dyer, Thomas Shepard, Mrs. Sparhawk, Brother Crackbone's wife, Mary Rowlandson, Barbary Cutter, and Cotton Mather (*BM* 4)—who lead her to the periphery of normative experience.

To Howe, the collective historical marginal is related to the individual, psychic marginal. That which is collectively repressed or forgotten is akin to that which the individual represses or forgets. Retrieving marginalized voices may, in fact, help to recover repressed parts of the self. This process of self-exploration may be triggered by feelings of love. Howe's subjective selection of voices follows intimations of love: "They walk in my imagination and I love them" (*BM* 4). Love, however, originates in the recognition of some quality in the other that one seeks to unfold in oneself: "Somewhere Coleridge says," Howe paraphrases, "that love may be a sense of Substance/Being seeking to be self-conscious" (*BM* 4). One feels drawn to voices when they awaken unconscious parts of the self. The logic underlying this analogy between collective memory and personal memory is that the same authoritarian principles that select what will go into the former also influence the formative processes of subjectivity. To give a concrete example from "Melville's Marginalia," if Mangan is exiled to the margins of the literary canon because he refuses to adhere to the rules of canon formation, similar rebellious impulses in a person's mind are repressed but can be recovered and made conscious through identification with Mangan.

The margins and the blank on Howe's pages endow lack with a more positive and valuable function; they serve the practice and representation of poetic memory. The margins form a transitional space between memory and oblivion. The white space imaginarily absorbs that which has been lost and escapes representation. So the uninscribed portion of the page creates a space of memory without necessarily fixating memory itself. Beyond this interpretation of the blank, it is obviously difficult to read what remains without representation. My first approach to the nonrepresented was to read Howe's poems as geopolitical cartography. The nonrepresented also has meaning with regard to textual subjectivity. The parts of subjectivity that, analogous to the poetic uninscribed space, withdraw from representation or are by definition unrepresentable can be explored by drawing on Freud's theory of the unconscious and Lacanian trauma theory. Devising a poetics that not only encompasses conscious, but also unconscious and lost memory, Howe practices poetic memory.

She rewrites subjectivity in a way that will result in its more comprehensive expression.

The white space on Howe's pages can be read as marginal or as blank, depending on one's perspective. Marginality implies that the margin functions as a border or a transitional space to a dimension beyond the page. In contrast, reading the white space as blank designates the white as already belonging to the other dimension that will continue beyond the page. Howe explicitly aligns the marginalia with Freudian concepts when, in analogy with the analysand's language, she thinks of them as immediate thoughts and associations. The Lacanian "Real," a dimension associated with trauma, recommends itself as an interpretive concept of the blank, which in Howe's poetics registers experiences of transgression and wilderness.

The marginal as that which has been repressed and is "close to the limit" is reminiscent of Freud's concept of the id, which in his *New Introductory Lectures on Psycho-Analysis* (1933) he defines as the unconscious mental region "that is foreign to the ego."[41] Peter Nicholls calls Howe's margins "something akin to the textual unconscious."[42] Similarly to Howe who is attracted by the marginal "dark side of history," Freud speaks of the id as "the dark, inaccessible part of our personality."[43] While reserving the margins for the repressed dimensions of history, Howe is particularly fascinated by marginalia as a "genre" of writing that, by definition, is practiced on the borderline position of the margin. Howe believes that Melville's marginal scribblings grant access to "fringes of consciousness or marginal associations" (*MM* 91). So the margin of a text designates the limits of consciousness. Howe's characterization of Melville's marginal annotations as "penciled single double and triple scorings arrows short phrases angry outbursts crosses cryptic ciphers sudden enthusiasms mysterious erasures" (*MM* 92) comes very close to a description of the characteristics of the id, described by Freud as a "chaos, a cauldron full of seething excitations." Like the id, the margin—filled with marginalia as the traces of the unconscious on the page— "is filled with energy reaching it from the instincts, but it has no organization." The encoded inscriptions and "mysterious erasures" that marginalia represent manifest "contrary impulses," in Freud's words, that "exist side by side, without cancelling each other out or diminishing each other." Therefore, "the logical laws do not apply in the id."[44]

Although Howe conceives of the written word as the record of history, the margins refer to time beyond the historical temporality. Freud, too, thinks of the id as characterized by a non-temporality. "There is nothing in the id," he declares, "that corresponds to the idea of time; there is no recognition of the passage of time, and—a thing that is most remarkable and awaits consideration in philosophical thought—no alteration in its mental processes is produced by the passage of time."[45] Devoid of time and its transformative effects, the id represents a space of memory in its vastest dimension imaginable. Id is memory unlimited. It lacks the ability to forget: "Wishful impulses which have never passed beyond the id, but impressions, too, which have been sunk into the id by repression, are virtually immortal; after the passage of decades they behave as though they had just occurred."[46] These characteristics of unconscious memory may explain Howe's insistence on the presence of the past and the pleasure of immersing herself in it.

Both Howe's margins and Freud's id take up space incomparably larger than that of print or of consciousness. "The space occupied by the unconscious id," Freud writes, "ought to have been incomparably greater than that of the ego or the preconscious."[47] Freud's hierarchy between the id and the ego is similar to Howe's inverted hierarchy of blank and print: "The ego is after all only a portion of the id, a portion that has been expediently modified by the proximity of the external world with its threat of danger. From a dynamic point of view it is weak, it has borrowed its energies from the id."[48] In writing, the margins have usually been perceived as secondary and as the mere by-product of print. Giving priority to print implies the assumption that language is the predominant vehicle for memory. Once words are resented as impediments to memory, they become secondary and merely the means "to lead us underground," literally to the white space on which print appears. Although Howe sometimes adheres to the primacy of print and the secondariness of the page as a projective surface, she mostly inverts their proportion into a few lines of print and a lot of white space. As the shelter of the "inapprehensible Imaginary of poetry" (*SM* 29), the margins are prior to words and anything but marginal. The margins are not the unconscious frame of poetry; they are the source and very condition of its existence. Howe laments the lack of interest in and concern for the margins, be it in editing books or in thinking about the past: "Sadly, if that were ever to be anthologized, the space will get lost; space always gets lost" (*K* 19).

Whereas the space of forgetting and marginality is rarely thought of as worth preserving, Howe is fascinated by this element of the page: "I would say that the most beautiful thing of all is a page before the word interrupts it" (*K* 7). When forced to choose between text and white space, Howe decides in favor of the margins: "When this poem ["Melville's Marginalia"; my insertion] was translated in France the thing that really upset me was the way the French language forced the line to be much longer, and I would change the line rather than to have the thing get spatially floppy. If there is no margin, it doesn't work for me and I can't figure ecstatic sound or vision."[49]

In poems such as "coffin the sea" (*MM* 123), Howe's page not only represents the psychic proportions of id and ego by assigning print and margins separate portions on the page, she also avoids the "linear outlines"[50] or clear lines of demarcation between print and white space, which, according to Freud, also do not exist between the ego and the id. Rather, ego and id must be imagined as "areas of colour melting into one another as they are presented by modern artists."[51] After having artificially separated the terrains of the id and the ego to simplify their analysis, Freud explains, "we must allow what we have separated to merge together once more."[52] Even writing unaware of the "politics" of print and margins never totally maintains their binary opposition because in conventional typography, too, the white fills the space inside and around the letters as well as the space between words and lines. In a sense, the white inside and around the letter contributes at least as much to the intelligibility of the letter as the material shape of the letter itself. In some of Howe's poems, the importance of the white space is amplified by the typographical simulation of its intrusion into the signifier.

Although both Freud and Howe take great interest in the phenomenon of the "marginal," their ideas about subjectivity and the marginal differ. In Freud's various models of subjectivity, the id is the domain most difficult to access. Although he unsettles the notion of the rational, self-determined subject by claiming that the id is a domain withdrawn from human self-consciousness, and although he divides the psychic apparatus into three domains, he never questions the unity of the subject as such. The unity of the subject is also guaranteed by the biological circumscription of his life, which starts with birth and ends with death. To Howe, subjectivity is marked by greater dispersion in time and space. It is not a consequence of biology but something that needs to be formed and is continuously in the process of formation. Subjectivity does not root within the one life alone but requires resonance with the past. It can be imagined as a thread, or as multiple threads, that bind a subject to figures in the past. Both Freud and Howe insist on the exploration of the marginal but for different reasons. Freud, the psychoanalyst, lays emphasis on cure. Along the lines of his famous dictum "where id was, there ego shall be," the aim of psychoanalytic therapy is to enable the ego to "appropriate fresh portions of the id."[53] For the sake of cure, psychoanalysis accepts that these portions of the id will "lose their importance and be deprived of their cathexis of energy, when they have been made conscious by the work of analysis."[54] Howe, the poet, does not aim at the exploration of the marginal to settle and appropriate it. She rather dwells in that transitory space between memory and forgetting, the represented and the nonrepresented to "figure ecstatic sound and vision." Whenever, in the process of writing, she positions herself on the borderline of the margin and wrests away an intimation of the wilderness, she laments that "Printing ruins it" (*MM* 147).

THE BLANK

Whereas, according to my reading of Howe's poetics of space, the marginal designates a zone between historiography and oblivion and qualifies as akin to the unconscious whose storage can be retrieved under certain conditions, the blank corresponds to the void and by definition defies representation. Analogous to Howe's understanding of the page as a map of history, the blank can be interpreted as the space reserved for traumatic experiences in American history. The association of the blank with pain has already been affirmed by Dickinson. Dickinson, Howe's worshipped poetic foremother, thinks of the blank as the domain of timelessness: "Pain—has an Element of Blank— / It cannot recollect / When it begun— or if there were / A time when it was not—." Dickinson not only associates the blank with a space beyond representation and historiography but also with suffering. The second and final stanza reads: "It has no Future—but itself— / Its Infinite contain / Its Past—enlightened to perceive / New Periods—of Pain."[55] Howe's and Dickinson's blank have in common that, despite its "infinite contain," recollection is inhibited. Impossible to be remembered and thus represented, such pain has "no Future—but itself—" or, in psychoanalytic terms, its own repetition and reexperience.

Some historical figures that "obsess" or "haunt" Howe experienced trauma. Howe transforms the page into a psychohistorical space capable of approximating the unrepresentability of trauma. A prominent group among the historical figures that attract Howe's interest are persons who had an experience of "wilderness," foremost Mary Rowlandson, who was captured by Native Americans, and Hope Atherton, who accompanied New England militia to counter an attack by Native Americans, lost his troop, and went astray in the wilderness.[56] Both Mary Rowlandson's and Hope Atherton's are experiences of "fright," as Freud calls it in *Beyond the Pleasure Principle*, defining the term as "the state a person gets into when he has run into danger without being prepared for it; it emphasizes the factor of surprise."[57] Because trauma is a sudden, violent blow inflicted on the psyche, the person could not prepare for this. "The traumatized," as Cathy Caruth clarifies the relationship between the present and a traumatic past, "carry an impossible history within them, or they become themselves the symptom of a history that they cannot entirely possess." The trauma amounts to "a pathology . . . of history itself."[58] Because the traumatic event has not, in the strict sense of the word, been "experienced" and remains an unpossessed portion of the past, it possesses the person. The symptoms of traumatization only show belatedly. The victim of trauma cannot narrate his traumatic experience, and any account narrated to him by a second party remains potential instead of verisimilar. He acquires no sense of conviction, Freud says, of the correctness of the narrative construction that has been communicated to him. Both Rowlandson and Atherton carry such an impossible history. She was "Invisible to her people. Out in a gap in the shadows" (*MR* 95). "For a time" she was "elided, tribeless, lost" (*MR* 95). Being captured, Howe claims, is to experience "impossible history" because it means to be "removed" from "Western rationalism, deep and deeper into limitlessness, where all illusion of volition, all individual identity may be transformed—assimilated" (*MR* 96). Returning to the colonies, the former captives face the difficulty of having to account for their experiences in captivity without shedding the slightest doubt on the preservation of their religious faith and integrity. This paradoxical task often results in passages such as the following, where biblical rhetoric checks the wilderness experience and brings it back in line with divine providence:

> There came an Indian to them at that time, with a basket of Horse-liver.
> I asked him to give me a piece: *What*, sayes he *can you eat Horse-liver*? I
> told him, I would try, if he would give a piece, which, he did, and I laid
> it on the coals to rost, but before it was half ready they got half of it
> away from me, so that I was fain to take the rest and eat it as it was,
> with the blood about my mouth, and yet a savoury bit it was to me: *For
> to the hungry Soul every bitter thing is sweet*. (N 21–22) (MR 125–26)

Howe points out the discrepancy between the literal "rawness" of the
captivity experience and the texts' inability to control it: "There she
stands, blood about her mouth, savoring the taste of raw horse liver.
God's seal of ratification spills from her lips or from her husband's pen"
(MR 126). Howe's judgment, its ironic tone and resistance to authorial
control, is, of course, anachronistic in the historical context of Rowland-
son's captivity, which occurred about three hundred years ago. Just as
Rowlandson imposes biblical order on her wilderness experience, the late
twentieth-century poet speaks and judges with the bias of her time,
which here is the analysis of power in discourse. But Howe is not inter-
ested in historicizing Rowlandson's testimony or in considering its func-
tion in Puritan culture. She is aware of her partiality, which she hopes
will be relativized by language itself: "Certainly my essays are often an-
gry, and the drive that propels me is some kind of feeling of righting a
wrong. But then language has its own message" (K 23). Howe's judgment
of Rowlandson's narrative as both reactionary and subversive must also
be received with the reservation of her own bias:

> Mary Rowlandson's thoroughly reactionary figuralism requires that
> she obsessively confirm her orthodoxy to readers at the same time she
> excavates and subverts her own rhetoric. Positivist systems of psycho-
> logical protection have disintegrated. Identities and configurations
> rupture and shift. Her risky retrospective narrative will be safe only if
> she asserts the permanence of corporate Sovereignty. Each time an
> errant perception skids loose, she controls her lapse by vehemently
> invoking biblical authority. "Not what the Selfe will, but what the Lord
> will," exhorted Thomas Hooker. Joseph Rowlandson warned, "If God
> be gone, our Guard is gone." (MR 100)

Howe concludes the essay: "Mary Rowlandson saw what she did not see
said what she did not say" (MR 128). Her implicit demand on Rowland-
son here is to come up with a "correct" testimony of her wilderness
experience, something which in her own poetics is admittedly impossible
and given to the blank. Howe only differs from Thomas Hooker and

Joseph Rowlandson in wanting a different version of greater "truth" from Rowlandson. Hope Atherton *did* attempt a truthful account of his wilderness experience, but "no one believed the Minister's letter."[59] In this letter, Atherton described how "he had offered to surrender himself to the enemy, but they would not receive him. Many people were not willing to give credit to his account, suggesting that he was beside himself."[60] Having been exposed to the strange, he himself "became a stranger to his community" and died soon after the traumatic exposure, which "earned him poor mention in a seldom opened book."[61]

Howe's "wilderness" evokes the Lacanian concept of the "Real," a domain that, when transgressed, causes trauma. Lacan elaborates on the Real when rereading Freud's account of the dream of the burning child. Lacan holds that the father is exposed to the realm of the Real upon the death of his child. The terror of this event is too enormous, he argues, to remain "experienceable" and therefore results in the father's missed confrontation with the death of his child. This confrontation is repeated in a dream the father has, in which the child, whose already dead body catches fire from a falling candle, speaks to him and asks: "*Father, can't you see I'm burning*?"[62] Lacan identifies three levels of reality, and the Real is implicated in all of them. It must be understood as the dimension beyond the screen of the dream and it drives the repetition.[63] In the story of the burning child, the child dies, strictly speaking, twice. In Lacan's interpretation, the foremost reality, which is traumatic and therefore "missed," is the actual death of the child. To "this not very memorable encounter—for no one can say what the death of a child is, except the father *qua* father, that is to say, no conscious being,"[64] the father literally falls asleep and leaves an old man at the vigil of the deathbed. The dream represents the second level of reality where, on one hand, the child's death is hidden from the father, because in the dream, the child is alive and speaks to him. However, on the other hand, in the dream the father is also informed about the actual fire. The dream repeats the missed reality belatedly and in a distinct way, that is, by showing the child's death through burning rather than as it really happened: from sickness. Lacan calls the dream "an act of homage to the missed reality—the reality that can no longer produce itself except by repeating itself endlessly, in some never attained awakening."[65] The third level of reality is represented by the father's awakening to the burning child and its "second death."

Susan Howe writes poetry that gives form to experiences of wilderness and approximates the unrepresentability of trauma. Trauma and symbolic representation are incompatible. Either the trauma is reexperienced, remains untranslated into symbolic form, and can be "witnessed," or, once translated into symbolic form, the trauma yields its power and makes full witnessing impossible. Cure in psychoanalytic terms may, to many survivors of trauma, be connoted negatively for it implies "the giving-up of an important reality, or the dilution of a special truth into the reassuring terms of therapy."[66] Ironically, narrative is the medium that allows for forgetting. "The possibility of integrating the lost event into a series of associative memories, as part of the cure," Caruth writes about Freudian trauma theory, "was seen precisely as a way to permit the event to be forgotten."[67] Howe is aware of the dynamics between trauma and representation and maintains that "Remembering a wild place, there is no forgetting" (*MR* 124). Yet writing a wilderness experience has an element of "killing" it: "You find it and you're trying to make it as beautiful as you can possibly make it, but you have to kill it to find it. You kill the thing into words."[68] She seeks to minimize forgetting by limiting, or rather adapting, textual representation. The stuttering and stammering language of the poems represents the broken accounts of victims of trauma. The "wild" arrangement of the lines symbolizes the interference of voices from the many layers of human consciousness. Howe carefully approximates the wilderness experience by means of a poetics that avoids the unifying persona or lyrical *I* but weaves a multitude of voices into the texture of the page. Instead of associating words on the basis of grammatical prescription, they are often associated on the basis of sound. She withstands the desire to "witness the event fully . . . at the cost of witnessing" itself.[69]

Seeking to undermine the restrictive mechanisms of language from within, Howe assigns the nonverbal or immaculate and uninscribed blank space on the page a crucial role. The role of the blank in the poems, I suggest, corresponds to the function of blankness in trauma, such as Cathy Caruth perceives it: "If repression, in trauma, is replaced by latency, this is significant in so far as its blankness—the space of unconsciousness—is paradoxically what precisely preserves the event in its literality. For history to be a history of trauma means that it is referential precisely to the extent that it is not fully perceived as it occurs; or to put it somewhat differently, that history can be grasped only in the very inaccessibility of its occurrence."[70] Howe represents the unrepresentable, traumatic past by accentuating the blank that surrounds and intrudes into her lines. Not spelling *it* out spells *it* out as much as possible and "preserves the event in its literality." Both "the phenomenon of trauma" and Howe's past before narrative "urgently . . . [demand] historical awareness and yet . . . [deny] our usual modes of access to it."[71]

Caruth envisages the possibility that "historical truth may be transmitted . . . through the refusal that is also a creative act of listening."[72] The blank, through its very lack of inscription, holds historical truth. Howe's poetics shifts the emphasis from product-oriented "knowing" to process-oriented "listening." She substitutes the model of received, ready-made memory with the processes of memory construction itself. The traumatic event, which derives its force precisely from its delay and incompletion, cannot be re-membered or re-presented but is re-experienced. Howe's focus on the process of memory construction is closest to the reexperience of the event that is unrepresentable. Limiting signification on the page and transposing it into the reader's mind is the poetic strategy most adapted to the "surprising literality and nonsymbolic nature" of traumatic dreams and flashbacks. Howe poetically renders a fragmented language from an experience of wilderness or transgression and, by inviting the reader to dwell in this prenarrative state of experience, conveys an impression of the past before its translation and its concomitant transformation into symbols. Seizing its greatest possible freedom, Howe, "through its breathless gasps," as Shoshana Felman argues with regard to Mallarmé's poetry, makes language "speak ahead of knowledge and awareness and break through the limits of its own conscious understanding. By its very innovative definition, poetry will henceforth speak *beyond its means*."[73]

The obscenity of acquiring historic memory may be the pivotal issue in Howe's *Nonconformist's Memorial*, and learning how to accept forgetting and loss is the red thread through the book's four long poems. This struggle for insight into the qualities of forgetting that do not make it a disaster per se is the concluding concern in this chapter. A line from the introductory poem "The Nonconformist's Memorial" spells out the imperative to forget. Jesus's order to Mary Magdalene is "Don't cling to me" (*NM* 11). The poetic speaker associates this line with the term *pivot*, as if the sentence were the pivot of the whole biblical scene. Howe, who believes that the association of words is not mere coincidence but represents a path "underground," adheres to her method of defining terms and comparing their definition. The onomatopoetic "cling" makes one think of the metal pivot. Pivot means "literally the unmoving point around which a body / . . . / turns" (*NM* 11). "Don't cling to me" is translated as "Literally stop touching me." The verb *turn*, which is set off from the definition of "pivot," gains another dimension in meaning as it follows the line "Literally stop touching me." In combination with the preposition *around*, "turn" would have meant to move around the pivot without ever touching it. However, because "turn" follows the line "Literally stop touching me," the reader is inclined to add the preposition *away* to the verb. No matter "Whether the words be a command / words be a command issuing from authority or counsel" (*NM* 8), they urge the addressee to let the loved person go. Even clinging to the line "Don't cling to me" is not permitted because the obsession to fathom the meaning of the line leads to the unambiguous conclusion: "Turn."

Howe believes that Mary Magdalene and Jesus loved each other, and if love incited Mary Magdalene to "stumble out on the great meadows," the death of the loved person sends her back from the "remote field" she suddenly found herself in:

> Love may be a stumbling
>
> out on the great meadows
> Prose is unknown
>
> You have your names
>
> I have not read them
>
> Coming from a remote field
> abandoned to me
>
> (*NM* 14)

The death of the loved person leaves the speaker utterly alone. She is alarmed by the fact that attempts to remember are like "Spirit snapping after air" (*NM* 27). In her "Court of interior recollection / . . . / There I cannot find there / I cannot hear your wandering prayer / of quiet" (*MM* 31). All she breathes is absence, but still, she does not abandon her hope for the eventual transformation of absence into presence: "Who is this distance / Waiting for a restoration / a righteousness" (*NM* 26).

While "The Nonconformist's Memorial" pronounces the imperative to remember without clinging, the "Silence Wager Stories" deal with the persona's attempts to adhere to it. Having been left "on an open field" now "abandoned" to her, the poem relates how the speaker lives through the experience of a full and fulfilling presence suddenly turned into utter absence: "Having a great way to go / it struck at my life / how you conformed to dust." The loss of a loved person seems to be aggravated by "lies" that had been exchanged between them. Mourning is therefore strongly tinted with anger: "Theme theme heart fury / all in mutiny." "Who goes down to hell alive / is the theme of this work." The speaker longs for peace: "Let my soul quell / Give my soul ease"; "Peace be in this house / Only his name and truth." Her conflicting emotions do not yet allow her to stop clinging:

> Far thought for thought
>
> nearer one to the other
>
> I know and do not know
>
> Non attachment dwell on nothing
>
> Peace be in this house
>
> Only his name and truth

> Though lost I love
>
> Love unburied lies
>
> No echo newlyfledge
>
> Thought but thought
>
> the moving cause
>
> the execution of it
>
> Only for theft's sake
>
> even though even
>
> perturb the peace
>
> But for the hate of it
>
> questionless limit
>
> unassuaged newlyfledge
>
> A counter-Covenant
>
> (*SWS* 36, 38–39)

Forgetting seems impossible because, as Howe writes in "The Captivity and Restoration of Mary Rowlandson," "Remembering a wild place there is not forgetting" (*MR* 124). She confronts her distress by pondering words: "Language a wood for thought / over the pantomime of thought / Words words night unto night" (*SWS* 39). Once again, words represent the path of memory. Howe ascribes words the capacity to follow the deceased person, because both words and mortality "drift" alike: "Drift of human mortality / what is the drift of words / Pure thoughts are coupled" (*SWS* 39). Instigated by the same "drift" of mortality and words, the persona takes words in as her daily food: "I feed and feed upon names" (*SWS* 40). Because, however, the word *drift* implies being carried along by currents of air or water, the word forever escapes the one searching for it. Eventually words will also prove fallible and cannot bestow final knowledge on the speaker ("I know and do not know," *SWS* 36). Words do not improve knowledge or memory, and the speaker's confidence in them breaks: "Words are an illusion / are vibrations of air / Fabricating senselessness" (*SWS* 38). Still, thinking goes on. Its movements are as inevitable as the movements of the sea, stirred by the absence of love:

> Half thought thought otherwise
>
> loveless and sleepless the sea
>
> Where you are where I would be
>
> half thought thought otherwise
>
> Loveless and sleepless the sea
>
> (*SWS* 42)

Reading the four poems of *The Nonconformist's Memorial* in their order, a transformation of the speaker's attitude toward that which cannot be remembered can be observed. Having struggled with the precariousness of remembering a loved person, the poetic speaker in "Eikon Basilike" and "Melville's Marginalia" grows interested in historical figures who refuse to be clung to. Some of these figures explicitly request more space. In "Eikon Basilike," for example, King Charles I ascended the scaffold, admonished the people to "remember," and "desired he might have *Room*" (*EB* 58). To Howe, this not only signifies that he needed room from his oppressors to speak his final words, but also that he wants room on the page. It is understood that the forged *Eikon Basilike* and the ensuing debates did not leave his memory the "Room" he had requested. "The Eikon is an imposture" (*EB* 66) because the King's memory is forced into a text of which, Howe believes, he would not have approved. Celebrating the dubious literary legacy Charles I did or did not bestow in the form of "The King's Book," Howe dedicates her "Eikon Basilike" to him as a poem practicing and enticing nonconformist memory.

Although "Melville's Marginalia" is written *in memoriam* of Melville and although Howe hopes to encounter Melville purely and immediately through his marginal annotations, the poet is aware of the impossibility of urging the loved author into full presence. She knows she occupies an "outside" position: "It just seems that I end up with this place that I wish I could belong to and wish I could describe. But I am outside looking in" (*TI* 166). Whereas absence in "The Nonconformist's Memorial" and in the "Silence Wager Stories" was intensely mourned by the speaker, it becomes an inevitability and almost normalcy in "Melville's Marginalia." The new quality Howe ascribes to absence is underlined by the "eternal wanderer" passage she quotes from Mangan's "My Bugle, and How I Blow It" (*MM* 104) and from Melville's letter to Hawthorne detailing the impossibility of writing back to the same person. Melville and Mangan describe themselves as innately escapist. This quality aligns them with the mourned person in "The Nonconformist's Memorial" and the "Silence Wager Stories." In Mangan's case, even the few traces he left are precarious: "All other simulacra / marked then ERASED," and again: "object is something erased"; "He put a veil on his face," and a little further "They are always masked." Howe insinuates that such "natural" escapism of otherness cannot be tolerated by authority. Authority makes the other "tractable" through means of oppression:

> The salary coyly said yes
>
> Drag handcuff along fence
>
> or you in it all tractable
>
> Awry pulled up by cinchstrap
>
> yes buckled to the capital
>
> green worth say yes English
>
> (*MM* 112)

The "capital" to which Mangan is supposedly tied punningly refers to London as the capital of the British Empire and to the word spelled with a capital letter, that is, "English." Mangan, the Irishman, counters (British) authority with "a certain mock hobo bravado" and stays essentially "untractable in darkness." To avoid the authoritarian grasp and to allow for true alterity, writing must be "author-evacuated." In sum, Howe transforms the precariousness of memory that she laments in "The Nonconformist's Memorial" and the "Silence Wager Stories" into a celebration of the intractability of the individual (writer) in "Melville's Marginalia." Whereas in the beginning the speaker's peace is disturbed by insufficiently stable knowledge, she sings the impenetrable alterity of the other toward the end of her book (*MM* 111–44).

"How to remember a nonconformist?" was the initial question of this chapter. Poetic memory encompasses the awareness that any form of representation cannot do the nonconformist justice, would be one answer. Poetic memory is an ongoing process without final results. It is, for Howe, the continuous reconstruction of fragments. In that, the process of memory formation runs analogous to the process of constructing subjectivity. The self, in Howe's poetic practice, is not only the sum of that which can be written, but also that which cannot be written. She demands an empty place reserved for the unknown: "We admirers of Faust / so inexpressibly wary / have no room for emptiness / in the sense of rest" (*MM* 140). Forgetting undergoes a change of meaning in *The Nonconformist's Memorial*. Rather than a pathology and unbearable condition, it becomes a form of insight and wisdom.

To Plath, the overwhelming persistence of the past in the form of fragments is threatening, particularly because the fragments were those of a civilization fallen into pieces in the Second World War. In poems like "The Colossus" and "Daddy," Plath's poetic speakers cannot appreciate the intrinsic value of the fragments because they still strive for completion. They want their labors of memory to have results. In contrast, Howe seizes on poststructuralist theory to criticize the desire for "resultfulness" in the form of textual articulateness, coherence, and order. She can experiment with the remains of literary memory more optimistically because, instead of seeking to draw a subject-status from personal memory, she assigns the collective remains of the past personal significance. Drawing on collective or marginal memory for personal reasons, Howe conflates the personal-collective binarism and opens up the collective for the practice of poetic memory. Howe's practice of poetic memory endows the textual remains of the past with subjective quality. The conflation of personal and collective memory coincides with Howe's dissolution of the present-past binarism and her assertion that she dwells in the past. Indeed, subjectivity in Howe's poems *depends* on the mnemonic amalgamation of past and present. Whereas Plath struggles with the ever incomplete subject-in-process, Howe reconstitutes it by integrating what seemed obstacles to Plath (fragments, gaps, incoherence, blanks). Howe's seemingly compromising poetics of only partial memory can be interpreted as a more comprehensive representation of memory and forgetting: poetic subjectivity encompasses memory even to the extent of its fragmentation and final loss.

Ellen Hinsey, as I will show in the following chapter, seeks yet other poetic approaches to questions of memory. While Plath struggles with mnemonic fragments that resist being fit into an aesthetic whole and Howe seeks subjective "wholeness" by representing conscious, unconscious, and lost memories, Hinsey poetically confronts a situation in which the purpose of the remains of the past has become questionable and in which the present seems to ignore their existence. Her concern is how to make the past meaningful to a present that, with increasing speed, disconnects from the past.

NOTES

1. Peter Quartermain, *Disjunctive Poetics: From Gertrude Stein and Louis Zukofsky to Susan Howe* (Cambridge: Cambridge University Press, 1992).

2. Susan Howe, "Statement for the New Poetics Colloquium, Vancouver, 1985," *Jimmy and Lucy's House of "K"* 5 (1985): 15.

3. Critics focusing on the relationship of Howe's work to history include Marjorie Perloff, "'Collision or Collusion with History': The Narrative Lyric of Susan Howe," *Contemporary Literature* 30, no. 4 (1989): 518–33; Susan Schultz, "Exaggerated History," *Postmodern Culture* 4, no. 2 (January 1994); Peter Nicholls, "Unsettling the Wilderness: Susan Howe and American History," *Contemporary Literature* 37, no. 4 (1996): 586–601; Kathleen Crown, "'This Unstable I-Witnessing': Susan Howe's Lyric Iconoclasm and the Articulating Ghost," *Women's Studies* 27, no. 5 (1998): 483–505; Paul Naylor, *Poetic Investigations: Singing the Holes in History* (Evanston, IL: Northwestern University Press, 1999).

4. Mangan recalls how as a student he answered the schoolmaster's question as to the meaning of *parenthesis* quite to the latter's satisfaction: "I should suppose a parenthesis to be something included in a sentence, but which might be omitted from the sentence without injury to the meaning of the sentence" (*MM* 93). Mangan refuses to

take credit for defining the term *parenthesis* in front of his schoolmates: the teacher wants to award him a seat up front in the class but Mangan politely declines, arguing that the boy who could not answer the question had at least studied it and that he himself just defined it spontaneously without having invested any effort (*MM* 93). Thus, Mangan performs the meaning of the term *parenthesis*: He defined it and thereby included it in the course of events at school, but it could have been as well omitted and would not have changed anything. He does not allow the act of defining *parenthesis* and of satisfying the schoolmaster to have any meaning or consequence. He cunningly hints at the pointlessness of the schoolmaster's question while hiding behind a chivalrous response.

5. "Roisin Dubh," or "Little Dark Rose" in English, is a poet's song to his beloved and has also been interpreted as a love song to Ireland.

6. Quartermain emphasizes the necessity of reading separate parts in the context of all of Howe's writing because, he points out, "her work is . . . all of one piece." Quartermain, 183.

7. This refers to Massinger's real epitaph. At the time, not being a member of the parish in whose graveyard he was buried made him a "stranger."

8. Susan Howe, interview with the author, May 22, 2003.

9. Howe talks about her studiousness when, for example, she gathered information on Mary Rowlandson: "I became totally obsessed with her, and that piece I wrote was so urgent . . . and I was up in the stacks at Sterling Library searching for information on various Native American raids near Deerfield and Hadley during the French and Indian Wars" (*TI* 167).

10. Howe believes that Hawthorne, too, doubted the "originality" of writing and that therefore he called his collection of stories *Twice-Told Tales*: "Michael Colacurcio thinks Hawthorne may have felt many of his stories were ironic repetitions of already familiar ones, and this is why he called the first book he signed his name to *Twice-Told Tales*" (*BM* 5).

11. Harold Bloom, *The Anxiety of Influence: A Theory of Poetry*, 2nd ed. (New York: Oxford University Press, 1997).

12. Fiona Green, "'Plainly on the Other Side': Susan Howe's Recovery," *Contemporary Literature* 42, no. 1 (2001): 81.

13. Susan Howe, "These Flames and Generosities of the Heart: Emily Dickinson and the Illogic of Sumptuary Values" (*BM* 143).

14. In my interview, Howe says she is obsessed with the question of when English became American English.

15. Susan Howe, "Thorow," in *Singularities* (Hanover, NH: University Press of New England), 41. Quote from Gilles Deleuze's and Félix Guattari's essay "1914. One or Several Wolves?," which is the second chapter in *A Thousand Plateaus: Capitalism and Schizophrenia*, trans. Brian Massumi (Minneapolis: University of Minnesota Press, 1987).

16. Michel Foucault, "What Is an Author?," in *Modern Criticism and Theory*, ed. David Lodge and Nigel Wood, 2nd ed. (New York: Longman, 2000), 175.

17. Nicky Marsh, "'Out of My Texts I Am Not What I Play': Politics and Self in the Poetry of Susan Howe," *College Literature* 24, no. 3 (1997): 125, 128.

18. Foucault, 181.

19. Ibid., 182.

20. *K* 11: "The Gospel when it becomes gospel, when it is written, grasps (this is all vaguely sexual, but then think about all the meanings of the word 'conception'). Mary,

the disciple, the first one who witnesses the resurrection, the one whose story we go by, gets dropped away almost at once."

21. While Howe's critique of historical and literary texts could be accused of anachronism for measuring them against late twentieth-century standards, this critique of the genesis of literature and the interference of mechanisms of ideological control could be legitimated as Howe's version of feminism. Anachronism is inherent to all feminist readings of historical texts, yet this problem would not justify dispensing with feminist critiques.

22. Foucault, 175.

23. Ibid.

24. Susan Howe, *My Emily Dickinson* (Berkeley, CA: North Atlantic Books, 1985), 13. Howe also distances herself from Foucault in the following passage: "'What is an author?' asks Michel Foucault in the essay that directly inspired and informed my writing about Anne Hutchinson, Thomas Shepard, John Winthrop, Anne Bradstreet, Mary Rowlandson, James Savage, and Emily Dickinson. Foucault's influence is problematic. This wide-ranging philosopher and library cormorant's eloquent, restless, passionate interrogation of how we have come to be the way we are remains inside the margins of an intellectual enclosure constructed from memories, meditations, delusions, and literary or philosophical speculations of European men" (*SM* 37).

25. Schultz, "Exaggerated History." The feminine, Schultz thinks, thus becomes the threatening "headstrong anarchy thought," which counters the "single" and coherent "thread of narrative" of, for example, the Gospel. "The woman's voice, upside-down as it is," Schultz elaborates, "does appear, and shows up (quite literally) the masculine voice, for all its typographical certainty about itself. Woman is figured as an impasse to narrative, but this impasse does not create incoherence so much as re-coherence." "A page like this one . . . forces an old impossibility, that of woman's speech, into possibility."

26. Quartermain, 183.

27. Susan Howe, "Articulation of Sound Forms in Time," in *Singularities*, 23.

28. The pairing of the terms *sea* and *coffin* may make reference to Susan Howe's loss of her husband David von Schlegell, whose element, she says, was the sea. *The Nonconformist's Memorial* is dedicated to him. In the interview with Lynn Keller she explains: "David was like a wall against the world to me. I felt I could do anything as long as the shelter and nurture he provided were there. . . . And it wasn't only his companionship and love but his work and his nature. He was of the sea. He was a wonderful sailor, and toward the end of his life when he couldn't sail because of the pain he was in, he could still row. He always had some kind of boat, and they were always beautiful ones. Now I feel that the sea went with him. The sea and poetry— actually for me they are one and the same" (*K* 29). David von Schlegell died on October 5, 1992. Howe: "I haven't been able to write poetry since then" (*K* 28).

29. Howe, "Statement for the New Poetics Colloquium," 15.

30. Julia Kristeva, "The Semiotic and the Symbolic," in *The Portable Kristeva*, ed. Kelly Oliver (New York: Columbia University Press, 1997), 37.

31. Ibid., 38.

32. Ibid., 46.

33. To Kristeva, the semiotic counters what Lacan called the signifier's dominance, also projected in the formula "the signifier enters the signified." See Jacques Lacan, "The Agency of the Letter in the Unconscious or Reason Since Freud," in *Ecrits: A Selection*, trans. Alan Sheridan (London: Routledge, 1977), 161–97. Lacan refers to the

idea that experience does not exist independently from language but that language is already involved in the perception and the assimilation of experience. Besides the lexicon, it is the grammatical structure of language—referred to by Kristeva as the level of "meaning" not *"Bedeutung"*—that exercises a strong effect on the human psyche, for "the dramatic transformation that dialogue can effect in the speaker" is caused by the power of grammatical structures, Lacan maintains (170). He has, for example, the introductory signifier of a sentence in mind which "by its very nature, always anticipates meaning by unfolding its dimension before it" (169). Beginnings of sentences like "'I shall never . . . ,' 'All the same it is . . . ,' 'And yet there may be . . .'" are "not without meaning, a meaning all the more oppressive in that it is content to make us wait for it" (169).

34. Margaret Homans, *Bearing the Word: Experience in Nineteenth-Century Women's Writing* (Chicago: University of Chicago Press, 1986), 7.

35. Kristeva, "The Semiotic," 38.

36. Marianne Moore, *Complete Poems* (New York: Macmillan, 1994), 49–50. Moore's influence on Howe also figures in "Melville's Marginalia," where she is mentioned explicitly: "If I be clear what is Moore / derision half-seriously" (*MM* 130).

37. Julia Kristeva, *About Chinese Women*, trans. Anita Barrows (London: Marion Boyars, 1977), 39–41.

38. Detailing the relationship between postmodern poetics and art, Howe and Smithson, would exceed the scope of this study. But the similarity between Smithson's notion of the blank and Howe's should not go unnoticed. A lot of Smithson's work is inspired by his interest in entropy, the tendency of all matter and energy in the universe to evolve toward a state of inert uniformity. The result of entropy is blankness. Due to the anachronisms they exhibit, museums, Smithson believes, also represent voids or blanks. Entropy, he holds, satisfies the human "desire for spectacle" and the "hope for disaster." Howe's blank is not a form of nothingness, but a screen that invites mnemonic contemplation. See Robert Smithson, "Entropy Made Visible: Interview with Alison Sky," in *The Collected Writings*, ed. Jack Flam, 2nd ed. (Berkeley: University of California Press, 1996), 301–9.

39. Howe, "Thorow," 40.

40. Howe, "Statement for the New Poetics Colloquium, Vancouver, 1985," 15.

41. Freud conceptualized two models of mental topography. The earlier topographical model, first presented in chapter 7 of *The Interpretation of Dreams* (1900), consists of conscious, preconscious, and unconscious; the second "structural" model, described in *The Ego and the Id* (1923), comprises id, ego, and superego. The id does not fully overlap with the unconscious because parts of ego and superego are also unconscious. Sigmund Freud, "The Dissection of the Psychical Personality" (hereafter, DPP), in *New Introductory Lectures on Psychoanalysis*, trans. James Strachey (New York: Norton, 1965), 71–72.

42. Nicholls, 593.

43. Freud, DPP, 73.

44. Ibid.

45. Ibid., 74.

46. Ibid. Freud's optimistic notion of the unconscious as the faculty authentically preserving all memory is certainly a bias typical of early psychoanalysis, which based its methods of cure on the availability of the patient's past. Meanwhile, we have become aware of phenomena showing that memory and also unconscious memory do not preserve experience in a near-authentic state. Memory can falsify the past to the

extent of inventing memories. "False" memories may then become part of the uncon-
scious as much as other impressions or experiences.

47. Ibid., 79.

48. Ibid., 76.

49. Interview with the author.

50. Freud, DPP, 79.

51. Ibid.

52. Ibid., 80.

53. Ibid.

54. Ibid., 73.

55. Dickinson, 323–24.

56. Susan Howe, "Hope Atherton's Wanderings," in *Singularities* (Hanover, NH:
Wesleyan University Press, 1990), 6–16; "The Captivity and Restoration of Mrs. Mary
Rowlandson" (*BM* 89–130). For a more detailed reading of "Hope Atherton's Wander-
ings," see Crown, "'This Unstable I-Witnessing.'"

57. Sigmund Freud, *Beyond the Pleasure Principle*, trans. James Strachey (New York:
Norton, 1961), 11.

58. Cathy Caruth, ed., *Trauma: Explorations in Memory* (Baltimore: Johns Hopkins
University Press, 1995), 5.

59. Howe, "Articulation," 4.

60. Ibid., 5.

61. Ibid., 4.

62. Jacques Lacan, *The Four Fundamental Concepts of Psychoanalysis*, ed. Jacques-
Alain Miller, trans. Alan Sheridan (London: Vintage, 1998), 59.

63. Ibid., 60.

64. Ibid., 59.

65. Ibid., 58.

66. Caruth, *Trauma*, vii.

67. Ibid. The producer of the Holocaust documentary *Shoah*, Claude Lanzmann,
calls the attempt at understanding this genocide "obscene": "It is not enough to for-
mulate the question in simplistic terms—Why have the Jews been killed?—for the
question to reveal right away its obscenity. There is an absolute obscenity in the very
project of understanding. Not to understand was my iron law during all the eleven
years of the production of *Shoah*. I had clung to this refusal of understanding as the
only possible ethical and at the same time the only possible operative attitude."
Quoted in Caruth, *Trauma*, 154.

68. Interview with the author. From a feminist point of view, Kristeva would equate
that which eludes the symbolic order with truth, and her elaboration of this thought
resonates again with Howe's poetics: "When Truth is stripped in order to be presented
as itself [a reference to Tiepolo's painting "Time Unveiling Truth"], 'truth' is lost
within itself; for in fact it has no self, it only rises between the cracks of an identity. But
once it is given form—as a woman, for example—the 'truth' of the unconscious passes
into the symbolic order, it even over-shadows it, as fundamental fetish, phallus-substi-
tute, support for all transcendental divinity" (Kristeva, *About Chinese Women*, 36–37).

69. Caruth, *Trauma*, 7.

70. Ibid., 8.

71. Ibid., 151.

72. Ibid., 154.

73. Shoshana Felman, "Education and Crisis," in Caruth, *Trauma*, 30.

THREE

Spacing the Past in Ellen Hinsey's *Cities of Memory*

As the title of her first collection of poems suggests, Ellen Hinsey conceives of her poems as *Cities of Memory*.[1] How does a poem compare to a "city" or, more precisely, a "city of memory"? Hinsey elaborates on this question: "Poems are archeological, and each contains many layers, like the many layers of Troy. There are infinite 'cities' in them, which are discovered as one goes down through the layers."[2] By the "many layers" and the "infinite cities" Hinsey points to the poem's references and dimensions of meaning that the reader may never exhaust entirely. These semantic dimensions acquire a particular "archeological" or mnemonic quality when the poet explores the texture of the past. The poems in *Cities of Memory* can be considered as mnemonic palimpsests that need to be "fathomed," which is the dominant image in a dream from which Hinsey derived the title of the book:

> The title *Cities of Memory* comes from a dream I had in which a close friend and I were descending through water toward sunken "cities of memory"; in the dream, it was not clear whether we would have enough oxygen to make the trip all the way to the bottom, and stay as long as we needed to "down there" in order to examine that underworld. (Since to explore the difficult past requires a specific type of "oxygen" which one cannot live in or breathe all the time). The dream ended with the anxiety of the unfinished, impossible, and poignant nature of the task.[3]

The past is visualized as a "sunken" city on the bottom of the sea reminiscent of Atlantis. Similar to Plath's poem "Full Fathom Five," the image of the sea is associated with processes of memory. As in Howe's poems, poetic memory approximates a limit or borderline. The space beyond that borderline—to Howe, the "wilderness," and to Hinsey, the city on the bottom of the sea—can be inhabited only momentarily; intimations wrested away from it are the poet's inspiration. Hinsey's sea world is infinitely enchanting but inherently unconquerable. Writing or remembering these cities is a task destined to remain "unfinished, impossible, and poignant." Because the poems (as cities) simulate the underwater cities, the reader must dive into, fathom, and explore them. Reading them is to breathe a different type of oxygen and destined to remain "unfinished." As Hinsey's poems share certain characteristics with a city, so does language. Structural linguists have described language in terms of its temporal and spatial—or horizontal and vertical—dimensions. Roman Jakobson identifies two methods of interpreting a sign: its "horizontal" position in the syntactical and grammatical context, which he calls "contiguity," and its "vertical" comparison with synonyms or near-synonyms, which he calls "similarity."[4] Analogously, from the walking perspective the city can be traversed and explored successively (temporally), following one item after another, or in depth (spatially), exploring one element of the architecture in its different layers. Language, to Ludwig Wittgenstein, is "a maze of little streets and squares, of old and new houses, and of houses with additions from various periods."[5] Language, like the city, is a space that can be inhabited; it evolves and changes over time and reflects the changes of history.

The comparison between language and cities or houses is a common topos in literature too. Henry James characterizes the novel as a "house of fiction." The house disposes, above all, of many windows for the reader or viewer to look inside and gain "an impression distinct from every other." In a novel, as Leon Edel, the editor of James's critical essays, elaborates on the distinctive individual reading experience, "the observers might watch the same show, but what they saw was never the same. One would see more while the other would see less; one would see black while the other saw white; one would see big, where the other saw small. And, not least, one would see coarse, where the other saw fine."[6] Preceding James and his image of fiction as a house, Emily Dickinson describes poetry as

A fairer House than Prose—
More numerous of Windows—
Superior—for Doors—

Of Chambers as the Cedars—
Impregnable of Eye—
And for an Everlasting Roof
The Gambrels of the Sky—[7]

While James's "house of fiction" is conceived as a closed system whose inner life changes according to what perspective or "window" one looks into, Dickinson's "house of poetry" refers beyond itself, to the woods ("cedars") and to the sky. As a specific language construct, the poem complicates the horizontal and vertical dimensions of language. The poem's material shape on the page constitutes a spatial construction and therefore an artifact in itself. Its temporal characteristics figure in the form of a succession of lines and stanzas as it becomes manifest in reading. The poem reinforces the vertical element of language: to a greater extent than narrative, it employs figurative language to create multilayered meaning. Its many references echo different periods of the past. Figures of speech, repetitions, and sound patterns make back-and-forth references within the poem and emphasize its spatial dimension. The spatial aspect of the poem halts its temporal continuity and complements linear modes with recursive modes of reading. Deciphering a poem involves both its spatial and temporal planes, because the reader must explore its metaphorical depth but also link its elements in consecutive order. City and poem are both "places" to be visited, explored, and lived in. They are temporal-spatial constructions through which the walker or the reader finds his own way.

The title *Cities of Memory*, which refers to cities remembered and cities made of remembering, implies that memory is solidified through its attachment to a "city." Throughout the history of Western conceptualizations of memory, memory has been thought together with material objects that would guarantee its persistence in time. The two most traditional models of memory are "inscription," an incision in a surface, and the "storehouse" from which particular items can be retrieved at will.[8] Ancient and medieval mnemotechnique projects items to be recalled on a spatial surface, "relying upon an association of places—a house, a space between columns, an arch and the like—and images."[9] The classical tale illustrating this mnemotechnique is Cicero's account of how the Greek

poet Simonides of Ceos was able to recall everybody's name thanks to the
seating order at the table after the house to which they had been invited
had crashed down on them.[10] *Cities of Memory*, too, continues the mne-
monic tradition of providing memory with material support against its
inherent deficiencies. In Jakobsonian terms, Hinsey creates a metonymic
relationship between memory and the city by "attaching" it or placing it
in contiguity to the city. In the sense of *pars pro toto*, the poet extracts
selected and exemplary memories from her exploration of the undersea
"city." She does not attach memory to real or imaginary urban topogra-
phies, however, but to the poem as a quasiphysical topography. Al-
though its spatial-temporal characteristics make it a suitable memory lo-
cus, the specific openness of the poem also makes it a comparatively
elusive and precarious carrier of memory. The formal flexibility of poetry
recommends it to the specific kind of memory I call poetic.

Unlike the cities of antiquity whose fall in history initiated the burial
of their physical remains in the ground, Hinsey's textual "cities of memo-
ry" are created as bulwarks against the "abyss of history" threatening to
devour the past. Their bulwark function is implied in the epigraph to the
first part of *Cities of Memory*, which comes from Paul Valéry's *Crisis of the
Mind*: "We had long heard tell of whole worlds that had vanished, of
empires sunk without a trace, gone down with all their machines into the
inexplorable depths of the centuries . . . but the disasters that had sent
them down were, after all, none of our affair. We see now that the abyss
of history is deep enough to hold us all" (*CM* 1). By quoting Valéry,
Hinsey laments "our often diminished relationship to 'history.'"[11] Hinsey
observes this development in American culture but also on a global level.
"When one lives in the US," she points out, "it is possible sometimes to
have the impression that history—that is, history with a capital 'H'—is
something distant from us."[12] Hinsey comments on the massive histori-
cal changes brought about by the end of the Cold War: "While the years
preceding and following 1989 were particularly charged in this respect
[historically conscious; my insertion], our present global situation seems
to indicate that an awareness of history is ever more critical. I think about
how Goethe said 'he who cannot draw on three thousand years is living
from hand to mouth.' Reading the news one often has the impression that
the world is living from hand to mouth."[13] In pretending the downfall of
past worlds has no relevance for the present, there is acute danger that
we may perceive the past as "other." The faculty that enables the percep-

tion of the past as similar to the present, or of the historical *other* as similar to the *self*, is memory.

Hinsey practices and represents poetic memory by shifting the paradigms that mark historic modes of assessing the past. Her poetic approaches to the past mend its temporal, spatial, sensual (acoustic), public, and private dimensions to renew our mnemonic abilities. The various dimensions of the past that the poems seek to capture also make up their "archaeological layers." The poems I will discuss in the first section of this chapter all remember specific "events," most of them from military history: Beethoven's death ("March 26, 1827"), a moment before the German invasion of Paris in World War II ("The Approach of War"), the Roman battle against the Veii and the German invasion of Poland in 1939 ("Lebensraum"), as well as the Spanish War against Napoleon as depicted by Goya ("The Disasters of War, Spain, 1810"). Her techniques for imagining and recreating the texture of an event vary from poem to poem. In "March 26, 1827," set on the day Beethoven died, she shifts focus away from the moment of his death by dilating (hence spatially expanding in the poem) the moments *before* and *after* the event. In "The Approach of War," she does not focus on a precise moment, such as the "outbreak" or "climax" of war, but rather looks at a *stretch* of time: war's approach. She also abandons the apparent center of the event (the Nazi conquest of Paris) to explore its impact on a peripheral location. In "Lebensraum," Hinsey avoids narrating events of World War II altogether, depicting instead a European conference on music occurring in a parallel "living space": the space of music and art. "Lebensraum" rescues an event blocked from collective memory by other events of 1939, regarded as more important. In "The Disasters of War, Spain, 1810," she complements Goya's drawings with a temporal or successive representation in (poetic) language.

The second part of this chapter consists of analyses of poems that are more explicitly reflective of the time-space amalgam constituting our reality ("The Roman Arbor," "Tones Overheard on Monastery Grounds"). Here, Hinsey explores the texture of the past by metaphorically dissecting and merging the dimensions of time and space that are differentiated conceptually but that, in the experience of the world, form an entity. While Howe moves the historical lens to the marginal and the forgotten, Hinsey personalizes our gaze at the past. In her "portrait poems" on Freud ("The Stairwell, Berggasse 19, Vienna") and a nameless woman escaping East Berlin before the completion of the wall ("The Jumping Figure"), Hinsey writes the intersections between individual biography and major events of history. In "Paula Modersohn-Becker at Worpswede," "Night in Clamart," and "Canticle in Grey," she poetically contrives the mnemonic conflation of self and other. In these three poems, Hinsey inquires into the enduring significance of the lives of Modersohn-Becker, Marina Tsvetayeva, and Anna Akhmatova.

SPACING THE PAST

The elegy for Beethoven, "March 26, 1827," composed in three parts, is the opening poem in *Cities of Memory*. In the first stanza, at the hour of his death, Beethoven is surrounded by friends who fear that, when the composer dies, sound will pass out of the world with him: "agitated voices betrayed // their fear that, with his passing, / the last of sound would be carted off—." Beethoven's nearness to death forces them to acknowledge that mortality is real: "They had to admit, in retrospect, / he had only ever been borrowed. / Now he was being taken back." One last time, Beethoven half regains consciousness:

> In the final hour the pallid frame
> offered to explain a thing or two
>
> if only in the register of dreams:
> *Do you hear the tolling?*
> *Change the scene!* In an alley
>
> of memory with light dimming,
> the opera's curtain rose out of habit,
> falling to the sound of trumpets.

Beethoven's final words, which he spoke to the basso Luigi Lablanche, conflate his approaching death with his habits as a regular visitor to the theater.[14] By drawing on the language of the theater, Beethoven both signals his preparedness for death and makes of his last instant a composite of many instances. The third and final part of the poem jump-cuts to the composer's funeral:

> When over, all Vienna came,
> Death had called them in their
> best. So black-gloved with

>   lilies on their northern shoulders,

>   they followed dutifully the
>   funeral bier, four abreast.
>   The opera chorus, then the friars,
>   the conductors and the socialites.

This account of the event reproduces historically precise images: people at his deathbed, Beethoven's last utterance, the funeral procession. Significantly, however, Hinsey leaves out what others might regard as the climactic moment: the instant of death. Experiences that resist representation (and mortality is surely one of them) are often frozen into tropes that shape our thinking about the experience or, worse, limit the experience itself. Images of death tend to be "deathly" in that they rigidify into clichés.

Gaston Bachelard memorably emphasizes the deadening effect of mnemonic formulas: "If memories are too often repeated, 'that rare phantom' is no longer anything but a lifeless copy. The 'pure memories' endlessly repeated become old refrains of the personality. How often can a 'pure memory' warm a remembering soul? Can't the 'pure memory' too become a habit? In enriching our monotonous reveries, in revitalizing the 'pure memories' which repeat themselves, we receive great help from the 'variations' offered to us by the poets."[15] While Bachelard endows "reverie," which to him is a form of daydreaming, with the capacity to renew memory, Hinsey draws on the potential of the poem. She perceives the depiction of death as a dried-out mnemonic reflex and endeavors to renew it by introducing a second line of "narrative" into the poem. She replaces the dramatization of death with a reflection on its nature, as suggested to her by the nature of a musical note. The poet subverts narrative structure by filling the middle part of the poem not with its expected climax but with a space in which to meditate on temporality:

>   That music is not the note
>   but the interval —
>   that it is not the note but
>   the possibility that lies between,

>   the sparrow in the field
>   and the silence after,
>   the approach of rain and the road's
>   washed shadow.

> The world with eighty-eight
> tones that wait to tell us of agony
> and agony's lifting,
> the done and left undone.

This part of the poem is moreover a meditation on the nature of poetry. For poetry, like music, comes into being through a shift of focus away from the "note" to the "interval." Poetry is the "possibility" of the "between," of that which the notes or words cannot say but only hint at. The poet's subject is not an event, not the sparrow's song or falling rain. She imagines the sparrow in the field *before* its song and the silence *after*, the *approach* of rain and the "washed shadow" that *remains*. This shift of focus is conditioned by Hinsey's concept of the moment as a composition of intricate confluences:

> Each moment is made up of an incalculable number of factors. We are bordered by physicality, thought, other matter, the impress of circumstance. Each moment exists at the center of an incalculable confluence of things. Some of these factors we have singled out and called by different names (sociological factors, political, psychological, spiritual, etc.) but some remain nameless. In the same way that physicists have not yet determined all the components that make up matter, we do not actually completely know what creates and makes up "the moment." What we do know is that the moment has a texture, and that in memory it can also be experienced as a weight—can press against the flesh.[16]

To disentangle, identify, and represent this "incalculable number of factors" that the moment is, Hinsey amplifies the "event" by imagining the moments before and after. The poem registers the cohesive elements that link events or musical notes to one another. The poet contrasts the definitiveness of the event with the possibility offered by its margins. Beyond the superficial stratum of linear time, deeper layers remain to be explored in the temporal palimpsest. Hinsey's interest in the marginal resembles Howe's. In contrast to the first and last parts of the poem, its meditative center is devoid of narrative development. The middle part of the poem has the space between as its subject matter and is, in itself, a space between. Avishai Margalit, in writing about "the experience of radical evil," has suggested that "one way of expressing the ineffable is by recourse to describing the-moment-before and the-moment-after the real horror takes place but avoiding the moment of horror itself."[17] Trauma is a representational gap that the reader risks filling with common images and clichés. The gap reminds the reader of the inappropriateness of whatever he has imagined.

Hinsey draws a parallel between Beethoven's death and musical resonance. Once emitted, where do these temporal phenomena go, the poet wonders, and how do they affect the world?

> Trombones sounded, but once
> emitted, music sank to the soil,
> as on the coldest day, when a shout
> disappears quickly as vapor
>
> dissolved in the air's oceanic vast.
> Beyond, it was sound
> that wept, and played a march
> in the loved octaves,
>
> knowing the future's empty
> shape, seeing events and figures
> in the angled glass—dark times
> would henceforth call it back.

Music and death affect the world like sound waves in growing, rotating circles. To make the event "felt," Hinsey metaphorically attaches time to space: "music sank to the soil" and disappears "in the air's oceanic vast." Music's absorption by the soil and the shout's dissolution in vapor simulate the numbing and choking sensations of sorrow and mourning. The span in time called "March 26, 1827" is described in terms of the effect of Beethoven's death on space. A "day" is not only a temporal unit but also "soil," "cold," "sound," "vapor," "air," "beyond." The poem suggests that music and time engrave themselves in space and leave traces in the matter. Although *music* passes quickly, *sound* remains: "Beyond, it was sound / that wept." Hinsey conceives of sound as the Platonic and eternal element from which music is created. Because it is part of the "beyond" and closer to the gods, it can foresee the future in the "angled mirror."[18] The dark ending of the poem foreshadows the oncoming events of the following poems.

The omission of the pivotal moment of death and the focus on the instant immediately preceding and following slow down the flow of time and the thought process. The otherwise habitual repetition of mnemonic patterns is interrupted, and a temporal span and imaginary space are

created for the exercise (and failure) of personal memory, of the mne-
monic imagination. Bringing time to a halt is a vital need for the writer
who, as Walter Benjamin holds, "cannot do without the notion of a
present which is not a transition, but in which time stands still and has
come to a stop. For this notion defines the present in which he himself is
writing history. . . . He remains in control of his powers, man enough to
blast open the continuum of history." [19] The Benjaminian historian and
the remembering poet need "cities of memory," away from the storm of
events, to meditate upon the past. Benjamin reminds us that "thinking
involves not only the flow of thoughts, but their arrest as well." [20] The
practice of poetic memory requires the capacity to pause.

The poem not only incites remembering via its subject matter, but also
through its structuring of the reading and the thinking process. In a time
of visual overstimulation and information overload, the "space necessary
for withdrawal and reflection—related to Maurice Blanchot's 'espace lit-
téraire'—is now more difficult to attain," Geoffrey Hartman believes. He
emphasizes the importance of delayed understanding as enabled by the
arts. [21] Hinsey's "cities of memory" not only shelter things past but also
provide a place for the reader to dwell in and grant him the personal
experience of the past. The space for poetic memory that Hinsey creates
amid the tumult of history initiates and enriches the reader's memory.
That which has already been prefigured by narrative merely incites re-
production (historic memory), whereas that which is left out stirs the
imaginative forces of memory (poetic memory). Widening the silences of
history amounts to poetic method: once the "events" have been pushed
apart and a space has been created in between, the poet's imagination is
drawn into this vacuum. Wolfgang Iser designates the text's silences and
gaps as the very features that trigger the reader's activity and set his
memory and imagination in motion in accordance with his own life or
reading experiences. The reader is thus enabled to assimilate the textual
or temporal other to his own subjectivity. [22]

Memory in "March 26, 1827" evokes Benjamin's differentiation be-
tween two models of history writing, which are ways of describing his-
toric and poetic memory: "telling the sequence of events like the beads of
a rosary" and the "tiger's leap into the past." [23] In a conventional and, one
could say, Plutarchian mode of imagining the past, historical events are
aligned in linear, temporally progressive order like the beads of a rosary.
In Benjamin's words, this mode of "Historicism contents itself with estab-

lishing a causal connection between various moments in history."[24] Whereas his preferred historical mode, the "tiger's leap," regards the division between past and present as artificial and thus seeks a link between recurring historical principles (or "monads," as Benjamin calls the smallest, indivisible, basic constituents of history), this latter kind of history is "the subject of a structure whose site is not homogeneous, empty time, but time filled by the presence of the now [*Jetztzeit*]." As an instance, he points to Robespierre's idea of the French Revolution as a reincarnation of the Roman republic; costumes of the past translated for present fashion are another example that Benjamin cites. The historian's "tiger," in these and similar cases, leaps into "a past charged with the time of the now . . . blasted out of the continuum of history."[25] Identification of the disruptive monads that render history nonsequential is the authentic goal of historiography, Benjamin writes, and draws us toward what he terms "Messianic time."

Hinsey's reconstruction of Beethoven's death is a tiger's leap into the past. She shares Benjamin's suspicion of the uniformity of the "beads" out of which most historians see the past as constructed, and she is no happier than he is about the automatism with which they are said to follow one another. The rosary beads evoke associations of ever-repetitive cycles of prayer and thus narrative and mnemonic schemata that Hinsey counters resolutely. Unlike Benjamin, however, Hinsey does not find "monads" or historical topoi; indeed, she misses these deliberately. Benjamin would select and order events differently from standard approaches to history, but he accepts the concept of events as such. Hinsey, in contrast, doubts that any event (or historical monad) is representable. The event, she assumes, will be remembered most vividly if one does *not* insist on its meticulous representation.

In her poem "The Approach of War" (*CM* 6), a shift of temporal focus—like the shift in "March 26, 1827," but historical rather than biographical in scope—generates a shift of spatial focus, from the geographical centers of history to their peripheries. Hinsey has explained that the poem describes the moment when a metropolis is declared an "open city," no longer defended by its government. Specifically, in this poem, she is thinking of the suburbs of Paris after the French government was moved to Vichy and the capital awaited the arrival of German troops. In a sense, then, it is history itself omitting the event, while the poet omits the geographical, the spatial, center. The suburbs of Paris spatialize what,

in the Beethoven elegy, are the suburbs of his death—the before and after
of the event. Finding the unity of event and site already undone, the poet
of "The Approach of War" imagines the impact of what is to come pe-
ripherally:

The Approach of War

That morning, daylight was the same.
            Everyday rituals, observed by no one,
        left the bedroom door open as a jaw in sleep.
        The faucet's three-four time went unnoticed.

At midday, a ragged curtain shifted in the breeze.
            The paper's checkered voice quietly yellowed.
        When afternoon arrived, there was soot in the air,
        and birds stayed nested in the dark, thatched groves.

Across an open field, a querulous voice called once
            and received its answer.
        The road was empty. A car, wrapped in dust,
        swept the lane, vanished.

The willows were still. A door mated a latch.
            At dusk the smell of pears rose,
        and a mist trawled the lake.
        A match was cupped under the dome of a palm.

Night, not yet soiled, made its way across
            the lake and into the arms of branches.

Focused on space, this poem has the temporal structure of four quatrains
and a couplet, in which stanzas or individual lines regularly indicate the
time of day: "That morning," "At midday," "When afternoon arrived,"
"At dusk," and "Night." These temporal attributes do not refer to specific
events but reflect ever-repeating cycles of time.

Thus embedded in spans of time, the approaching war is understood
in terms of its atmospheric impact on place. The massiveness of war is
contrasted with the depiction of minute details, which Hinsey imagines
as indications of disquiet. The poem is written from the perspective of a
belated observer—a civilian who knows war is approaching and per-
ceives the scenery as if it were preparing for the dangers to come. Set up
in this way, the poem allows the reader to experience a moment in the

past as a person present at the time might have done. This approach attempts to make up for our temporal distance from events by sharpening the reader's senses, in particular our hearing and sight. Simultaneously, this approach allows the reader to perceive what no one perceived at the time; we are shown what there is to be seen when no one is seeing it. Apart from subtle indications of disquiet, the poem unfolds as if the situation were normal—and most people, if asked how they experienced a historic event, report ordinary details. Such accounts, sometimes criticized as lacking in historical awareness, reflect the capacity of personal memory to avoid "totalizing" versions of what has occurred. The civilian's perspective on political events reveals that, at the moment of their occurrence, events are never historical in themselves but are assigned historical relevance retrospectively and tendentiously. Hinsey argues that "'History' and concepts of history attempt to describe this progress of moments, but because of the overwhelming number of factors involved, we are forced to choose that which is seen as most essential (economic, social, scientific) to relate, although most things fall outside of our analysis." [26] Recreating the past on the basis of components disfavored by approved historiographical approaches, the poet looks askance at our conventional biases about the past and at how these limit our memory of it. "Our 'category' of 'history,'" Hinsey writes, "is itself historical and 'created' and therefore subject to the limitations of cognition." [27]

Seeing the past from untried angles is difficult, but Hinsey has of course not been alone in attempting to do so. W. G. Sebald, among other writers, has shared in the effort—although, according to what he writes in his novel *Austerlitz*, it is unlikely that original and authentic memory can ever be made accessible. Most of it is buried too deeply under a heap of stock images and "set pieces":

> All of us, even when we think we have noted every tiny detail, resort to set pieces which have already been staged often enough by others. We try to reproduce the reality, but the harder we try, the more we find the pictures that make up the stock-in-trade of the spectacle of history forcing themselves upon us: the fallen drummer boy, the infantryman shown in the act of stabbing another, the horse's eye starting from its socket, the invulnerable Emperor surrounded by his generals, a moment frozen still amidst the turmoil of battle. Our concern with history, so Hilary's thesis ran, is a concern with pre-formed images already imprinted on our brains, images at which we keep staring while the truth lies elsewhere, away from it all, somewhere as yet undiscovered. I

myself, added Austerlitz, in spite of all the accounts of it I have read, remember only the picture of the final defeat of the Allies in the battle of the three Emperors. Every attempt to understand the course of events inevitably turns into that one scene where the hosts of Russian and Austrian soldiers are fleeing on foot and horseback on to the frozen Satschen ponds.[28]

Like Sebald, Hinsey resists "pre-formed images" and concerns herself with remembering the "as yet undiscovered" past—hence, her focus on the "approach" of war. She is also aware, however, that although the poet may choose other "vectors" than the historian, her choice likewise signifies limitation. Seizing on factors peripheral to—in the suburbs of—an event, a poet risks losing its singularity.

The poem "Lebensraum" in *Cities of Memory* (CM 7–10) associates two wars, both of which were motivated, according to standard histories, by the need and search for "living space." The poem is divided into two parts, of which the first, entitled "Rome," addresses the Roman war against the Veii, while the second, "Europe, 1939," addresses the onset of the Second World War. Although, formally, the two-part structure of the poem represents the temporal separation of two events and their linear succession, several components are common to both, bridging the divide between the two wars and the two parts of the poem, as if spatially. Conventional historiography would more likely represent different historical eras as occupying different spatial universes. Relating the two wars in a single poem, Hinsey reminds us that Roman and National Socialist imperialism, temporally two thousand years apart, took hold on the same European soil—and this perspective will reappear and inform other poems in the collection.

In "Lebensraum," Hinsey employs three primary linking strategies. Present in both sections of the poem is a single observer of events: the Roman god Janus, whose two faces—one looking forward, the other backward—can see both past and future, and thus realize the repetitiveness of history. Janus is a mythological figure whose cultural connotations, as evoked by the poem, make him akin to the poet:

>   in the center, two-doored, prescient,
>
> lay the temple of Janus. In the web
>   of evening's shadow, the dual face
>
> watched both doors, as the young,

> their bodies strung like lyres, passed by
>
> on their way to war. Janus, seer
> > of future and past, foreseer of all
>
> human folly, marked each breath
> > as if the last, knowing how sword or
>
> ash-carved bow might come to take
> > the final note.

Like the poet, Janus relates historically distant events by occupying the space between, condensing two times into one mental space. But Janus is the poet's disillusioned counterpart, observing historical repetitions, while the poet searches history for openings and alternatives.

Another feature linking the two wars is the poem's title, which implies that both were motivated by a search for "living space." The word *Lebensraum* is famously associated with German National Socialism and World War II, but an epigraph taken from Michael Grant's *History of Rome* indicates that the Roman war to which the poem refers was similarly motivated: "The Romans now felt ready to move against the Veii, and they were all the more eager to do so because they themselves . . . stood in urgent need for land." Hinsey extends the semantic scope of the word *Lebensraum* beyond its Nazi and thus modern associations. *Lebensraum* was a euphemism or code word for the Germans' hegemonic aspirations, and as such its use in the poem contrasts ironically with events: *dying* space is all the room that the poem's wars generate. Hinsey also extends its semantic scope by taking the word literally. Searching 1939 for genuine living space, the poet recovers a music conference from the margins of collective historical memory. Granting a euphemistic term its literal meaning triggers a change in historical perspective.[29] Insisting on the proper, denotative sense of *Lebensraum*—expanding space for life, rather than for death—makes room for historical possibility.

The third link between parts one and two of "Lebensraum" is formed by the implied narrative analogy of the two wars. Because the events of war have been presented in the first part, the pattern for the second war has already been laid out. The narrative or temporal line of the first part of "Lebensraum" is introduced with Janus who witnesses the Romans setting off to battle against the Veii in search of new land. Hinsey refers to the legend of Romulus and Remus when she calls Rome a "place of marred beginnings" that consequently only seems to generate marred events. The bodies of the "young" are "strung like lyres," and Janus "marked each breath / as if the last, knowing how sword or // ash-carved bow might come to take / the final note." The battlefield turns into a cemetery, the families grieve privately, and "When together the voices rose, a sorrow // thick as smoke hung above the houses, / the city covered as with a terrible net, // and by the wind's syncopation, leaves / framed and unframed the marble head." Instead of simply reiterating the narrative pattern and stressing the temporal succession of events, Hinsey depicts "Europe, 1939," the second part of the poem, spatially. Leaping from the Roman era right into the twentieth century, the poet's immediate association with "Europe, 1939" is an image of mechanical urban bustle: "Traffic pulsed under leaden skies, / at corners where crowds, paralyzed // by go or stop, waited for a sign / to turn them again to the daily task" (*CM* 9). The speaker leaves the crowds to follow the movement of "daylight" and to enter the halls where a conference on "standard musical pitch" is held.

The poem plays with the clichés and patterns, the "pre-formed images," of our historic memory. The title of the second part, "Europe, 1939," encourages readers to expect a poetic version of the first year of World War II. Hinsey disappoints this expectation, reminding us instead that, while preparing for war, five European nations convened to settle musical matters:

> I found great irony in the fact that, right before the onset of World War II, which would tear Europe apart, a conference was held in May 1939 that would, for the first time, standardize the pitch at which orchestras around the world would tune their instruments. Up until this time there was no standard pitch (although other pitches had been less officially observed, such as the Vienna standard of 435). In an official document describing the event it is noted that in May 1939 in London, "Five countries (France, Germany, Great Britain, Holland and Italy) sent delegates, while the official views of Switzerland and the United States of America were before the conference." A440 was adopted.[30]

This conference is observed, in Hinsey's text, from the perspective of "light," which, as the poem's anonymous conscience, illuminates the meeting place (beneath a "marble . . . dome") and searches it for possibilities alternative to war:

Beyond them, daylight wound its path—
> pausing on bridges where taxis passed,

and below, on the cargo of rusted barges;
> and entered, finally, a still-dark hall,

quiet beneath the marble of its dome.
> Here the hopeful gathered, and opened

the door to sound. For somehow there
> lingered the shape of a thought not

yet debased

Daylight leaves the scene of the "paralyzed crowds" for the "still-dark" hall of a "dome" that hosts the conference on musical pitch. Daylight functions as a metaphor for thought, and when thought works on the space of the past, light becomes the metaphor to represent the inward seeing of memory. While traversing the city, light shifts its horizontal orientation to the vertical and explores the spatial instead of the linearly temporal plane or, to extrapolate from the musical metaphor, investigates the interval instead of the succession of notes. The space apart from the mechanical bustle holds a historical alternative. The shift of attention to alternative space breaks up the apparent cogency of the historical narrative. The historical alternative is represented metaphorically; the "vehicle" *"unity of / the forces"* has two "tenors"—the tenor "orchestra" and the tenor "army"—suggesting that either the orchestra or the army "could warm its notes to the / same verdant plain." Time is a dimension characterized by the contiguity of events (or temporal strands). This poem is energized by the utter incompatibility of the temporal strands it depicts: the countries of Europe arm for war while simultaneously attuning their orchestras. Ernst Bloch called this form of contiguity the "synchronicity of the nonsynchronous"—the parallel existence of differing strands of history.[31] The dimension allowing for the "synchronicity of the nonsynchronic" is space, for space enables divergent histories to occur together.

It is in this way that space in "Lebensraum" harbors the poem's historical alternative; space *is* "Lebensraum." We are prompted to conclude that, if our *historiography* shifted its spatial focus, then our *history*—to the extent that history is memory—would be different and, not inconceivably, more to our liking. Space inspires narrative, and alternative space

inspires alternative narrative. There are always historical alternatives be-
cause there is always alternative space. In the poem's language, the factu-
al existence of alternative space apart from the mechanical urban bustle
commands the escape from historical "predetermination."

Withstanding the depiction of "Europe, 1939" in terms of the Roman
war, Hinsey resists that which memory researchers refer to as *schemata,*
that is, the principle that one event is conceived and remembered in
terms of another previous event.[32] The psychologist and early memory
researcher Frederic Bartlett explains the term *schema* as "an active organ-
isation of past reactions, or of past experiences, which must always be
supposed to be operating in any well-adapted organic response." Sche-
mata represent one mode in which the past exercises a strong influence
on the experience of the present: "Determination by schemata is the most
fundamental of all the ways in which we can be influenced by reactions
and experiences which occurred some time in the past."[33] Hinsey refrains
from modeling World War II on the Roman war, but baffles readers'
expectations when depicting the music conference as the focal event in
1939. She confronts readers with their mnemonic predispositions, or with
their propensity for historic memory and the fixated mode of thought it
entails.

Similar to the meditative space of the Beethoven elegy, the "bustle" of
time is also stopped in "Europe, 1939," and seemingly marginal events
can be discovered and expanded. Again, Hinsey's poetic reinvestigation
of the past evokes Benjamin's conceptualization of "Messianic" history.
As Benjamin claims, stopping the flow of time may bring forth the "op-
pressed past" and generate moments of "true" historical insight:

> Where thinking suddenly stops in a configuration pregnant with ten-
> sions, it gives that configuration a shock, by which it crystallizes into a
> monad. A historical materialist approaches a historical subject only
> where he encounters it as a monad. In this structure he recognizes the
> sign of a Messianic cessation of happening, or, put differently, a revolu-
> tionary chance in the fight for the oppressed past. He takes cognizance
> of it in order to blast a specific era out of the homogeneous course of
> history—blasting a specific life out of the era or a specific work out of
> the lifework.[34]

The moment of the music conference Hinsey "blasts out of the continuum
of history" could exemplify Benjamin's concept of the "monad." In the
dome, arguably a "configuration pregnant with tensions," Hinsey stops

the flow of the linear narrative. She inflates a moment from the past that, due to its neglect by historiography, may constitute a portion of the "oppressed past" or of a past that, due to the more "pressing" event of the war, came to be ignored. The music conference that is being held in the dome could also be attributed with "Messianic" connotations, because it stirs the hope for a better course of history that eventually will have to yield to the barbarism of war. The time that elapses between such "monadic" instances of hope is of secondary importance, because it is merely Janus's time of repetitive historical atrocities. In this sense, the Benjaminian "monad" is the very opposite of the event of conventional historiography. Benjamin contrasts the "monad" with the "rosary beads" as the repetitious, schematic, and uniform constituents of linear time. Rosary bead historiography, to Benjamin, is the account of the "historically understood" and therefore "contains time as a precious but tasteless seed."[35] In the poem, Janus is depicted as a character whom the ongoing repetition of "human folly" leaves languid and indifferent. His simultaneous vision of the past and future deprives him of all curiosity, because he is used to witnessing the periodical reenactment of war. As in "March 26, 1827" and "The Approach of War," the poetic spectator sets out to explore space in between the "beads" of historiography. But analogous to the comparison between poet and Marxist historian in "March 26, 1827," the correspondence between the poet's memory of the 1939 music conference and Benjamin's historical "monads" is only approximate. As far as Benjamin's somewhat elusive "Theses on the Philosophy of History" allow for such clear-cut statements, he advocates a form of historiography whose selection of historical events follows principles different from that of the "ruling classes." The "oppressed past" he seeks to recover is thus also tied up with the "oppressed classes." Being neither a Marxist historian nor Benjamin's contemporary, Hinsey does, of course, not share his specific political aims. Rather than seeking to wrest the "oppressed past" away from the historiography of the "ruling classes," she aims at wresting it away from the deadening patterns of mnemonic schemata.

Although Hinsey expands and blasts open the spatial periphery of history and points out historical possibility, she remains within the confines of historical fact. In "Europe, 1939," the course of history proceeds differently from the way the speaker would have it. The space of possibility is abandoned when the poem's ancient scribes venture a glance at the "real world." Hinsey's Janus opened the door of night, and watched

as those few hopeful fled—as any music that
might have sounded fell to the grass

as the dew was drying under the hoofs
of the fallen Polish cavalry.

The historical catastrophe takes its course, despite which Hinsey by no means grants the irrelevance of poetry to history. Rather, she emphasizes that (and shows how) art can preserve alternatives that were once available and one day may be reactivated.

Memory feeds on the remains of the past and depends on the mediation of the past through means of representation. The poem "The Disasters of War, Spain, 1810" (*CM* 11) takes its title from the early nineteenth-century series of eighty-three etchings by Goya. To Susan Sontag, Goya's "Disasters of War" represents "the preëminent concentration of the horrors of war and the vileness of soldiers run amok."[36] In the tradition of Walt Whitman's elegiac "When Lilacs Last in the Dooryard Bloomed," the speaker in "The Disasters of War, Spain, 1810" imagines herself walking across a deserted battlefield at night. It is covered with the dead or half-dead bodies of the fallen soldiers: "dark bodies lay like slate in that empty / cleft of night. All the world's passion / spent, left to rot on the ground." The poet's sight traverses the field with the speaker and her lantern, "as one would a ruined place." The reader is offered a personal experience of the scene as the lantern captures the battlefield in a succession of images and the poet registers them in the form of words, lines of words, and stanzas of words on the page. She cuts up Goya's depiction of historical atrocities into a sequence of smaller images and translates them into an ordered narration. His spatial depiction is temporalized.

Instead of turning away from the bloodshed, the speaker witnesses the fallen soldiers' prayers when "a hand reached up, lit // for a moment in its dreaming." Even in their pitiable condition ("your hands entwined, your jaw gone slack") they are still "praying face down in the mud." The speaker feels her way into the scene by identifying with a river that winds its way through the battlefield: "I / pieced through bodies as a river goes, / threading myself, as if around rocks." The identification with the fallen soldiers ("There perhaps I // lay with you, as only my empty lantern / knew") becomes possible through the speaker's imaginary insertion into their space. The breach between present and past, "I" and "them," is bridged by the constant of space. With her "censer of light," the poet resembles an ecclesiastic who ritually acknowledges the soldiers' deaths and thereby pulls the anonymously slaughtered men from the "abyss of history" back into the realm of memory. The soldiers' recovery into the poem and into memory is redemptive. Emphasizing that the poet's lantern is "not Diogenes'," who is said to have carried a lantern through Athens at daytime searching for an honest man, the poet refuses to cynically dismiss history as a space devoid of "honest men," but confronts it with compassion and sincerity. The poem concludes with the citation of one of Goya's captions: *"Para eso habéis nacido. / (For this you were born.)"* (*CM* 11). Whereas Goya sarcastically referred to the mutual slaughtering of men in war, Hinsey redefines being human positively as the ability and ensuing obligation to remember. Acts of memory not only benefit the remembered, but also strengthen the rememberer: "But far from theoretical, this way of 'remembering' is an essential act. Everything which is remembered is salvaged, and contributes in some way to the essential nature and estate of endurance."[37]

The poem is a classical case of ekphrasis, the translation of one medium, here the painterly, into another, the poetic. Whereas in the previously discussed poems Hinsey complements the narratives of history with the spatial dimension of the past, she verbalizes and thus adds a temporal plane to Goya's already spatialized, painted depiction of the Spanish war against Napoleon. Fathoming the texture of Goya's drawing consists of reimagining the events as a witness and devising a personal, narrative approach to it. Sontag calls Goya's massive "assault on the sensibility of the viewer" a "turning point in the history of moral feelings and of sorrow." At Goya's time, his mode of representing the war and influencing its remembrance was effective, and the captions below the drawings, such as "No se puede mirar" ("One can't look") most likely true. It is questionable, however, if in our time of visual overstimulation the atrocities in Goya's etchings can still produce the same strongly repulsive effect. Arguably, Goya's drawings, although opposed to mnemonic standards and clichés of his time, may meanwhile have become a cliché themselves. Hinsey writes against such petrification of memory and employs ekphrasis to enable a renewed perception of the past in her own medium.

Transforming the painting into poetry is ethically motivated. Refusing the morbid totality of the drawing, Hinsey searches for "a recognizable face among the carnage." To Hinsey as well as to Emmanuel Lévinas, the face of the other is an ethical imperative:

> But this facing of the face in its expression — in its mortality — summons me, demands me, claims me: as if the invisible death faced by the face of the other — pure otherness, separated somehow from all unity — were "my business." As if, unknown to the other whom, in the nakedness of his face, it already concerns, it "regarded me" before its confrontation with me, before being the death that looks me square in my own face. The death of the other man puts me in question, as if in that death that is invisible to the other who exposes himself to it, *I*, through my eventual indifference, became the accomplice; and as if, even before being doomed to it myself, *I* had to answer for this death of the other, and not leave the other alone in his death-bound solitude. It is precisely in this call to my responsibility by the face that summons me, that demands me, that claims me — it is in this questioning that the other is my neighbor.[38]

Whether in the form of a drawing or a poem, art grants experience and urges the spectator or reader to enter into a relationship with it. The poet's experience of the drawing becomes manifest in her poem. Ekphrasis is her active and transformative response to the human atrocities suffered by the other in Goya's drawing. The poem responds and it disseminates; it manifests experience and it wants to generate more. The "I" in the poem is both the speaker and reader. The poem's sensual resuscitation of the past incites the reader's experience of the past. Memory of the Spanish war is not contemplation but practice; it requires the speaker's, and invites the reader's, insertion into the scene.

THE PASTNESS OF SPACE

In "The Roman Arbor" and "Tones Overheard on Monastery Grounds," Hinsey is less interested in events and their "texture," but explores places. Whereas in "March 26, 1827," "The Approach of War," and "Lebensraum" she complemented the events with their spatial dimension, she seeks, in these poems, the temporal elements in the mnemonic palimpsests of space. Sites of memory stabilize and validate memories and provide memory with the continuity and longevity that humans, eras, and even cultures have to a lesser extent.[39] Space as the carrier of memory gains increasing importance in times of rapid social and cultural change. Pierre Nora speaks of the substitution of *milieux de mémoire* by *lieux de mémoire* in the twentieth century, when communities and traditional forms of life fell apart due to the acceleration of historical change.[40] As Aleida Assmann defines it, a site of memory is that which remains of that which is not any more.[41] Sites of memory are both actual physical sites but also representations of history, and this is also the case of the ancient arbor and the monastery in Hinsey's poems. As representations, they are not immediately decipherable but require prior knowledge, and if the visitor brings his cultural memory and, I would add, his capacity for poetic memory to the site, it may grant him the reexperience of the past. This was the purpose that Renaissance humanists already pursued on their travels, and Assmann relates the example of Petrarch and Giovanni Colonna who traveled to Rome because they felt that the city mysteriously preserved what time had annihilated. Places have the capacity to densify time, and, to adopt Assmann's pithy formula, historical chronology becomes historical topography. History can be retrieved through examination of its topographical sites.[42] In Hinsey's two poems, the space of the past only becomes meaningful through its experience by the poetic subject. In "The Roman Arbor," the poetic speaker retrieves the past from her encounter with an ancient statue, and in "Tones Overheard on Monastery Grounds," she contemplates the transformation of time into topography.

The poetic speaker visits "The Roman Arbor" (*CM* 43–44) in the tradition of humanist travelers like Petrarch. The past does not remain confined to the ruins but is actually experienced in a quasiphysical encounter with a statue.

> So when you met, face to face between the
> columns, you were not prepared—
>
> he stood greater than you, his stone locks
> worn smooth as the tide's back,
>
> his breast four times the hand's compass.
> Breathless before his bulk, you
>
> failed to notice that afternoon was gaining
> territory.

The speaker's quasi-alive encounter with the artifact can be interpreted as the reversal of mnemotechnique. While the sculptor who created the statue in ancient times incised his image or memory of a specific person or god into the stone, the protagonist reads off the presence of this person or god from the sculptured statue. Like Petrarch's Rome, Hinsey's ruins are doubly encoded signs, referring to the vanished parts of history of which they are the remains, but also to the enlivening capacities of poetic memory.[43] Even a place utterly detached from the present and from its original state gains presence and expression through the memory of the witness.

In contrast to Petrarch, Hinsey's speaker does not possess the authority of decoding the physical remains of the past. While Petrarch can read the historical topography of Rome because he already knows its history and because he thus projects a "cover memory" on the actual ruins, the poetic persona is "not prepared." The "face-to-face encounter" takes her by surprise, and she engages with the statue not on the basis of her historical preknowledge but on the basis of their epiphanic communion. The control of the remembering self over the past other still exercised by Petrarch is lost. The encounter leaves the persona "breathless" and removes her from any spatial ("his breast four times the hand's compass") or temporal ("you / failed to notice that afternoon was gaining / territory") measure. The past is experienced as an eruptive force and evokes associations with the eruption of the unconscious. The unconscious or, to use another Freudian term, the "repressed" returns as an expression of grief:

> Then, slowly under
>
>   the heat, a thought crept along the stone sills,
>   leaving behind a thin trail of grief.
>
>   Who is not like him—you asked—your words
>   sifting in the striated light,
>
>   and turning as the sand lifted once in
>   the hot breeze, you said:
>
>   *Who is not a witness of ruined places?*

The meditation on, or rather, the encounter with the statue takes the form of communication, triggering "a thought," the recognition of mutual "grief," and finally a rhetorical question designating both speaker and statue as "witnesses of ruined places." The image of the "thought . . . leaving behind a thin trail of grief" may have been inspired by a snail's moist trail but in the context of the poem also suggests that this "thought" causes both the speaker and the petrified other to weep.

Significantly, the poem does not make clear who speaks or feels or weeps. This effect is mainly achieved by Hinsey's use of pronouns. The dominant pronoun of the poem is "You," encompassing the speaker and the reader. Although throughout the poem the speaker refers to the statue as "he," the final question could be spoken by the speaker and also by the statue. The poem confuses the binarism between speaker and reader, subject and object. The reader is immediately implicated in an encounter with the past. In addition to the speaker and the statue, the reader becomes a witness to the "ruined places." The term *ruined places* refers literally to the topographical remains of the past and also metaphorically to the destruction of social structures. Speaking with Nora, physical sites of memory indicate the loss of *milieux de mémoire,* that is, the breakup of human relationships. "Ruined places" harbor the memory of the damage inflicted on human bonds. The witness alleviates the separation between past and present. He pulls the remains of the past into the present and thus mends their discarded condition as ruins. Witnessing holds the possibility of reconstruction and reconciliation. The poet as witness transforms the ruined place into a poem and thus accomplishes an act of healing. The scars of space are sublimated within the crafted space of the poem.

Whereas in "The Roman Arbor" the discarded and disconnected past suddenly gains immediate presence, the opposite is the case in "Tones Overheard on Monastery Grounds" (*CM* 62-63). While "The Roman Arbor" describes how presence can be retrieved from monuments that appear as accidental leftovers from the past and as entirely unrelated to the present, Hinsey follows the impregnation of time into space in "Tones Overheard on Monastery Grounds." Whereas in the previous poem the past suddenly erupts from its storage place, the speaker in "Tones Overheard on Monastery Grounds" observes how sound as the sensually perceptible form of time is "stored" by the physical environment in the first place. Hinsey attempts to deepen our understanding of the relationship between time and space by observing how the present moment is absorbed into space and leaves its mark. This poem, with its emphasis on sound, can also be read as self-referential, for imagining the relationship between sound and space implicitly reflects how the sounding of poetry may affect the (material) world.

The sounds listened to by the speaker point beyond themselves to times past and time's ongoing penetration of space. The monastery grounds have been marked by time or, to speak with the image from the poem's title, penetrated by sound for centuries. The fleeting of time, which in the poem is equated with the evasiveness and irretrievability of sound, causes feelings of nostalgia:

> Sound penetrates, holds in the distance. And then—
> the intermittent brush of April against the transept.
> We listen. A child's voice fades through a back door
> like day through a velvet cloth. This, a rhythmic

> motif that will never be heard again, ever. And these:
> chance light, sound, the movement of bodies,
> are joined for a moment like the final section
> of a symphony heard only once, and then, in sleep.

The poet makes the implied question explicit: "But what is lost?" Do these rhythms, these accidental variations "attach themselves to candlesticks"? In other words, where does the instant made tangible by the chance confluence of sounds disappear to? "Tones Overheard on Monastery Grounds," the penultimate poem of *Cities of Memory*, echoes the question already asked by the first poem of the book, "March 26, 1827." Although one differentiates between the dimensions of time and space conceptually, the imagery in the poem suggests that they can only be experienced in symbiosis; they never represented separate entities in the first place. The imagery approximates the time-space amalgam when projecting how they affect one another: the transept stops the "brush of April" and is also gradually eroded by the wind, as the image of brushing implies. The back door diminishes the child's voice and makes it "fade." The "day" penetrates the "velvet cloth" to a certain degree, but is simultaneously muffled by it and "fades." The speaker continues to reflect on whether sounds—or poems—"attach themselves to candlesticks" or to "the base of a lone saint, worm-eaten," and whether they "stay in the form of a shadow." She analogously ponders words, which are sounds that require the presence of an other. The speaker wonders whether words "register / in the mind, like weather not to be repeated" or if a "sentence penetrating like a ray through clouds // above monastery grounds, angling in such a way / it seems it will never again fall so." Following sounds and words, "a glance," another temporal phenomenon, is imagined as "mimicking the green of a branch / by an ancient door." The symbiotic moments between time and the monastery grounds can only be witnessed momentarily: "Even these exchanges that make / the heart rise, dissolve like light on weathered ground / that humbles and exalts." But only because the heart's rise is not permanent and the poet's X-ray gaze cannot be maintained longer than for the instant of an epiphany, time is not lost: "Yet as day's hand caresses / again the forlorn saint, so too are we changed: // the touch of time stays with us as we look." The poem in conclusion soothes the speaker's *tempus fugit* nostalgia and invites memory to work on the physical remains of the past to recover what is no longer forced to be *temps perdu*.

The poem overthrows the conventional hierarchy of time and space, according to which time leaves its mark on space. The poet ascribes space a much more active and transformative role, for space also works on time. The images imply that time is partly obstructed by spatial matter and transformed by it. Hinsey's notion of space as absorbing time is reminiscent of Susan Howe's emphasis on (white) space as the poet's means of representing what has not been or cannot be "marked" by history writing. Both share the idea of the palimpsestic nature of space, which is always more than what the eye can see and must be fathomed in its past dimension. But while Hinsey seeks to reconnect past and present civilizations, Howe is interested in the space beyond the borderline of civilization.

The site of memory is both a physical body of the past and in the present. This temporal hybridity, this simultaneous otherness and sameness, gives Hinsey's ruins and monasteries their particular aura. The aura of sites of memory, Assmann writes, is generated by their strange conflation of temporal proximity and distance. Like memory, these sites bring something distant very close and remove something very close into the far distance.[44] Benjamin calls "aura" a "sonderbares Gespinst aus Raum und Zeit,"[45] a strange fabric of space and time, and this is also true for the auratic site of memory. Aura, he elaborates, is "the unique phenomenon of a distance, however close it may be."[46] To Benjamin, "aura is never entirely separated from its ritual function,"[47] and a monastery's aura is marked by its function as a transitory space between man and God.[48] By making time felt and observing in analogy with the present how time must have transformed the place and must have endowed it with the touch of distance, Hinsey bridges the gap between past and present and depicts the present as an extension of the past rather than its disruption.

COLLISIONS OF SMALLER AND GREATER HISTORIES

If so far the archaeological texture of Hinsey's poems has been explored in terms of the time-space alloy, the following portion of my chapter will be concerned with poems in which Hinsey remembers people. In her poem on Sigmund Freud and on the nameless female witness of the construction of the Berlin Wall, Hinsey is interested in the conflation of personal and collective history. Like time and space, personal and collective history do not figure as separate entities in our experience, even if conceptually they tend to be distinguished.

The poem "The Stairwell, Berggasse 19, Vienna" (*CM* 35–38) depicts Freud's confrontation with rising Nazism. The historical facts underlying the poem are quickly summarized, here in the poem's epigraph: "*From 1891 to 1938, Berggasse 19 was the location of Freud's consulting rooms and, one flight above, his private quarters. On March 15, 1938, the household was invaded by Brownshirts. In June of the same year, the Freuds left Austria for England.*" Hinsey attempts to capture the sense of a person's lingering presence when visiting the places they lived in, and in Freud's house the staircase caught her attention:

> When I was working on "The Stairwell," I visited both Freud's house in Vienna and his house in London. One of the most impressive things about his house in Vienna was that there was almost nothing there. The apartment itself is almost entirely empty, since all of Freud's objects were taken with the Freuds when they fled to London. After the war, Anna Freud did not think it fitting to return these objects to the city which her father had been forced to flee. So in the apartment in Vienna, there was—or at least when I visited it in the mid 1990s—a sofa, a hat rack, a pack of Tarock on a table (in the days waiting to leave Vienna, Freud would play Tarock with those few friends remaining in Vienna). In his consulting rooms they put up a mural of what the room would have looked like (with his statues, etc.) but little remains of "the spirit of the place." The only location I found that retained a "sense of the past" was the stairwell—with its inlaid marble floor, and its circular balustrades, and that is the motif I situated the poem around.[49]

The stairwell in the poem becomes the symbol of transition. The stairs were climbed daily by Freud's patients and led them into "the idol-heavy dark" of his consulting rooms. Freud himself would pause "on the stairs, a hand would grasp / the simple rail, and wonder how the branches / bent beyond the inlaid window's frame." The stairs were the liminal space between his work and his living quarters "where the hearth's warmth flickered." The daily routines centering around the staircase are described in the first part of the poem, whereas the intrusion into the house by brownshirts and the Freuds' subsequent departure for England are addressed in the second part. The stairs allow the Nazis to invade Freud's privacy, and the stairs lead Freud's way out of the house and away from Vienna.[50] The staircase constitutes a material link between the outside historical world of Nazism and the inside world of a temporality and a space seemingly detached from the outside. It materializes the link between collective history and the private life; it is a site loaded with the past.

Although the raid of brownshirts dramatizes the clash between Freud's personal world and the outer world of rising Nazism, Hinsey inserts quotations from Freud's own writings to complicate this tentative binary contrast between inner and outer. These quotations are excerpts from rather disparate writings by Freud, such as his *Interpretation of Dreams* and the essay "Group Psychology and the Analysis of the Ego." They are absorbed into the poem, but they also form their own line of narrative, suggesting that the collision between external and internal worlds, political reality and intellectual contemplation, is only superficial. Hinsey reminds us that, on a deeper level, they are connected by the dimension of the unconscious. Entering Freud's "idol-heavy dark" cabinet, the patients come into a world different from that of daylight and the waking state. They arrive as if in a trance, "like water drawn up // from a source." The Rorschach pictures in the card box facilitated association and the exploration of the patients' unconscious:

> Left behind, in the corner, a box of cards,
> with images like those that later
>
> came to mind: an acrobat whose skirt is
> blown like the skin of glass around a lamp,
> and the man whose fingers clutch
> laurel as if in drowning hands.

Hinsey's memory of Freud's daily routines feeds on the physical remains of the house in Vienna and the objects inside of it. It is also enriched by his writings on unconscious processes as another form of material (and intellectual) legacy. The first quotation from his *Interpretation of Dreams* is inserted in the passage on Freud's patients who wait to be admitted to the consulting rooms: "*Dreams are disconnected, they accept / the most violent contradictions without / the least objection.*" It is continued two stanzas further: "*they admit impossibilities, they disregard / knowledge which carries great weight with / us in the daytime.*" These quotations can be interpreted as a description of what happens after the patients have lain down on Freud's couch, or they can be read as comments on the discrepancy or "most violent contradiction" between Freud's world of "pure bourgeoisie" and the gathering of the "primal horde" in the outside world. Formally, the first quotation on the nature of dreams interrupts a sentence in the poem and can be interpreted as a sudden interference of the unconscious. The quotations emphasize the coexistence of "theory" and "poetry" as well as the interreferentiality between these two forms of discourse. As quotations, they are hybrid text forms in the sense that they are "collective" and belong to anyone, but they are also "personal" insofar as they are endowed with a specific meaning in the context of the poem. Although strongly reminiscent of Howe's use of quotation, in Hinsey's poem they serve the complication of the personal and collective element in Freud's life. In Howe's poetics, they are indicative and expressive of the poet's voice.

The unconscious is also accountable, Hinsey implies, for the maelstrom effect of Nazism in the outside world. She quotes from Freud:

> *In a group the individual is allowed to throw off*
> *the repression of his unconscious instinctual*
> *impulses. The apparently new characteristics are*
> *in fact manifestations of this unconscious in*
> *which all that is evil in the human mind is*
> *contained as a predisposition.*

The group effect is grounded on the precariousness of civilized control over the primitive impulses. Collective history, like the individual life, is driven by unconscious forces. Freud's concept of the unconscious serves Hinsey as a joint between personal and collective history, allowing her to explore their relatedness.

On March 15, 1938, Freud's home became subject to a raid by Hitler's *Sturmabteilung*: "brown-shirted figures climbed / the stairs. Their heels, like // spades on the floor, crushed the inlaid flowers / underneath." Hinsey imagines that, at this moment, Freud remembers a biblical line that helps him interpret the meaning of the assault:

> Through the shifting
> silt of fear knowledge fragmented then
> coalesced — here new threats borrowed
> from ancient tongues,
>
> repeating the well-known litany: *The enemy*
> *said, 'I will pursue, I will overtake — my desire*
> *shall have its fill of them.'*

Memory enables Freud to recognize that the biblical quotation holds personal truth. This epitomized merging of the collective with the personal through memory is the climax of the poem. To recapitulate: first, the poem combines personal and collective history on the semantic level by remembering how Freud, toward the end of his life, was affected by Nazism. Second, it merges two forms of discourse: the "poetic" text as the conventionally more "personal" form of discourse and the passages from Freud as the "scientific" and conventionally more "objective" text format. Third, the quotations themselves becomes monads of personal and collective truth.

Freud can avert further damage during the raid by suffering *"violent contradictions without / the least objection,"* an ability formerly attributed only to dreams. He pretends that things go their normal course: "But it was natural // to let the visitors in, natural to use the daily set / of words: *Meine Herren, wie geht's uns denn / heute abend?"* And indeed, things do go their "normal" cause because, as a theorist of human instincts, Freud cannot be surprised by the threatening political form they have taken. In a letter to Lou Andreas-Salomé from July 30, 1915, he writes, "I cannot be an optimist and I believe I differ from the pessimists only in so far as wicked, stupid, sense-less things don't upset me because I have accepted them from the beginning as part of what the world is composed of."[51] Freud's theory partially anticipates and coincides with the political events outside, because both involve the archaic dimensions of the psyche.

Associating Nazism with the archaic and the mythical, Hinsey implies that European society was in a state of regression. While Freud still lives in a "state of grace," simply "life's common / backdrop," the "primal horde" gets ready: "Faustian elements gathered force, / massed like dark water under bridges; / thirsty as the primal horde, they bent / together and lit their torches." The "Faustian elements" represent forces of a dark, mythological underworld; the "primal horde" evokes associations with Freud's own mythmaking in *Totem and Taboo*. Myth is the narrative link between civilization and primitivism and indicates the transition from one to the other. The stairwell symbolizes the ascendance of the archaic forces of history to the "first and second stories" or higher states in the evolution of civilization. Hinsey suggests that events are not only driven by their causal relationship to prior events, as historiography claims, but also by the primitive components of the human psyche. Historiography, like other disciplines claiming scientificity, assumes rational patterns at work in history, but is more reluctant to account for—and therefore participates in—the repetition of the irrational patterns that are equally part of the history of man.

Not a famous male intellectual but an unidentified, nameless woman in her mid-thirties[52] is the speaker in "The Jumping Figure" (*CM* 48–49). The poem is a dramatic monologue about the construction of the Berlin Wall on August 13, 1961. The speaker is one of the persons who jumped out of their windows to the western side before the wall was finished. Situated temporally between the speaker's perception of, on the one hand, sirens and the noise of approaching tanks that now "move slowly through the / dust that's had barely fifteen years to rest" and, on the other hand, her leap out of the window and into another segment of history, the poem depicts a moment of intense remembering.

Leaping into another life figures as a form of suicide. If the woman leaves the rooms she has become accustomed to, it will be a final departure ("If I falter / it's that the past holds me so, in these rooms / where each night I have laid my / head"). She takes a final glance at photographs, saying good-bye to the people of her past and also finding herself reflected in their gaze as they perceive her ("It's just that faces / in this room profess a perfect innocence— / the photographs lean in like a pious chorus / exacting these ultimate confessions"). She hesitates because she fears she might not survive the leap ("I . . . know enough to fear the peace of those / who've missed the net: for as their faces / were free, their limbs were grasped / in such calligrams of despair").

The speaker remembers her life as inseparably entangled with the turns and twists of history. She feels like a plaything of time, tossed about by events she was not able to control: "I am the figure in the clock / that hourly appears on the ledge, then / retreats from that beleaguered edge into / the close and shuttered dark." She identifies with a figure pulled out into the bright light of history at regular intervals, but is otherwise left in the dark of a different temporality. She never rebelled against her "object" status: "Patience had been my guiding star." However, her passivity and lack of resistance when being "swept / with the rest down the avenue" has tired her out, and she is "fatigued by choices . . . [she] didn't make." But she immediately questions whether not making choices was not a choice in itself, as, for example, when she harbored a girlish fancy for the leading men of Nazi Germany: "But can / I say I didn't choose to feel a certain / ecstasy in that first, long-ago spring, or feel / my girlhood bloom under the voices of furious / power?" She remembers the immediate postwar period as "time scattered on barren ground—," as if time together with place—Germany had temporarily ceased to exist as a state and had its territory divided into occupation zones governed by the Allies—had lost its structure, order, and cohesion. At nineteen, "the year that might have been my glory," she worked as one of the so-called *Trümmerfrauen* who rebuilt the destroyed cities and "passed bricks hand over hand." The sequence of displacements is continued at the present moment ("Today, again displaced"), and once more she feels as if her "body has been pledged to a dynasty / perched a third time on the edge."

Regardless of their divergent social status and intellectual achievement, Freud and the woman share the experience of being overpowered by history. Both escape their annihilation by adverse political regimes, but their price is loss of memory. Leaving one's home poses a particularly drastic threat to one's memory. "One of the most interesting observations in the study of the social framework of memory by Maurice Halbwachs," writes Peter Burke, who elaborates on the dependence of memory on space, "concerned the importance of a fifth medium in the transmission of memories: space." Burke portrays relocation as a common practice, when the identity and social cohesion of certain groups was to be destroyed.[53] Hinsey's anonymous Berlin woman must have an intuitive anticipation of her loss of memory and, at this moment of rupture, pulls her life together through memory. In both her case and Freud's, leaving their homes also poses a threat to their lives: Freud only lived another year in his London exile, and Hinsey's Cold War refugee experiences her leap over the wall as a form of suicide. She declares, "I have not grasped the nature of things, / but remember how velocity adds its hand / to that which drops from a height." Because she did not "grasp" she *was* "grasped" by "the nature of things" once more. Memory makes her understand her jump more pessimistically as a fall, as "drop[ping] from a height." Hinsey imbues with a tragic element a story that Western historiography might have written as a tale of individual triumph over a totalitarian state and its attempt to lock its citizens in. Anticipating the leap as a fall is devoid of an experience of agency and initiative. Likewise, the speaker feels pushed into the next world or life just as she felt pushed into worse historical eras before, and she cloaks her decision in the habitual passivist rhetoric: "I must accept the path my feet dictate." Notice that despite her denial of agency, she does defy those who want to "seal her fate." Also, the poem is mainly written in iambic "feet," rhythmically supporting the persona's "forward" movement.

"The Jumping Figure" is one of the rare poems by Hinsey that are spoken by a lyrical *I*. Writing about Freud, Modersohn-Becker, Tsvetayeva, and Akhmatova, she mostly addresses them as "you," as if in conversation with them. Hinsey argues against overusing the self-centered, therapeutic *I* so common in contemporary American poetry and against using poetry as a merely idiosyncratic space:

> Psychoanalysis, insofar as it bases its technique on a scientific method, has isolated the self as a way of rendering it "a comprehensible object." The self, so considered as object for the goals of psychoanalysis, has thereby revealed a wealth of data that allows for psychological intervention. However, the poem which employs the therapeutic "I" has at its base a goal of self-analysis and self-revelation, for which the poem acts as testimony. The process of the poem is one of identifying—often within a scope of predefined categories such as childhood trauma, abuse, or sexuality—certain "memories," and then finding a form of their expression. . . . Rather than communicating directly with the reader or working from an implied relationship, the poem asks the reader to understand and sympathize with the author's relationship to his or her own history. As a result, the poem becomes a hermetic space of personal experience. Under these conditions the scope of poetry undergoes the stultifying transition from communication to transcript.[54]

Hinsey prefers the *I* that seeks a relationship with the reader: "The traditional or axiomatic relationship of the writer to the reader involves a fluid, less clearly defined and more generous 'I.' This 'I,' while naturally originating with the author, nevertheless contains within it an opening towards multiplicity. It is this second sort of relationship which Martin Buber describes in his famous work *I and Thou*. For Buber, any 'I' that does not include a corresponding 'thou' turns both the self and the other into objects, eliminating the possibility of real communication in the present." [55] Hinsey recurs to the lyrical *I* when it serves the "affirmation of the complexity—yet necessity—of shared human experience." [56] As the representative of "shared human experience," the *I* in "The Jumping Figure" exemplifies the common experience of critical political events as infinitely less transparent than affirmed through their belated analysis, interpretation, and assimilation by historiography.

The preference for the first- and second-person singular indicates the personal involvement of the reminiscing poet with the person she remembers. When a poet writes about an admired literary figure, as Hinsey does in the poems discussed in the final section of this chapter, the pronouns *I* and *you* indicate a high degree of subjective identification. The historian is officially not allowed identification with his subject and, by his choice of third-person pronouns, underlines his aspiration to the greatest possible degree of objectivity. The use of the pronouns *I* and *you* implies that that which is remembered is not an entity independent from the rememberer but exists only in relation to him or her. As Martin Buber claims, self and other cease to be separate entities when these pronouns are spoken. To Buber, *I* and *you* are always interrelated: "If *Thou* is said, the I of the combination *I-Thou* is said along with it." [57] Moreover, the *I* needs the *you* to be, or, in Buber's words, "I become through my relation to the Thou; as I become I, I say Thou." [58] In contrast to Buber who conceives of the epiphanic encounter between *I* and *you* in the present, Hinsey situates this encounter within a mnemonic realm where the *you* is only present thanks to the memory of the *I*. While many *I-you* encounters in the present never attain the quality Buber imagines, the mnemonic *I-you* encounter is triggered by an intimacy often missed in the present. As Howe would agree, the reading process opens the hermetic closure of the *I-you* encounter and addresses any *you* willing to answer. Although the *you* is the immediate invocation of the person remembered, it simultaneously addresses the reader and invites his identification with the person from the past.

ALTER EGOS

Subjectivity in the previous poems depends on the poetic remembering of the many merged dimensions—spatial, temporal, collective, personal—that compose reality. The self explores these confluences and positions itself within the texture of each moment. The self realizes the interconnectedness of the present with the past, the individual with the collective, and the random with the central. It also needs to deviate from mnemonic schemata and must seek a personal approach to this conflation of "vectors." In Hinsey's poems on the German painter Paula Modersohn-Becker and the Russians Marina Tsvetayeva and Anna Akhmatova, subjectivity becomes manifest in the mnemonic encounter with a beloved writer. In the manner of Howe, a person is remembered on the basis of the affinities the remembering poet feels to her. The following poems, in this sense, are "double-histories"[59] of the speaking poet and the addressed writer. Remembering personally meaningful writers, the poet establishes an idiosyncratic tradition and creates her poet-self.

The poem "Paula Modersohn-Becker at Worpswede" (*CM* 53–54) sympathetically retraces the reasons for the painter's departure from her German *Landschaft*. As Hinsey explains in the introduction to the poem: "*Paula Modersohn-Becker began her career as a painter in the small German art colony of Worpswede. In an attempt to break with the prevailing visual idiom there, she made four trips to Paris, the last in 1906. She died following childbirth after returning to her husband in Worpswede.*" The departure is necessitated even though "You loved the idiom / of the place," for the artist needs a stimulating environment to enter into the creative process:

> You loved the idiom
> of the place. But as a foot cannot retrace
> its step in ground grown cold
> since its passing, so repetitions bear
>
> their weight on one who takes them
> on day after day: a palette like a landscape
> can grow too small, and fade, failing
> to tell how noon lay bright or fallow,

>   or how it turned pressed on by imagination's
>   weight . . .

The artist needs the lucky combination of certain circumstances to be able to create. If circumstance and tradition bring her to a standstill, the poet must leave for other environments and materials to work with. The effect of seeing "daylight, finally, over the Seine, / and Cézanne's colors found in a gallery," Hinsey claims, can be felt in Modersohn-Becker's paintings: "your *Landschaft* / could not bear up under a red that / seemed to speak in tongues, and a pink / that rose up, an island, untamed"; "you gave up twilight, the pastoral figure // in half-light, to pass into knowing."

Modersohn-Becker's story resonates with Hinsey's own and also, as she explains, with her mother's. Hinsey's interest in a woman artist who felt the need to leave her home to explore and develop her art may allude to her own decision to leave her native New England and live and work in Paris instead. Hinsey writes: "A poem like 'Paula Modersohn-Becker at Worpswede' is also the story of my mother's (a painter) near-death experience in childbirth, and her 'death' as a painter due to the sexism of the era."[60] Modersohn-Becker did die from childbirth, but unlike Hinsey's mother, she had managed to escape the limited social boundaries set for women. The poet herself seems to continue and simultaneously transcend the lives of these two women by living and working as an artist in Paris.

Hinsey can retrace Modersohn-Becker's history so empathically because her feelings of affinity transcend the dividing line between memory of the self and memory of the other. Remembering favors the poet's imaginary merger with the predecessor and weakens the borderline between self and other. While remembering oneself in an earlier period of time may sometimes feel like remembering a different person, remembering another person from the past may sometimes feel like remembering oneself. Ideally, remembering is not a one-way process in which the rememberer acts on the remembered, but through remembering, the rememberer herself is acted on. As in poems by Howe, the past is projected as acting on the present in Hinsey's. This is the case in "The Roman Arbor" and is also hinted at in Hinsey's unpublished essay "In Search of Paula Modersohn-Becker." She describes her trip to the small art colony of Worpswede in northern Germany and her meeting with an elderly man who calls himself the "Worpswede Archive." The poet relates an epiphanic "encounter" with the admired painter when the "archive" leaves her with a photo album:

> Suddenly other people have arrived and our reverie has been broken. Our "archive" sees that we still have strange wanderlust in our eyes, and looks for something more he can tell us. Instead, he hands us a thick album and sends us outside, so he can attend to his guests. There, under a small grove of birch trees are two white chairs and a table, and we take the bulging album and place it on the table. As if still surrounded by the marvel of his voice, the album continues to breathe his story, as in it, with astonishment, we find postcards and correspondence between Rilke and Clara and Paula, simple day to day missives, details of lives lived as all are, in the everyday, in the real. We rarely speak as we turn the pages, beneath the shifting leaves, and it seems that something from "all the green in the park" ("allem Grün im Park") has indeed crept near us, and circles around us, and the sky darkens to a mat grey. After the album is done a single envelope slips from it. On it, in careful handwriting, is Paula's name, and then after this, "akt" "nude." Respectful discretion has placed this one photo under covers. It slips into our hands like a secret benediction, and we know with trains to catch and the on-coming rain, this is the last real moment in this out-of-time place in this out-of-time moment under the birch trees, with Paula entrusted to our hands. The photo, far from "intimate," shows what Paula Modersohn Becker herself revealed in her paintings—the image of a woman who stares back with unflinching honesty, a being-with-herself that makes you the one who is challenged, and precludes your interpretation. It is you, also, who are seen—and must examine yourself.
>
> There in the grove, suddenly, for a moment, as if a spirit lifting from the papers, Paula is everywhere and nowhere.[61]

Hinsey experiences the album as more than the remains and the representation of the past: as it is opened, "the album continues to breathe his story." The past, as materialized in the album, is depicted as a living organism. Remembering "Rilke and Clara and Paula" is like time travel that transports the rememberer to an "out-of-time place" and into an "out-of-time moment." Instead of allowing the rememberer to simply "consume" the "akt" photograph, remembering Paula Modersohn-Becker "makes you the one who is challenged, and precludes your interpretation." Memory, Hinsey argues, casts the glance of the past on the present and reverses their agency. Remembering and embedding oneself in the past, "It is you, also, who are seen—and must examine yourself."

As in the poems on Freud and the woman leaping over the Berlin Wall, Hinsey imagines the "layering" of "personal-historical" and "historical-historical" time[62] in other portrait poems. However, the lives of the writers remembered in the following poems are more intimately related to that of the rememberer. In "Night in Clamart" (*CM* 39–40) Hinsey searches for Marina Tsvetayeva's traces in the dodgy Parisian suburb of Petit Clamart where Tsvetayeva lived under conditions of economic hardship. Hinsey admires the Russian poet for the assertion of spiritual wealth against all political odds from which she suffered in her home country. Tsvetayeva's art is compared to "hyacinths . . . speaking / color to the darkness" and to walking

> head down, head hung
> with stars,
>
> along roads written
> as afterthoughts,
> threatened with dissolution
>
> by dirty rains.

After her departure from France and her return to the Soviet Union in 1939, Tsvetayeva ended her life "under harsh government reprisals," as Hinsey explains in the endnotes to the poem. The poet's lot was "Contretemps"; her life was played on by "loss and circumstance" and betrayed by time,

> gutting you of
> all you had, making you
>
> ring out your sorrowful
> notes, in the dark of night
> and with no goodbye.

Hinsey complements Tsvetayeva's life by adding from the perspective of the present that part of history her life was so desperately missing: the liberation of the Eastern European countries after 1989.

> If one
> could call to you tonight!
> Tell you it's all beginning,
>
> the rivers starting again

from their sources, your
native homes, Moscow,

Prague, moving like
bridge ice into water.

The poet's memory links the Russian poet's life to the present and grants
it the happy ending it was not allowed in her own days. In retrospect,
memory of the dead endows their lives with the sense and purpose they
may, due to mere historical contingency, have missed in their own life-
time. Memory thus balances their lot in life's aftermath. The layers of
personal time and history that during Tsvetayeva's lifetime stood in utter
opposition, even combat, and ended with the annihilation of the individ-
ual life can finally be mended fifty years after her death. Hinsey changes
the record of the personal life by changing the ending, which was not the
capitulation before "*Contretemps*" but the contribution to its eventual
transformation. And the poet is rewarded for alleviating the tragic and
seemingly definite ending of Tsvetayeva's life: "For a moment there //
is laughter, and the / moon rises like a kite / on its narrow string."

In "Canticle in Grey" (*CM* 64–65), Hinsey remembers Anna Akhmato-
va and retraces her presence in the gardens at Tsarskoye Selo, the sum-
mer residence of the Russian royal family where Akhmatova spent the
first sixteen years of her life. The poem is, above all, an affirmation of the
redemptive power of poetry. This poetic self-assertion is supported for-
mally by the sestina: every stanza repeats the final words of the lines of
the first stanza or, to interpret this pattern, every stanza asserts the poetic
power and validity of the others. In contrast to Tsvetayeva who resigned
before Stalinist persecution, Akhmatova bore it all and serves as an exam-
ple of someone who, despite all reprisals and historically "dark" situa-
tions, held on to her art. She left an imprint of art and beauty on the
world and, more particularly, on her beloved town of Tsarskoye Selo.
Although her early life was already threatened by an "impending dark,"
Akhmatova learned her craft feeding on the spirit and beauty by which
her "master" Pushkin had marked the place:

Before evening's dark
you could walk along the verdant summer trail
gathering sounds: never knowing that for you
lay a sorrow of home equal to exile's reign.

Still, there was time. At Tsarskoye Selo, in the rain,
    you listened for your master along allées by the shore
        where he had passed. Among the gardens you
learned your craft. And if your eyes could still touch
    the golden spires, or swan's legs in flight left to trail,
        in dreams you heard the sound of an impending dark.

Akhmatova greatly admired Pushkin and dedicates poems to his memory in Tsarskoye Selo. Hinsey continues this line of "apprenticeship"—the pattern of indented lines imitates that of many poems by Akhmatova—and seeks intimations of Akhmatova in the gardens now.

Witnessing the incarceration of her son and enduring outside the prison walls become metaphors for a poet resisting political dictatorship: "Winter again: beneath frost's hand a spiraling trail / of bodies held to relentless queues. Undaunted, you / stayed, as the prison wall like a sightless shore / cast up its victims in the snow." This "sorrow of home" could not push Akhmatova into an outer exile, like Tsvetayeva's, but led her into an inner exile ("a sorrow of home equal to exile's reign"). She mastered the exile, Hinsey believes, by feeding on that early period of poetic nourishment: "And when the sky filled with a ravening dark / you stood"; "St. Petersburg was sunk as below a tide. Alone you / watched it." Akhmatova's art and memory are invincible and cannot even be annihilated by death, as the epigraph that introduces the poem affirms: "*And I can't return! But even beyond Lethe I will take with me / The living outlines of my gardens at Tsarskoye Selo.*"

In the second part of her poem "Requiem,"[63] titled "Epilogue II," Akhmatova ironically ponders the possibility of a monument erected to her memory:

And if my country ever should assent
to casting in my name a monument,

I should be proud to have my memory graced,
but only if the monument be placed

. . . here, where I endured three hundred hours
in line before the implacable iron bars

Hinsey grants Akhmatova a monument, which she finds in a bronze figure in the park at Tsarskoye Selo called "Girl with a Broken Jug." The sculpture was created by Pavel Sokolov in 1816 and is inspired by Jean de la Fontaine's fable "The Milkmaid." In the fable, a milkmaid on her way to the market dreams about future wealth. Jumping for joy, she forgets about the pitcher on her head: it falls, breaks, and spills the milk, whereupon the girl sits down by the road and mourns her misfortune. Akhmatova transcends her "monument" in Hinsey's poem: "And through the dark / you remained—a bronze figure softened by rain / who above a broken jug could praise the water's touch." Despite her state of "brokenness," Akhmatova can, in contrast to the milkmaid, still "praise the water's touch." Hinsey's sculpture is "softened by rain," indicating Akhmatova's receptivity to nature and its "gathering sounds" on the "verdant summer trail." Searching for her traces, the sculpture serves as a projective surface that awakens the poet's reminiscing associations. With Akhmatova's story in mind, Hinsey cannot help but see the sculpture as detached from its original context. The statue is assimilated to the rememberer's present need, which it also inspires. Akhmatova, Hinsey's poetic speaker testifies, left permanent traces on her gardens, endowed them with an aura, and bestows intimations of her presence on the poet: "Here, by the shore, figures pass slowly in the dark, / their thoughts trail like willow branches in the rain. / They stop. Is it you? Silently the updraft's touch."

Hinsey's attempt to expand our notions of the past is motivated by her conviction that the division of time into past and present, which is a variant of the division between self and other, simulates a separation that, in fact, does not exist:

> "History" is personal; it is not "out there" but "in here." It is in us. We exist with the past (as well as with the present and with the potential future). In this way "historical" events are personal; they are ours. Events which are seemingly distant are related in some intimate way; their seeming separation is reflective of our limited concepts of the nature of time, and the "sequence of events." All these "time-events" exist inside us simultaneously, and this is part of the fluid, encompassing, and complex engagement involved in the poetic journey.[64]

Overcoming the breach between present and past amounts to overcoming the separation of self and other. Whether Hinsey reconstructs the space of the past in analogy with space in the present, whether she traces the time-space symbiosis of events and places, whether she observes the reciprocal transformation of space and time, or whether, as particularly in the "portrait poems," she investigates the interaction of personal and historical temporalities and of self and other, she always bridges the "abyss" between past and present and pulls them into one poetic space of memory. All these poetic strategies are practices of poetic memory aimed at enhancing the self's experience and the experience of the self as self by changing the parameters of space, time, history, and the other.

Hinsey's method of poetic spatialization and its materialization into poems allows her to offer her readers the poems as "gifts." In *Cities of Memory*, Hinsey not only intends to provide memory with a more solid form, but also to invite the reader to carry the poem along as an artifact. The reader becomes a rememberer of and a traveler in the poetic cities. The poem is his companion. Hinsey conceives of the poem as a "guide" in critical situations and as an "energy" that sustains us:

> In *Cities of Memory* I was also preoccupied with the idea of a poem becoming a "poetic object," i.e. giving to the poem a "holdable" form. My reasons for this are deeply personal, and not particularly theoretical. I still think we have a need in modern life for poems we can "carry with us," which accompany us, and remain in our consciousness as a form of guide. A recent poem like Adam Zagajewski's "Try to Praise the Mutilated World" is a poem like this. Or a poem like John Donne's "Hymn to God, my God, in my Sickness" is a poem which for me has transmitted through its music, form and meaning some sort of critical energy, which is now situated in me, and also out beyond me (because the poem is also always voyaging out, independent of us, into time). And I do feel that this critical energy comes from its form. Sometimes the form is part of what allows the poem to become flesh, and allows us to carry it. In ways that are mysterious, it is my experience that through its form the poem becomes an *être*.[65]

NOTES

1. Ellen Hinsey was born in 1960 and has lived in Paris since 1987. She is the author of *Update on the Descent* (Northumberland, UK: Bloodaxe Books, 2009), *The White Fire of Time* (Middletown, CT: Wesleyan University Press, 2002), and *Cities of Memory* (New Haven, CT: Yale University Press, 1996), which won the Yale Series of Younger Poets award in 1996. Her work has appeared in the *New York Times*, *New Yorker*, *Poetry*, *Southern Review*, and *Poetry Review* (UK) as well as in French, Italian, German, Danish, and Serbian translation. Hinsey investigates modes of memory and history, particularly in her first book. *The White Fire of Time* is conceptualized as a study of *vita contemplativa* and it is complemented by *Update on the Descent*, a book on the *vita activa*.

2. Ellen Hinsey, first letter to the author, "Notes on *Cities of Memory*," August 17, 2003.

3. Hinsey, "Notes on *Cities of Memory*."

4. Jakobson equates these characteristics of language with the "two polar figures of speech," metonymy (as a matter of contiguity) and metaphor (as a matter of selection), and relates them to Freud's theory of the structure of dreams whose elements, like those of discourse, are either based on contiguity (Freud's metonymic "displacement" and synecdochic "condensation") or on similarity (Freud's "identification and symbolism"). Roman Jakobson, "Two Aspects of Language and Two Types of Aphasic Disturbances," *Language and Literature*, ed. Krystyna Pomorska and Stephen Rudy (Cambridge, MA: Belknap Press of Harvard University Press, 1987), 105, 113.

5. Aphorism 18 in Ludwig Wittgenstein, *Philosophical Investigations*, trans. G. E. M. Anscombe, 2nd ed. (Cambridge, MA: Blackwell, 1997).

6. Henry James, *The House of Fiction: Essays on the Novel*, ed. Leon Edel (Westport, CT: Greenwood Press, 1973), 11.

7. Dickinson, *Complete Poems*, 327.

8. Edith Wyschogrod, *An Ethics of Remembering: History, Heterology, and the Nameless Others* (Chicago: University of Chicago Press, 1998), 174.

9. Ibid., 181.

10. Simonides of Ceos (around 557–467 BC) had been ordered to write for the boxer Skopas a poem on a festive occasion in his house. But Skopas resented that Simonides did not dedicate the entire eulogy to him but reserved a passage for the gods. Sarcastically, he suggested to Simonides to ask the gods for the second half of his honorarium. Then, Simonides was called in front of the house by two strangers, Castor and Pollux, and the moment he was out of the building it crashed down and buried the host and his guests. Besides having thus received his "pay" from the gods, he was asked to identify the mutilated corpses. On the basis of their seating order at the table Simonides was able to render every deceased person his name so that they could be buried by their families. Besides illustrating mnemotechnique, this legend also affirms the prevalence of memory over death and destruction. See Aleida Assmann, *Erinnerungsräume: Formen und Wandlungen des kulturellen Gedächtnisses* (Munich: C. H. Beck, 1999), 35–36. Hinsey also understands this myth as a case of hubris where Skopas is punished and only memory remains (Ellen Hinsey, second letter to the author, February 23, 2005). In mnemotechnique, these so-called memory loci "may be real or fictional but must be numerous and arranged in order" (Wyschogrod, 181.) Frances Yates emphasizes that "the formation of the loci is of the greatest importance, for the same set of loci can be used again and again for remembering different material." Frances A. Yates, *The Art of Memory* (London: Routledge and Kegan Paul, 1966), 6–17.

11. Hinsey, "Notes on *Cities of Memory*."

12. Paul Holler, "A Conversation with Ellen Hinsey," http://international-poetry. org/hinsey/interviews/holler.html (accessed June 5, 2010). Binary notions of European inclinations toward the past and an American focus on present and future are still upheld in contemporary discourses. The German poet Durs Grünbein, for example, takes offense at the city pattern of Los Angeles, which to him figures as a diagram of amnesia, and its rampant territory, he finds, is a shock to city planners and historians. The city is framed by major garbage dumps, which are not created as an unfortunate civilizational by-product but with enthusiastic deliberateness, Grünbein believes (quoted in Assmann, *Erinnerungsräume*, 404).

13. Holler, "A Conversation with Ellen Hinsey."

14. Lablanche (or Labanche) came to visit Beethoven and unexpectedly found him in a coma. It was Lablanche to whom Beethoven whispered these words. In their biography *Ludwig van Beethoven* (Paris: Fayard, 1967), Jean and Brigitte Massin interpret his words as referring to the changing of the acts in the theaters of Vienna at the hour of Beethoven's death. See Hinsey, *Cities of Memory*, 67.

15. Bachelard, 106–7.

16. Hinsey, "Notes on *Cities of Memory.*"

17. Avishai Margalit, *The Ethics of Memory* (Cambridge, MA: Harvard University Press, 2002), 168. The extended passage reads: "The authority of the moral witness comes, among other things, from the ability to 'describe *this*.' The ability to describe does not preclude the idea that what the witness expresses is how 'ineffable' the experience of radical evil is. One way of expressing the ineffable is by recourse to describing the-moment-before and the-moment-after the real horror takes place but avoiding the moment of horror itself."

18. Hinsey, second letter to the author.

19. Walter Benjamin, "Theses on the Philosophy of History," in *Illuminations: Essays and Reflections*, ed. Hannah Arendt, trans. Harry Zohn (New York: Schocken Books, 1968), 262.

20. Ibid.

21. Geoffrey Hartman, *Scars of the Spirit: The Struggle Against Inauthenticity* (New York: Palgrave Macmillan, 2002), 204.

22. Wolfgang Iser, *Die Appellstruktur der Texte: Unbestimmtheit als Wirkungsbedingung literarischer Prosa* (Konstanz, Germany: Universitätsverlag, 1970), 15.

23. Benjamin, "Theses," 261, 263.

24. Ibid., 263.

25. Ibid., 261.

26. Hinsey, "Notes on *Cities of Memory.*"

27. Ibid.

28. Winfried Georg Sebald, *Austerlitz*, trans. Anthea Bell (London: Penguin, 2002), 101–2.

29. See Assmann, *Erinnerungsräume*, 50: "Eine wichtige Dimension, in der die empirische Erfahrung kulturellen Wandels gemacht werden kann, ist der Sprachwandel. Historisches Bewußtsein beginnt deshalb nicht selten mit einem Bewußtsein für Sprachwandel." (An important dimension where one can have the empirical experience of cultural change is linguistic change. Therefore the beginning of historical awareness may often coincide with the awareness of linguistic change [my translation].)

30. Hinsey, second letter to the author.

31. Ernst Bloch, "Nonsynchronism and the Obligation to Its Dialectics," *New German Critique* 11 (1977): 22–38.

32. Peter Burke, "History as Social Memory," in *Memory: History, Culture, and the Mind*, ed. Thomas Butler (Oxford: Blackwell, 1989), 102. Burke explains the term *schemata* referring to Bartlett, Warburg, and Lord.

33. Frederic C. Bartlett, *Remembering: A Study in Experimental and Social Psychology*, 1932 (reprint, Cambridge: Cambridge University Press, 1995), 201.

34. Benjamin, "Theses," 262–63.

35. Ibid., 263.

36. Susan Sontag, "Looking at War: Photography's View of Devastation and Death," *New Yorker* (December 9, 2002): 89.

37. Hinsey, "Notes on *Cities of Memory*."

38. Emmanuel Lévinas, *Entre Nous: Thinking-of-the-Other*, trans. Michael B. Smith and Barbara Harshav (New York: Columbia University Press, 1998), 145–46.

39. Assmann, *Erinnerungsräume*, 299.

40. Pierre Nora, "Between Memory and History: Les Lieux de Mémoire," *Representations* 26 (Spring 1989): 7.

41. Assmann, *Erinnerungsräume*, 309.

42. Ibid., 310–11.

43. Ibid., 312.

44. Ibid., 337–38.

45. Walter Benjamin, "Das Kunstwerk im Zeitalter seiner technischen Reproduzierbarkeit (Zweite Fassung)," in *Walter Benjamin: Ein Lesebuch*, ed. Michael Opitz (Leipzig: Suhrkamp, 1996), 318. This second version of Benjamin's essay is not translated in Hannah Arendt's English edition *Illuminations*.

46. Walter Benjamin, "The Work of Art in the Age of Mechanical Reproduction," in *Illuminations*, ed. Hannah Arendt, trans. Harry Zohn (New York: Schocken Books, 1968), 222.

47. Ibid., 224.

48. Assmann, *Erinnerungsräume*, 303.

49. Hinsey, "Notes on *Cities of Memory*."

50. Hinsey explains Freud's hesitation in the poem when leaving the house: "In a related way, 'departure' thus took on a part of speech, a declension, which included doors, hinges and stairwells. Upon leaving Vienna Freud apparently stated: 'We are between door and hinge,' quoting a saying that means being in a great hurry, like 'someone who wants to leave the room but finds that his coat is caught.' (From Peter Gay's *Freud: A Life for Our Time*)." Hinsey, "Notes on *Cities of Memory*."

51. Sigmund Freud, *Letters of Sigmund Freud*, ed. Ernst L. Freud, trans. Tania and James Stern (New York: Basic Books, 1960), 171.

52. In the immediate postwar period of 1945–1947, the speaker was nineteen, and the historical moment is 1961.

53. Burke, "History as Social Memory," 101–2. The passage continues: "One of the most interesting observations in the study of the social framework of memory by Maurice Halbwachs concerned the importance of a fifth medium in the transmission of memories: space. He made explicit a point implicit in the classical and Renaissance art of memory; the value of 'placing' images that one wishes to remember in particular locations such as memory palaces or memory theatres." Burke gives an example of what happens when space as a medium of memory is lost: "Some of the Catholic missionaries in Brazil, the Salesian Fathers, were apparently aware of the link between spaces and memories. One of their strategies for the conversion of the Bororo Indians, as Lévi-Strauss reminds us, was to move them from their traditional villages, in which houses were arranged in a circle, to new ones in which the houses were arranged in rows, thus wiping the slate clean and making it ready to receive the Christian message. I sometimes wonder whether the European enclosure movement may not have had similar effects (however unintentional) in wiping the slate clean for industrialization. Especially in Sweden, where the destruction of traditional villages and their relocation was even more complete than in England. Yet in certain circumstances, a social group and some of its memories may resist the destruction of its home. An extreme example of uprooting and transplantation is the case of the black slaves trans-

ported to the New World. Despite this uprooting, the slaves were able to cling to some of their culture, some of their memories, and to reconstruct it on American soil."

54. Ellen Hinsey, "The Rise of Modern Doggerel," *New England Review* 19, no. 2 (1998): 141–42.

55. Ibid., 142.

56. Ibid., 143.

57. Martin Buber, *I and Thou* (New York: Macmillan, 1958), 3.

58. Ibid., 11.

59. Hinsey, second letter to the author.

60. Hinsey, "Notes on *Cities of Memory.*"

61. Ibid.

62. Ibid.

63. Anna Andreevna Akhmatova, *Poems of Akhmatova,* trans. Stanley Kunitz and Max Hayward (Boston: Little, Brown, 1973), 99-118.

64. Hinsey, "Notes on *Cities of Memory.*"

65. Ibid.

FOUR

Psychoanalyzing Persephone

Louise Glück's Averno

Louise Glück's *Averno*[1] is a *memento mori* collection of poems, demanding that poet and reader remember they are mortal. In the title poem, Glück writes: "I wake up thinking / *you have to prepare.* / Soon the spirit will give up—" (*AV* 60). Averno, or Avernus in Roman times, is a crater lake west of Naples and, according to ancient Roman belief, the entrance to the underworld.[2] Paradoxically, *memento mori* asks us to remember death, which, however, lies beyond our personal memory. It is an appeal to our poetic memory: we are to recall something that will occur only in the future. To "remember death," the poet turns to the death of others, as-suming that death is a shared experience. In *Averno*, Glück evokes ancient mythology and the tale of Persephone who qualifies as an "expert" in dying because the cyclical repetition of moving between the world and the underworld, of dying and of being reborn, forms the core of her experience. The poet also investigates death, or the death drive, as it occurs as part of life. Her underlying assumption is that the last death is the final experience of the "death current" that has always been part of the stream of life.

Glück's poetics is psychoanalytic, and it is my concern in this chapter to investigate how psychoanalysis—both as a theory of memory as well as a model of speaking and writing—informs the *Averno* poems. The psychoanalytic approach to memory and the self is Plotinian. While Plu-tarch bases his mnemonic model on the conscious recollection of life,

179

psychoanalysis makes space for the existence of a larger self by conceptualizing an unconscious in the human psyche. In Freudian theory, the unconscious is the realm of the instincts, sensual perception not processed by the conscious ego, and repressed thoughts and memories. Unlike Plotinus's idea of the "truer" human self as our "divine" nature, Freud's concept of the unconscious is not religiously connoted. Yet, while the unconscious is the primitive and barely tamable part of the psyche, it is also our energy reserve. It represents a well of truth, and Freud often attributes it with omniscience.[3] Freud finds ancestral traces and universal psychic patterns in the unconscious, some of which, like the Oedipus complex, are externally preserved in mythology. Jung further associates the unconscious and the mythological by conceptualizing the archetypes and the collective unconscious. Both psychoanalytic thinkers conceive of the human psyche as mysterious and as extending far beyond the consciously accessible facts of life.

In the mythical tale, Persephone is a diminished figure, and the poet-analyst creates her as a character who through psychoanalytic and poetic method can be helped to remember and embody a fuller self. Freud's theory of neurosis as a form of suffering from reminiscences or their absence pertains to Glück's analysis of Persephone. The flow of thoughts and images in the poems is modeled on Freud's method of free association. These poems invite us to look at them with the kind of scrutiny psychoanalysis brings to language. Their prosody is full of the associations, hesitations, and interruptions valued by the psychoanalyst for the openings they may provide to the analysand's unconscious. Indeed, Glück may have named her book after such an opening: *Averno*, after all, is the gate to the underworld. The poet relates to Persephone in complex ways: she identifies with her as a surrogate and, at other times, stands back, observes, and analyzes her. Glück negotiates her relationship to Persephone not only as a mythical character, but also as an archetype, which, according to C. G. Jung, is an intrinsic component of the human unconscious. By augmenting our understanding of the manifestations of this archetype, Glück's poems enact the process of individuation as described by Jung. By remembering a self larger than the conscious ego, she practices poetic memory.

According to the myth,[4] Persephone amuses herself by plucking violets and white lilies in the idyllic landscape of the Sicilian fields of Henna, a valley of eternal spring. Suddenly, Hades, the god of the underworld, appears, ravishes her, and takes her with him to the underworld. Persephone's mother Demeter searches the whole earth for her daughter and, grief-stricken, lays waste to the land. She asks Persephone's father Zeus to force Hades to set Persephone free again, and Zeus consents on the condition that Persephone has eaten nothing that comes from the underworld. But Persephone tasted seven pomegranate seeds, and so will not be allowed to return fully to the earth. She will remain six months of the year with Hades and spend the other six months on earth.

The myth is strikingly silent about Persephone's existence in the underworld. This silence frustrates the poet who wants to learn about death, but it also intensifies her need to know. Ovid concentrates on plot: he describes in detail how Hades goes about Persephone's abduction and how Demeter vengefully searches for her daughter. Persephone, the figure inspiring the tale, is, however, a cipher. It is ironic that the myth, which by generic definition preserves information of the deep structure of the human psyche, is incomplete. To address this gap, Glück approaches the myth in the form of a psychoanalytically minded investigation. If a crucial dimension of the narrative is missing, she assumes it may have been repressed into an unconscious space. Glück free-associates on the basis of the elements that the tale provides, thereby connecting her personal unconscious with the mythical unconscious. This mutually enhanced memory of poet and myth constitutes the substance of *Averno*.

Glück enrolled in psychoanalysis instead of going to college. At the same time, she attended poet Léonie Adams's workshop at Columbia University. She views psychoanalysis as an education in its own right and holds that "it would be impossible for . . . [her] to speak of education without speaking of this process." In her essay "Education of the Poet," Glück details the influence psychoanalysis had on her thinking and writing:

> Analysis taught me to think. Taught me to use my tendency to object to articulated ideas on my own ideas, taught me to use doubt, to examine my own speech for its evasions and excisions. It gave me an intellectual task capable of transforming paralysis—which is the extreme form of self-doubt—into insight. I was learning to use native detachment to make contact with myself, which is the point, I suppose, of dream analysis: what's utilized are objective images. I cultivated a capacity to study images and patterns of speech, to see, as objectively as possible, what ideas they embodied. Insofar as I was, obviously, the source of those dreams, those images, I could infer these ideas were mine, the

embodied conflicts, mine. The longer I withheld conclusion, the more I saw. I was learning, I believe, how to write, as well: not to have a self which, in writing, is projected into images. And not, simply, to permit the production of images, a production unencumbered by mind, but to use the mind to explore the resonances of such images, to separate the shallow from the deep, and to choose the deep.[5]

Glück's understanding of the process that informs her writing is apparent in *Averno*. Glück, for example, aims at transforming Persephone's paralysis into insight. The myth furnishes her with images that, because of their archetypal nature, are both objective and personal. She uses doubt about the myth and its articulated ideas. To fathom its missing dimension, she examines it for its evasions and excisions. She withholds conclusion to see more, and her continuous investigation entails multiple revisions of the myth to find "the deep."

The structure of *Averno* is inspired by Persephone's cyclical experience of life and death. The book is organized as a half-cycle, starting out from the world of the living, leading into and traversing the underworld, and ending with the announcement of Persephone's rebirth and return to the earth. The stream of poems picks up while the speaker is still in the world and facing the end of her life. The first two poems of the collection, "The Night Migrations" and "October," set the tone of *memento mori*. In "The Night Migrations," the arrival of winter is signaled by the red berries on the mountain ash and the birds' migrations, and the speaker grieves that dying means taking leave from these beautiful sights. "October" presents a frightened speaker who knows another winter is near but is in disbelief because the last just seems to have ended:

> Is it winter again, is it cold again,
> didn't Frank just slip on the ice,
> didn't he heal, weren't the spring seeds planted
>
> didn't the night end,
> didn't the melting ice
> flood the narrow gutters
>
> wasn't my body
> rescued, wasn't it safe
>
> didn't the scar form, invisible
> above the injury

> terror and cold,
> didn't they just end, wasn't the back garden
> harrowed and planted

> (*AV* 5)

This enumeration of rhetorical questions without a question mark expresses both the speaker's surprise at the inevitability of the cycle and her certainty of it. The lines seem to be spoken in such haste and urgency, the speaker is already in the grips of the changing seasons. Both poems remind the speaker that "the light of autumn . . . has turned on us" (*AV* 12); both prepare for death, which in the book figures as the descent into *Averno*. Although the speaker resists the necessity of the cycle, the cycle will enable her to remember the future.

The book is framed by two poems that are both called "Persephone the Wanderer" and that can be understood as gateways marking the entrance into the underworld and the exit from it. Their containing function also shows in their identical length of twenty-nine stanzas. The first Persephone poem follows "The Night Migrations" and "October," which set the tone of *memento mori*, and the second one concludes the book. My close reading will focus on them because they revise the Persephone myth most explicitly, and by comparing Persephone at the beginning and at the end of *Averno* they reveal the "changes effectuated" by the poet-analyst in the course of the book as a whole. In between these two poems, *Averno* consists of fourteen other poems, of which six are designed as poetic sequences (plus "October," number seven) constituting their own smaller cycles of living and dying. The book encompasses other currents and whirlpools forming smaller time cycles and mnemonic bubbles. These lyrical and reminiscing sequences comprise between three and twenty-two sections, and they follow, for example, the cycles of the seasons ("October"), cyclical movement through space ("Landscape"), or the cyclical changes of a lifetime ("Prism").[6] Like a continuous undercurrent, the Persephone topos runs through all of them. Cycles are forms of movement that are repetitive and yet proceed forward. Arguably, cycles represent the most common temporality of the analytic process: analysands work through their materials repetitively, yet move ahead through different versions of the same stories toward greater understanding of their psychic life. Like Persephone, who suffers the change of seasons passively, the analysand is subject to her or his feeling states and only develops greater awareness and control gradually.

The first poem, "Persephone the Wanderer" (*AV* 16–19), begins with the facts of the myth: Persephone "is taken from her mother / and the goddess of the earth / punishes the earth." The speaker interprets Demeter's devastation of the earth not as evidence of her grief, but of her passion for destruction. "Scholars" are still working on their understanding of the myth, and they cannot decide whether Persephone cooperated in her rape or not. Amid this uncertainty, the speaker perceives one truth: "the return of the beloved / does not correct / the loss of the beloved." Persephone returns to the earth blemished, and the consequences of her abduction cannot be undone. One such consequence might be that, because Persephone has been in "the bed of the god," the earth is not "home" to her anymore. She may also be a "born wanderer" and never have had a home. Having offered different interpretations, the speaker reminds the reader not to take sides in this mythical drama. Rather, the characters should be understood as "aspects of a dilemma," comparable to the "ego, superego, id," that is, "aspects" of the Freudian model of the mind. While Demeter's rage has turned the earth into a barren and cold place, Persephone is "having sex in hell." The speaker wonders what might be on Persephone's mind. Does she still have an "idea / of mind," or do such concepts not apply in the underworld? Persephone must know, the speaker claims, that mothers run the earth and that she is not "a girl any longer," who, as she implies, could be run by her mother. The speaker bluntly asserts an insight: Persephone believes "she has been a prisoner since she has been a daughter." The speaker predicts that Persephone's "passion for expiation" will subject her to a future of "terrible reunions," leaving ambiguous whether she refers to the reunions with Demeter or with Hades. Persephone does not choose her own way of life, but drifts "between earth and death." In Demeter's and Hades's ongoing battle, "the daughter is just meat." The speaker speculates that there is a "rift in the human soul," which alienates one from life and which mutes Persephone's "maidenly songs / about the mother's / beauty and fecundity." At the end of the poem, the speaker's and Persephone's voices merge in their address of the soul:

> My soul
> shattered with the strain
> of trying to belong to earth—

> What will you do,
>   when it is your turn in the field with the god?

Death is imbued with complex connotations: it comes as a relief; it is a traumatic turning point; it is an erotic encounter; it is a crisis calling for a decision; it is a moment with the divine.

While the first "Persephone the Wanderer" poem is a meditation on her wandering between the world and the underworld, Persephone "is dead" in the second poem, and "we don't expect to know / what Persephone is doing" (*AV* 73–76). Rather, the speaker, in Persephone's stead, retrieves the mother's strange thoughts and memories. The mother views the child as a "cipher," hinting at the mystery the daughter represents and the mother's lack of relationship to her. She looks at the infant and thinks: "*I remember when you didn't exist.*" The mother's gaze at her child, the poet suggests, is responsible for the void at the center of the myth. Because of the mother's ambivalence, "the infant / is puzzled." The child will defend against this confusion by later forming the "opinion . . . / she has always existed." She will remember her mother as many mothers are remembered: waiting for the child at a bus stop, "an audience for the bus's arrival." It is "a morning / in early spring, in April" and life could begin. But the speaker sets limits to such hopefulness, stating that Persephone's life is going to be short. It is impeded by the "deep violence" and "hostility" of the earth, which does not want to "continue as a source of life." The mother represses her aggression against the life she created. After her daughter has been taken away by death, the mother feels guilty and fears blame. She prepares her defense but only reveals her envy of Persephone. She searches for the daughter because she cannot tolerate her independent existence. Demeter promises Zeus to end winter on earth, if he in turn will get their daughter back from Hades. But Persephone has gotten used to death and resists returning to the earth. Yet the mother is merciless and "over and over . . . hauls her out again." Persephone beseeches her father and asks him how she is to "endure the earth." Zeus consoles her, reminding her that forgetting will facilitate the transition, and that she will return to the underworld. In the meantime, winter on earth will end and "those fields of ice will be / the meadows of Elysium." These are the final lines of *Averno*, and they announce Persephone's rebirth to life on earth.

UNCERTAIN WANDERING

The two "Persephone the Wanderer" poems are called a "first version" and a "second version" (*AV* 16 and 73). Derived from the Latin verb *vertere*, the poem as "version" represents an instance of turning. Figuratively speaking, the poems also represent different "versions" or interpretations of the Persephone myth. The first poem announces Persephone's "turn" to the underworld, the second her "turn" back to the earth. Depending on where Persephone turns, a new myth comes into being. "Versions" withhold conclusion, and each version's lack of closure allows for more insight to emerge. Glück believes that the enormity of the unknown demands such resistance to completion: "It seems to me that what is wanted, in art, is to harness the power of the unfinished. All earthly experience is partial. Not simply because it is subjective, but because that which we do not know, of the universe, of mortality, is so much more vast than that which we do know. What is unfinished or has been destroyed participates in these mysteries. The problem is to make a whole that does not forfeit this power."[7] By affirming the "power of the unfinished," Glück also advocates the practice of poetic memory, which presupposes that all memory is partial. Rather than clinging to a firmly circumscribed record that preserves memory but also restrains its practice, poetic memory is dynamic. Glück keeps the myth of Persephone radically open and grants it the "power of the unfinished" by conceiving of Persephone as a "wanderer" between the realm of the living and the realm of the dead. Glück's Persephone frustrates those who want to assign her static, singular meaning.

To evoke wandering of thought in the poems, Glück relies on the psychoanalytic method of free association. Here is what this associative mode looks like in Glück's first Persephone poem. It begins:

> In the first version, Persephone
> is taken from her mother
> and the goddess of the earth
> punishes the earth—this is
> consistent with what we know of human behavior,
>
> that human beings take profound satisfaction
> in doing harm, particularly
> unconscious harm:

we may call this
negative creation.

Persephone's initial
sojourn in hell continues to be
pawed over by scholars who dispute
the sensations of the virgin:

did she cooperate in her rape,
or was she drugged, violated against her will,
as happens so often now to modern girls.

(*AV* 16)

In this associative sequence, Glück first personalizes the mythical fact
("Persephone / is taken from her mother / and the goddess of the earth /
punishes the earth") by pronouncing a moral judgment on the mother
("this is / consistent with what we know of human behavior // that hu-
man beings take profound satisfaction / in doing harm"). This general-
ized moral judgment pronounced by a "we" that includes the speaker
leads her to other "general" or "objective" opinions, like those expressed
by "scholars" who investigate the myth. The speaker appropriates their
judgmental tone by reproaching them for lewd motives: they "paw" over
Persephone and take keen interest in the question of whether she instigat-
ed her rape or not. Unmasking the perverse interest of the "scholars" in a
rape fantasy, she then alludes to Persephone's loss of innocence in the
underworld, where she is "stained with red juice." As this short passage
shows, the speaker adheres to Freud's prescription to practice free associ-
ation in a mode of "dispassionate self-observation" and by "communi-
cat[ing] everything that occurs to . . . [her] without criticism or selec-
tion."[8] Her thought is "wandering," as she swiftly changes topics and
perspectives, often from stanza to stanza. She does not shy away from
anything "disagreeable," "nonsensical," or seemingly "unimportant."[9]
She discusses taboo topics, pays attention to what appears to be eclectic
detail, and presents herself as an ideal Freudian self-analyst.

   The space of the poem is as verbal and open as the analytic space. By
immersing herself in free association, the poet lets Persephone be a wan-
derer and gives her much space for walking about and for turning here or
there to learn about herself. Both poetic and psychoanalytic spaces must
be undetermined if language is to yield a glimpse of unconscious pro-

cesses and deeper truth. The poet, like the analyst and the analysand, places faith in the formative and expressive powers of the unconscious.

Wandering between the world and the underworld, Persephone does not exist in deliberate or purposeful cycles of being, but seems in the grip of a repetition compulsion of which she knows neither the origin nor reason. The speaker comments:

> You do not live;
> you are not allowed to die.
>
> You drift between earth and death
> which seem, finally,
> strangely alike.
>
> (*AV* 18)

Persephone is characterized as remarkably passive, indifferent, and unaware in this life that is supposedly hers. According to psychoanalytic theory, repetition replaces recollection when memories are repressed. Impossible to be remembered and verbalized, they will show in a person's behavior and be enacted. In Freud's words, "sometimes, the patient does not remember anything of what he has forgotten and repressed, but acts it out. He reproduces it not as a memory but as an action; he repeats it, without, of course, knowing that he is repeating it."[10]

One way, then, of describing Persephone's compulsion to wander is to call it a gap in her memory. For Freud, the therapeutic effect of psychoanalysis is essentially bound up with filling the gaps in the patient's memory, and Glück borrows from psychoanalytic method to "retrieve" Persephone's missing memories. Freud conceived of pathological symptoms as representing the affect that had been dissociated from the repressed idea (or memory). His treatment of hysterical patients showed that if only the patient could remember and verbalize the first time the symptom had occurred, and thereby reconnect affect and idea, the symptom would disappear. Similarly, one could argue that Persephone is in the grip of an affect, which shows in her apparently meaningless wandering. Glück sets out to find the forgotten idea hinted at by her wandering, which is required to release Persephone from her repetition.[11]

As in the process of analysis, Persephone's wandering is transformed in the poem from a state of confused dislocation into a more positive form of ontological questioning (Where is her home? Does she have a mind in the underworld?) and into sudden insight. Glück highlights the importance of Persephone's insight by placing it in a stanza of its own: "Regarding / incarceration, she believes // she has been a prisoner since she has been a daughter" (*AV* 18). Persephone comes to understand that she felt attracted to the underworld because "at home," she had been subjected to her mother. The poet twists the myth by associating incarceration not only with her abduction to the underworld, but also with having a mother in her life on earth.

PSYCHE DIVIDED

As she begins to recognize the conflicts in the relationship with her mother, Persephone discovers that her psyche is divided. Developing awareness of the divisions, lifting the repression, and further integrating the mind is to practice poetic memory. Glück proposes several ways in which the divisions in Persephone's psyche can be related to psychoanalytic models of the mind. One is Freud's structural model of the id, ego, and superego; the other Glück calls the "rift in the human soul," suggesting the existence of opposite forces—a life and death drive—in human nature. Glück does not favor one model of explanation over the other, and the poems will disappoint the wish for theoretical consistency. At its best, poetry is play, dense with ambivalence and conceptually mobile. Poems keep knowledge in suspension.

In the first Persephone poem, Glück makes us aware that the characters in the myth represent the components of Freud's structural model:

> You are allowed to like
> no one, you know. The characters
> are not people.
> They are aspects of a dilemma or conflict.
>
> Three parts: just as the soul is divided,
> ego, superego, id. Likewise
>
> the three levels of the known world,
> a kind of diagram that separates
> heaven from earth from hell.
>
> (*AV* 17)

Persephone, Demeter, and Hades are in conflict with each other in the myth just as ego, superego, and id are in conflict with each other in the mind. The addressed "you," presumably the reader, is advised not to side with any of the mythical characters. Since they are components of one and the same psyche, favoring one over the other would only aggravate internal conflicts. Glück also associates superego, ego, and id with the "three levels of the known world" or "heaven," "earth," and "hell." The superego is the "ego ideal" and is endowed with higher aspirations one could associate with heaven. The ego represents the intermediary between superego and id and, topographically, one could think of it as the earth situated between heaven and hell. (The earth could also be interpreted as "reality" and representative of the reality principle.) The id, which Freud characterized as a "cauldron full of seething excitations,"[12] is reminiscent of hell. Persephone, representing the ego function, mediates between Demeter (superego) and Hades (id). Demeter displays a form of unquestioned authority and moral self-righteousness similar to that ascribed to the superego. With the force of a drive, Hades reaches out for Persephone from the dark, unknown realm of the underworld. He takes her with him against the mother's and against her own will, but partly also to her great pleasure.

In addition to struggling with the conflicts between id, ego, and superego, Persephone is torn between life and death:

> They say
> there is a rift in the human soul
> which was not constructed to belong
> entirely to life. Earth
>
> asks us to deny this rift, a threat
> disguised as suggestion —
> as we have seen
> in the tale of Persephone
>
> (*AV* 19)

The "rift in the human soul" becomes manifest as Persephone's periodic withdrawal to the underworld. Persephone is alternately in the grip of the life drive and the death drive, or eros and thanatos. The "rift" in her soul is the suture between these two opposite, yet closely intertwined, forces. Is this "rift" a "threat"? Glück plays with this question through syntax and enjambment and generates the ambivalence in meaning explored in the analytic space. "Threat" first appears to be in apposition to "rift," signifying that the "rift in the soul," that is, the desire not only for life but also for death, is a threat to the speaker. "Threat" also turns out, in the next line, to be in apposition to the phrase "asks us to deny," which makes the demand the earth places on the speaker the actual threat. This syntactical ambivalence nicely differentiates what Persephone is supposed to believe from what is actually true. It contains both the acceptable belief held on to by the ego and the repressed knowledge that pushes through in poetic language. Demeter expects Persephone to reject Hades, the death drive incarnate. The poet suggests that Persephone's soul is "shattered" by this expectation, "the strain / of trying to belong to earth—" (*AV* 19). The myth implies that Demeter and Hades do not represent the life and death drives in a pure form. Rather, both gods are endowed with both drives. In the myth, Demeter, the goddess of life and fertility, also devastates the earth, and Hades, the god of death and the underworld, falls violently in love with Persephone. In Glück's poems, Persephone's soul does not crack from living or dying, but from having to deny the mother's ambivalence, from having to pretend that life and death are unrelated forces.

The speaker's voice is marked by changing fusions of eros and thanatos. The cohesive force of the life drive seems at work when the speaker declares:

> the goddess of the earth
> punishes the earth—this is
> consistent with what we know of human behavior,
>
> that human beings take profound satisfaction
> in doing harm, particularly
> unconscious harm:
>
> we may call this
> negative creation.

(*AV* 16)

The voice, when driven by eros, emphasizes consensus; it speaks for the unified plurality of a "we." It is reminiscent of the voice of the "knowing analyst," one of whose tasks it is to represent the life drive to the patient. Yet while the energy of the voice is derived from eros, the content of these lines manifests the simultaneous activity of thanatos. The speaker elaborates on the goddess's destructiveness and her propensity for "negative creation." This phrase alone suggests a fusion of life and death drives. So too does Demeter's, or anyone's, "profound satisfaction / in doing harm." There is a passion for violence in human nature.

The psychoanalyst Oscar Sternbach reminds us that while eros and thanatos are forces "constantly participating in every human action," they are mixed and fused not only "in various proportions" but also "in various rhythms."[13] This holds true for Glück's Persephone poems too, where life and death drives are not only fused vertically, that is, in various proportions at one given point in the poem, but also horizontally or in changing rhythms as the poem proceeds. The unified and forcefully assertive semantics of the first stanzas are gradually undermined by a carefully designed ironic subtext that fragments meaning. First, Glück ventures a skewed and questionable comparison of Demeter's conduct with "human behavior." Second, the apparently compelling interpretation of the goddess's "profound satisfaction / in doing harm" becomes dubious in the light of the more conventional interpretation of her as a mother acting on her grief. Third, taking "profound satisfaction" in "unconscious harm" has an oxymoronic quality, for how can one actively take satisfaction in something one is unconscious of? The poet rather seems to put her finger on the mother's pretense of unconsciousness and ignorance. It turns out that the argument put forward so confidently by the "we" lacks stringency and is subtly compromised at a deeper level of the poetic texture.

If the life drive in language and poetry becomes manifest as poetic form, semantic cohesion, and condensed imagery, the death drive predominates when language decomposes and turns into silence. In the first Persephone poem, the tone, just as in analysis, can change drastically after the speaker has labored toward insight and understanding. Having exercised its force maximally by laying out the theory of the ego, superego, and id components of the psyche, by producing the insight that Persephone has been at the mercy of "forces contending over" her, and by reaching awareness of Persephone's inner division ("where / the rift is, the break is"), eros tips over into thanatos. In terms of drive theory, the increase of tension is relieved by a pleasurable decrease of tension. The speaker drifts off in her thoughts: "White of forgetfulness, / of desecration—"; "White of forgetfulness, / white of safety—"; "Song of the earth, / song of the mythic vision of eternal life—" (*AV* 17–19). In these three two-line stanzas, the syntax is fragmented. Thoughts are alluded to but lead into silence. The dash may be viewed as representing the "rift" or the "break" in the soul. At the same time, thanatos remains fused with eros, because the poem never entirely disintegrates and the page does not turn blank. Also, in these short stanzas, the proportions between thanatos and eros gradually change in favor of the life force: the break from Persephone's life on earth toward her life in the underworld is first compared to a form of "desecration," then more positively envisioned as a form of "white safety," and eventually celebrated as the "mythic vision of eternal life." The dashes are not only symbols of rupture but also of transition. Reminiscent of the dashes in Emily Dickinson's poetry, they signify the thought's unfinished state and its continuance beyond the printed word and the page.

In her essay "The Dreamer and the Watcher," Glück argues that forgetting, which one could consider another manifestation of the decomposing forces of thanatos, signifies not only loss but also renewed possibility: "The drive toward oblivion seems to me (as to many others) not a symptom of sickness but a true goal, and this wish of the self to do away with the very boundaries it has struggled to discover and maintain seems to me an endless subject, however we may try to subvert its grandeur."[14] This is an apt description of the poetics employed in the Persephone poem: having struggled toward understanding, the poet undoes the self-imposed boundaries of her insight and starts anew. Just as forgetting is necessary for new thought to emerge, the death drive can enable the creation of new life.

SETTING THE EARTH ON FIRE

Between the two "Persephone the Wanderer" poems, Glück continues, more or less explicitly, to associate on the Persephone theme, resting at moments of insight only to continue the journey the next instant. Images—stars, night, ice, snow, river, sea, lake, birds—reappear; they can be compared to threads of memory that are dropped, picked up again, and weaved further into a poetic texture that is always growing denser. The poems materialize a psyche fathoming and construing its own depth.

The motif of the burning fields of wheat is such a thread woven through the poems "Landscape," "A Myth of Innocence," and "Averno." It is an image that evokes the fused forces of life and death: the wheat (life) is destroyed (death) by fire (life and death). This act of destruction is also a common farming practice intended to produce ash as fertilizer for

new growth. Burning the fields is the motif most expressive of the rela-
tionship between Persephone and Demeter: Demeter is identified with
the field and the earth's procreative power. She is the goddess honored
for bestowing the gift of the harvest and often depicted holding a sheaf of
wheat. In "Landscape" (*AV* 44–45) a "young girl"—by implication Per-
sephone—is identified as the person who sets the fields on fire. Glück's
Persephone stops being her mother's appendage when she discovers and
acts on her own potential for destruction and turns it against the mother.
The third, middle section begins:

> In late autumn a young girl set fire to a field
> of wheat. The autumn
>
> had been very dry; the field
> went up like tinder.
>
> Afterward there was nothing left.
> You walk through it, you see nothing.

Setting the fire was easy, conditions ideal: after a dry fall, "the field went
up like tinder," as if the wheat had wanted to be burnt. The emphasis on
the "nothingness" produced by the fire resonates with Persephone's sud-
den and untraceable disappearance after she has been abducted by
Hades, singed by his fiery desire. Double harm has been inflicted: the
earth's harvest and the mother's daughter have been taken. The girl's
lashing out at the earth has negative repercussions for herself and also for
a "farmer," whom, hopefully, "the insurance will pay."

> It is like losing a year of your life.
> To what would you lose a year of your life?
>
> Afterward, you go back to the old place—
> all that remains is char: blackness and emptiness.
>
> You think: how could I live here?

The farmer, the girl, and the earth have lost a year of life and labor. The
girl lost some life to death; Persephone lost some life on earth to the
underworld. The girl made her home inhospitable and cannot imagine
having lived there or living there again in the future. She turned outward
what she had held inside: her death impulse changed a field of wheat
into "blackness and emptiness." She proved the earth mistaken, who

"even last summer . . . behaved / as though nothing could go wrong with it." Setting the field on fire was an act of defiance against the mother. The girl demonstrates her power by setting limits to the earth's omnipotence.

At the same time, the speaker suggests that the girl only had the power to destroy because the seed of death had already been sown into that dry field of wheat:

> One match was all it took.
> But at the right time—it had to be the right time.
>
> The field parched, dry—
> the deadness in place already
> so to speak.

The earth contained her own potential for self-destruction, which the girl only had to dip into to set off. The mother's death force finds its equivalent in the daughter: there is a very small difference between the "field parched, dry" (a synecdoche representing the earth or mother) and the "wheat" (an image for the daughter). The one's deadness translates into the other's; parched dry soil generates parched dry wheat.

In Glück's book, "Landscape" is followed by "A Myth of Innocence" (*AV* 50–51), a poem in which Persephone reflects on the role she played when captured by Hades. Glück puns on the myth of Persephone being a tale of innocence and on Persephone's innocence being a myth in the sense of a lie. This Persephone is aware of the intricate interplay between libidinal and destructive drives within herself and debates whether she "was abducted" by Hades or whether she "offered" herself, "wanted to escape . . . [her] body," and "willed this." Depending on the perspective, loving action turns into hateful deed and vice versa: offering herself to Hades implies rejecting her mother, and holding on to her mother amounts to rejecting Hades. "A Myth of Innocence," if read as a commentary on "Landscape," underlines that the girl is responsible for setting the fire just as Persephone participates in her abduction. The images resonate with the ones in "Landscape":

> One summer she goes into the field as usual
> stopping for a bit at the pool where she often
> looks at herself, to see
> if she detects any changes. She sees
> the same person, the horrible mantle
> of daughterliness still clinging to her.

Persephone is the "young girl" in the field who examines and questions herself, using the surface of the pool symbolically as a mirror. A "mantle" is a cloak and something that covers and conceals, and it is also the zone of hot gases surrounding and containing a flame. This Persephone feels suffocated by her mother's constricting protection and is ready to show her "fire," which, presumably, lays the field of wheat ablaze. As if commenting on the previous poem, Persephone stipulates that "everything in nature is in some way her relative"; she makes explicit that the wheat represents herself and the earth the mother. Persephone remembers Hades's beauty when he appeared suddenly, the "sunlight flashing on his bare arms." Both the images of the mantle and the flashing sunlight visually recall the blazing fire laid by the girl in "Landscape." Persephone's and Hades's desire for each other singed the earth, wounded the mother.

The fire-setting incident finds its continuation in the title poem "Averno" (*AV* 60–69). In the second of five sections in this poetic sequence, the speaker revisits the field in winter and marvels at the apparent lack of consequence of the disaster:

> I didn't go back for a long time.
> When I saw the field again, autumn was finished.
> Here, it finishes almost before it starts—
> the old people don't even own summer clothing.
>
> The field was covered with snow, immaculate.
> There wasn't a sign of what happened here.
> You didn't know whether the farmer
> had replanted or not.
> Maybe he gave up and moved away.
>
> The police didn't catch the girl.
> After awhile they said she moved to some other country,
> one where they don't have fields.
>
> A disaster like this
> leaves no mark on the earth.
> And people like that—they think it gives them
> a fresh start.
>
> I stood a long time, staring at nothing.
> After a bit, I noticed how dark it was, how cold.

> A long time—I have no idea how long.
> Once the earth decides to have no memory
> time seems in a way meaningless.

The vivid, emotional, and suspenseful picture the field offered in the summer and fall has decomposed. People and color have fallen out of the tableau—the farmer and the girl presumably moved away—and only the white canvas is left. The earth covered the field with snow, an image that evokes repression and willful forgetting. If there were wounds, the earth concealed them under an "immaculate" blanket and appears remarkably unimpressed. For the moment, history has been undone and memory avoided. Glück implies that Demeter did not freeze the world to signify she was mourning the daughter's disappearance but to undo Persephone's deed and sink it into oblivion under a thick, cold, white surface.

In the second section of "Averno," the girl "moved to some other country, / one where they don't have fields"—by implication the girl is Persephone who descended to the underworld. Her existence becomes dubious altogether in the third section:

> Afterward, the girl was gone.
> Maybe she didn't exist,
> we have no proof either way.
>
> All we know is:
> the field burned.
> But we *saw* that.
>
> So we have to believe in the girl,
> in what she did. Otherwise
> it's just forces we don't understand
> ruling the earth.

Repressing the girl's destructive deed first leads to eliminating her from the field of mind and displacing her into some faraway country and then generates doubts about whether she existed at all. At this point of deepest negation, the speaker transforms lack of knowledge into the need for belief. When the drive toward decomposition climaxes, it tips over into the unifying force of the life drive. The girl's act of destruction is reinterpreted as a much-needed assertion of subjectivity. Charring the field is reenvisioned as a mode of leaving one's mark on an environment otherwise ruled by unknown forces; it is a mode of "leav[ing] . . . [one's] name behind" before falling into "the pit of disappearance."

Demeter heals the wounds Persephone inflicted on the field when "after the first winter, the field began to grow again." Yet the field cannot be changed back into the field before the fire. Now, "there were no more orderly furrows. / The smell of the wheat persisted, a kind of random aroma / intermixed with various weeds, for which / no human use has been as yet devised." The charred field may be overgrown, but the "wheat" remains polluted by "weeds." The near-homophone of *wheat* and *weed* represents the olfactory pollution ("a kind of random aroma / intermixed with various weeds") in terms of a slight phonetic deviation. The image of entangled wheat and weeds evokes the psychoanalytic idea of the "entanglement" of the life drive and the death drive, both of which can almost never be encountered in a pure form. Glück points out that "no human use has been as yet devised" for the weeds, implying that they are usually combatted by the farmer or gardener because they threaten the growth of the "good grain." In an analogous manner, the death drive is combatted by culture as a force in human nature that is antagonistic to civilization and pushes it toward disintegration. But there is hope that the weeds, too, serve a purpose, which has not been discovered "as yet."

In the context of *Averno*, the changes inflicted on the field of wheat resonate with the changes Persephone has undergone when she returns from the underworld. In the first Persephone poem, we learn that "the return of the beloved / does not correct / the loss of the beloved"; in "A Myth of Innocence," "the girl who disappears from the pool / will never return. A woman will return, / looking for the girl she was." Something has been lost forever: the loss of the beloved daughter is a fact, and it is not erased by her return; the child self has been lost to the woman who comes back; the crop grows back, but the wheat is polluted by weeds. Glück emphasizes loss by punning on *weeds*, which refers to an undesirable plant but also to a widow's black mourning clothes. The charred black fields were first erased by snow and then covered by a new crop; and still, the past has not been undone and memory persists. The fields of wheat are clothed in weeds of mourning.

Contrary to the speaker, the earth has no interest in memory:

> Nature, it turns out, isn't like us;
> it doesn't have a warehouse of memory.

> The field doesn't become afraid of matches,
> of young girls. It doesn't remember
> furrows either. It gets killed off, it gets burned,
> and a year later it's alive again
> as though nothing unusual has occurred.

The earth's astonishing reproductive capacity, which could be celebrated as the expression of her abundant and indestructible life drive, causes the speaker to feel deeply alienated from her. Because nature has no memory, it "isn't like us." Memory, in this poem, is connoted with the death drive: if, like nature, we did not have memory, we would move naturally with the seasons. But knowing that fields of wheat can be easily destroyed can take away our joy in the arrival of a new spring. Remembering death can spoil our joy in life. Unlike nature, the farmer

> thinks: *my life is over.*
> His life expressed in that field;
> he doesn't believe anymore in making anything
> out of earth. The earth, he thinks,
> has overpowered me.
>
> He remembers the day the field burned,
> not, he thinks, by accident.
> Something deep within him said: *I can live with this,*
> *I can fight it after awhile.*
>
> The terrible moment was the spring after his work was erased,
> when he understood that the earth
> didn't know how to mourn, that it would change instead.
> And then go on existing without him.

The farmer understands that, just as the earth did not mourn the destruction of the field, she will not mourn his death. While he survives the burning by bearing it, fighting it, mourning it, the earth will simply survive by "changing," barely taking account of the loss that occurred. Glück alludes to Eliot's famous opening of *The Waste Land*: "April is the cruelest month, breeding / Lilacs out of the dead land, mixing / Memory and desire, stirring / Dull roots with spring rain."[15] She echoes the despair in Eliot's poem over life proceeding regardless of which trauma needs to be survived. The earth is fundamentally "other" and her indifference toward human experience "overpowering." "The earth . . . / has overpowered me" is the translation of a German phrase Glück employed earlier in *Averno*. The speaker in the fourth section of "Landscape" asks, "why did I reject my life?" The reason is given promptly: *"Die Erde überwältigt mich:* / the earth defeats me." Life on earth is cruel: the speaker "had forgotten / how harsh these conditions are: // the earth not obsolete / but still, the river cold, shallow—" (*AV* 47). In "Averno," the earth is not only experienced as hostile because of its harsh seasons, but also because of its alien way of operating. Her inexorable life force is, ironically, not something by which the speaker feels nourished, but *"überwältigt,"* "overpowered," and "defeated." The experience of this difference between the earth, often referred to as "mother earth," and her "children" is profoundly disturbing.

DEMETER'S DARK SIDE

By burning the field of wheat and turning it into a charred wasteland, Persephone makes visible the earth's "dark side." The speakers in "Landscape" and "Averno" detect the aggression hidden within Demeter's fierce drive for growth and reproduction. She is unwilling to acknowledge her "dark side" even when it is put right before her eyes, and rather covers it up in snow. In Glück's version of the myth, Persephone is alienated from her own aliveness because of her mother's negation of her own destructiveness. In "The Theme of the Three Caskets," Freud argues that myths and fairy tales often represent evil as good, turn the goddess of death into the goddess of life, and serve the psyche's need for wish fulfillment. He attributes to the poet the capacity to see through these distortions and sense the original myth.[16]

While "Landscape" and "Averno" only metaphorically imply the relationship between mother and daughter, the second "Persephone the Wanderer" poem (*AV* 73–76) makes it explicit. Glück lets the analysis of the mother unfold, and sometimes verge on the polemical; she is not interested in the objectivity of multiple perspectives or in analytic theories of the mother, but in the expression of all the emotional rawness and subjective bias that drive this daughter's search for the truth.

Persephone's mother "looks into the infant's face. She thinks: / *I remember when you didn't exist."* Does the mother remember her life before the child was born? Does she threaten the baby, insinuating that its existence is precarious? Does she assert her dominance by reminding the child that her memory reaches beyond its existence? As if the mother's invocation of the past spoiled the future, the child's life is "unfortunately . . . going to be / a short life" and "She is going to know, really, // only two adults: death and her mother." Reminiscent of the preoedipal stage of life, Persephone's only acquaintances are Hades and Demeter; she lacks a father's presence and protection. Zeus only enters the stage after the daughter has already been lost to the underworld. Rather than speaking of "her husband and her mother," Glück deliberately chooses the asymmetrical configuration of "death and her mother" to suggest that "death" and "mother" are not separate opposites but components of the same unit. The poem continues:

> But two is
> twice what her mother has:
> her mother has
>
> one child, a daughter.
> As a god, she could have had
> a thousand children.
>
> We begin to see here
> the deep violence of the earth
>
> whose hostility suggests
> she has no wish
> to continue as a source of life.
>
> And why is this hypothesis
> never discussed? Because
> it is not *in* the story; it only
> creates the story.

Trying to empathize with the child's innocent perspective but incapable of reexperiencing the child's feeling, the speaker suggests sardonically that having two people in her life is not so bad since it is "twice what her mother has," being the mother of only *one* daughter. Rather than happiness and pride, the single daughter instills in the mother a sense of limitation and failure, for "as a god" she could have given life to "a thousand children." So, one is inclined to ask, what held her back? Although the mother consciously claims she would have liked to have had many children, the actuality of only giving a short life to one daughter is the manifestation of an unconscious wish: *not* to be "a source of life." The goddess

of life and fertility has an unconscious rampant with violence and hostil-
ity. The well-known myth of Persephone is a conscious version of the
tale; it also has a "narrative unconscious" that lies outside of the story
and yet "creates" it. The poet attunes herself to the myth as the analyst
attunes herself to the analysand's language; both are listening for the
repressed unconscious of the respective narrative.

Joyce McDougall writes that "a baby's earliest external reality is its
mother's unconscious."[17] Persephone is so deeply impressed with her
mother's repressed death drive that she becomes the queen of Hades. The
daughter acts out her mother's unconscious death wish by descending to
the underworld. This has repercussions for the mother whose steady
course is unsettled by the daughter's propensity for death. While Per-
sephone is in Hades, the mother becomes a wanderer in the daughter's
stead: "In grief, after the daughter dies, / the mother wanders the earth."
The daughter has forced the mother to share the "wanderer's symptom."
Demeter freezes life into winter and acts on the hostility and aggression
she had previously denied.

The mother's "grief" is not motivated by love but by feeling threat-
ened by the loss. Anticipating the need for self-defense, Demeter "is pre-
paring her case; / like a politician / she remembers everything and admits
/ nothing." But she slips and involuntarily reveals her envy: Persephone's
"birth was unbearable, her beauty / was unbearable." The parallelism
tricks the mother into admitting that she viewed her daughter as a rival.
Softer memories of "Persephone's / innocence, her tenderness—" lead
nowhere, as the dash concluding the line implies. The mother resists her
loving feelings. Her desperate search for the daughter is "a warning
whose implicit message is: *what are you doing outside my body?*" Gripped
by her instincts of survival and control, the mother's actions are as natu-
ralistically determined as those of a tree:

> the daughter's body
> doesn't exist, except
> as a branch of the mother's body
> that needs to be
> reattached at any cost.

However, the analogy is faulty and makes us feel the unnaturalness of
the mother's love: a tree is not able to think it wants its branches reat-
tached. Losing her daughter is, above all, a threat to the mother's abso-
luteness. The daughter's detachment forces the mother to face her dou-

bleness, or the existence of both the life and death drives within her. The daughter becomes the mother's rival as the death drive is life's rival and Hades is Demeter's rival.

The mother makes a deal with Zeus that she will end winter on earth if he gets Persephone back from Hades. But Persephone has come to like her life in the underworld and does not care much anymore for "The small pestering breezes / that . . . [she] so loved, the idiot yellow flowers—" of her mother's realm. "Persephone / was used to death. Now over and over / her mother hauls her out again—." The dashes may indicate that the "breezes" and "flowers" are not so "pestering" or "idiotic" after all, and Persephone may also have more positive feelings about her mother's insistence on her return to life. But Persephone does not probe further into her ambivalence. In Glück's version of the myth, Persephone's resistance to life is actually her resistance to the mother, and she equates being alive with yielding to her. She fears being merged with the mother, who cannot tolerate her detachment.

Glück's revision of Demeter's role has a personal dimension. In her autobiographical essay "Education of the Poet," Glück describes her own mother's influence on her early life: "I was born into the worst possible family . . . I had a strong desire to speak, but that desire was regularly frustrated: my sentences were, in being cut off, radically changed—transformed, not paraphrased."[18] Glück's mother did not speak to create personal intimacy, but "to fill a room with ongoing, consoling human sound" or to act as the girl's severest critic. Yet she also read to her constantly, so that before Louise "was three, . . . [she] was well grounded in the Greek myths, and the figures of those stories, together with certain images from illustrations, became fundamental referents."[19] Glück's early introduction to mythology through her mother complicates what it means for her to remember Persephone and Demeter. Having been a passive receptacle for the world of myth, Glück reinvents the myth. Not having been allowed to detach from her mother in language, the poet ends up being the one to speak. Psychoanalyzing Persephone becomes an act of emancipation from the mother through poetry. Glück is fully aware of the powers of poetry and willing to use it as a vehicle for revenge:

> The poet, writing, is simultaneously soaked in his materials and unconstrained by them: personal circumstance may prompt art, but the actual making of art is a revenge on circumstance. For a brief period, the natural arrangement is reversed: the artist no longer acted upon but

acting; the last word, for the moment, seized back from fate or chance. Control of the past: as though the dead martyrs were to stand up in the arena and say, "Suppose, on the other hand . . ." No process I can name so completely defeats the authority of event. [20]

Revenge is achieved by symbolizing and sublimating the mother's negative unconscious. Glück seems to speak about conscious acts of revenge; yet the artist may not only be in control of the revenge, but also, like Persephone, in the grip of the revenge as an unconscious force.

ARCHETYPAL MEMORY

Among psychoanalytic writers, C. G. Jung (1969) devotes the greatest attention to Persephone and conceives of her as a female archetype[21] characterized by her identification with the mother and by her paralyzed "feminine initiative." This type of daughter perceives of her mother as a kind of "superwoman" and is

> content to cling to her mother in selfless devotion, while at the same time unconsciously striving, almost against her will, to tyrannize over her, naturally under the mask of complete loyalty and devotion. The daughter leads a shadow-existence, often visibly sucked dry by her mother, and she prolongs her mother's life by a sort of continuous blood transfusion. . . . The girl's notorious helplessness is a special attraction. She is so much an appendage of her mother that she can only flutter confusedly when a man approaches. She just doesn't know a thing. She is so inexperienced, so terribly in need of help, that even the gentlest swain becomes a daring abductor who brutally robs a loving mother of her daughter. Such a marvellous opportunity to pass himself off as a gay Lothario does not occur every day and therefore acts as a strong incentive. This was how Pluto abducted Persephone from the inconsolable Demeter. But, by a decree of the gods, he had to surrender his wife every year to his mother-in-law for the summer season. (The attentive reader will note that such legends do not come about by chance!)[22]

Inside of this confusedly fluttering girl, however, sleeps Kore, the queen of the underworld. Kore, Jung believes, is part of a woman's "supraordinate personality"[23] or "true self," the unconscious dimension or "dark side of the human psyche"[24] that needs to be uncovered for a more integrated person to emerge.

Jung expanded Freudian theory by postulating the existence of a deeper unconscious than the personal one; this "collective unconscious" contains all instincts and archetypes or primordial images, as he also called them. He specified Freud's idea of the conscious ego by developing the concept of the persona, a term originally referring to the mask worn by ancient actors, and in Jung's work meaning the constructed personal and social identity or, in his more provocative words, the "compromise role in which we parade before the community." In the terminology of this study, Jung's persona would be the product of historic memory. He contrasts the persona with the unconscious self and holds that the latter amounts to "one's real individuality." Bringing the personal unconscious to awareness and integrating the forgotten and repressed elements of the self are essential steps toward a person's individuation. This is Jung's variant of practicing poetic memory. By retrieving the personal unconscious, a person also gets in touch with the collective unconscious. Because the personal and the collective unconscious are not neatly separate from each other, "the conscious mind becomes suffused with collective material."[25] Glück's *Averno* poems exemplify this conflation of the personal and the collective unconscious: associations on the myth elicit personal poems, and poems evolving from personal memory illuminate neglected aspects of the myth. For example, in the first Persephone poem, the concluding question "What will you do, / when it is your turn in the field with the god?" (*AV* 19) connects Persephone's fate to the personal *memento mori* poems at the beginning of the book. In "October," which never mentions Persephone and precedes the more explicit mythical poems, the speaker replies to the world's tempting appeal to "Come to . . . [her]": "death cannot harm me / more than you have harmed me, / my beloved life" (*AV* 9–10). These lines clearly anticipate Persephone's rejection of Demeter and her submission to Hades. Glück lets the personal lead her to the mythical, and she uses the mythical to penetrate more deeply into the personal. This dialectical process allows her to retrieve material both from the personal unconscious and from the collective or archetypal unconscious.

Jung suggests that the "self" is too detached from the conscious ego to be recognized by it in a direct way: "The self is felt empirically not as subject but as object, and this by reason of its unconscious component, which can only come to consciousness indirectly, by way of projection."[26] Glück projects her unconscious self when she associates on Persephone and Demeter as archetypes, and she makes her projections conscious through writing. She also needs to differentiate the recovered part of her unconscious self from the archetype. The archetype, on one hand, is an inborn *form* of perceiving and apprehending life experience. Its *content*, on the other hand, is indeterminate and needs to be filled with the concrete experiential substance of the individual life.[27] This implies that individuation is a twofold process of differentiation. "The aim of individuation," Jung writes in "Relations Between the Ego and the Unconscious," "is nothing less than to divest the self of the false wrapping of the persona on the one hand, and of the suggestive power of primordial images on the other."[28] First, there must be what one could call "outward" differentiation from the persona or mask as the representative of social norms, and secondly, there must be "inward" differentiation from the archetypal prescriptions encountered in the unconscious. Both kinds of differentiation require trust in the existence of a larger and truer self that makes the journey worthwhile. Both necessitate the experience of poetic memory or a person's ability to remember and recognize truer forms of the self as they emerge.

As a poet, Glück is even more ambitious than Jung, because she rewrites the archetypes and preserves them in her poems. In *Averno*, not only is the poet-speaker's consciousness expanded, but Persephone's too. Both evolve from the fluttering or, in Glück's terminology, "wandering" girl with a mother complex to the adventurer who conquers the underworld in her quest for self-knowledge. By integrating the experience of the death drive, which in the tale is represented as the withdrawal from the earth and the existence in the underworld, the life drive can be embraced more fully. The influence between the archetype and the poet-speaker is mutual: the archetype incites the poet-speaker to explore that facet of her own self, and the speaker, by doing so, personalizes and enriches the archetype. The poet-speaker deepens her understanding of her personal unconscious by analyzing it as a concretization of the archetypal, and she projects the archetypal by abstracting it from the personal. The memory of this process of growth and of changing the unconscious is stored in the poems.

The archetypal unconscious may supply a person with contents that, when assimilated, can help her transcend narcissistic constriction. Jung presciently accounts for Glück's evolution as a poet when he expounds on the effects of this process of self-realization:

In this way there arises a consciousness which is no longer imprisoned in the petty, oversensitive, personal world of the ego, but participates freely in the wider world of objective interests. This widened consciousness is no longer that touchy, egotistical bundle of personal wishes, fears, hopes, and ambitions which always has to be compensated or corrected by unconscious counter-tendencies; instead, it is a function of relationship to the world of objects, bringing the individual into absolute, binding, and indissoluble communion with the world at large. The complications arising at this state are no longer egotistic wish-conflicts, but difficulties that concern others as much as oneself. At this stage it is fundamentally a question of collective problems, which have activated the collective unconscious because they require collective rather than personal compensation. We can now see that the unconscious produces contents which are valid not only for the person concerned, but for others as well, in fact for a great many people and possibly for all.[29]

Glück echoes Jung when she speaks about her desire to identify her personal poetry with collective human concerns: "It was clear to me long ago that any hope I had of writing real poetry depended on my living through common experiences. The privileged, the too-protected, the mandarin in my nature would have to be checked. At the same time, I was wary of drama, of disaster too deliberately courted: I have always been too at ease with extremes. What had to be cultivated, beyond a necessary neutrality, was the willingness to be identified with other. Not with the single other, the elect, but with a human community."[30] Although any act of memory changes what it retrieves by fusing it with aspects of the personal present, memory of the mythical has such personal transformation as its very goal. According to Jung, the reinterpretation of myth and its archetypes is a vital task of every age because it ensures the connection of contemporary consciousness with the ancient psychic past and counters the fragmentation and limitation of the psyche: "If we cannot deny the archetypes or otherwise neutralize them, we are confronted, at every new stage in the differentiation of consciousness to which civilization attains, with the task of finding a new interpretation appropriate to this stage, in order to connect the life of the past that still exists in us with the life of the present, which threatens to slip away from it."[31] Jung suggests that retrieving and reinterpreting the archetype is a potent and crucial act of memory that fuses the past and the present, the individual and the community. If the psyche wants to become ever more conscious, it must keep enlarging its binding force.

Poetry in *Averno* is writing *toward* the unconscious, and it is writing *from* the unconscious. Glück's associative method is a sort of fishing net sifting the deep waters of the psychic underworld for what they are willing to yield. Catching forgotten memories and making them conscious changes Persephone's story dramatically. As long as Persephone wandered repetitively and aimlessly between her mother's and her husband's realm, she had no future. When the past is frozen, so are present and future. When the past can be changed, it turns into fertile grounds for new life.

Both poetry and psychoanalysis aim at progressing from the common utterance to the brink of the ineffable. It is difficult for Persephone to speak from the depth of her being because, to find access to her unconscious, she needs to retrieve her mother's unconscious, too. The mother's soul, as Glück's Persephone comes to understand, has a dark side that complements the goddess's conscious desire to promote growth and fertility on earth. In the mother's realm, Persephone was expected to repress her death drive just as the mother did. The fused presence of both drives in mother and daughter was split between them, and while Demeter ruled on earth, Persephone made the underworld her domain. As long as this split is sustained, the daughter must feel "hauled out" of the underworld and forced back into life by the mother.

The poet's exploration of the mythical unconscious restores Persephone's subjectivity and lets her speak as an "I" in the final stanzas of *Averno*:

> I think I can remember
> being dead. Many times, in winter,
> I approached Zeus. Tell me, I would ask him,
> how can I endure the earth?
>
> And he would say,
> in a short time you will be here again.
> And in the time between
>
> you will forget everything:
> those fields of ice will be
> the meadows of Elysium.

(*AV* 76)

Persephone does not repress the memory of her mother's violence anymore, but has recovered it. Preparing her ascent to the earth, she confesses to her father Zeus her difficulty "endur[ing] the earth" or bearing the union with her mother. Zeus offers Persephone a tender and soothing reply: she will "forget everything," forget the battles with her mother and her withdrawal to the underworld. It will be spring on earth, and the wintry "fields of ice" will be the "meadows of Elysium." Elysium is the place in the underworld where the souls of the heroic and the virtuous find their peace. By connecting to her unconscious, Persephone has become one of them and more: she can take the blissful places she has discovered in the underworld with her to life. She has united the life and death forces within herself. Glück has freed Persephone from the repetition and opened up the myth's archetypal structure to new life.

NOTES

1. Louise Glück, *Averno* (New York: Farrar, Straus and Giroux, 2006).

2. See epigraph in *Averno*.

3. "A dreamer knows in his unconscious thoughts all that he has forgotten in his conscious ones, and that in the former he judges correctly what in the latter he misunderstands in a delusion." Sigmund Freud, *Delusions and Dreams in Jensen's "Gradiva"* (1907), in *Standard Edition*, trans. James Strachey (London: Hogarth Press, 1959), 9:83.

4. I am referring to Ovid's account of the Persephone myth in the *Metamorphoses* because of its canonical status and narrative detail. I deviate from Ovid by using the Greek names of the gods. Glück does not make reference to any mythical account in particular. In a private conversation with the author, she explained she deliberately avoided researching the myth so she could write entirely from memory. The source most vivid in her memory is *D'Aulaires Book of Greek Myths*, written and illustrated for children.

5. Louise Glück, *Proofs and Theories: Essays on Poetry* (Hopewell, NJ: Ecco Press, 1994), 12–13.

6. "October," for example, is modeled on the seasons and starts out with "winter again" (*AV* 5), moves through summer (*AV* 7) and spring ("In the thawed dirt, / bits of green were showing," *AV* 9), and ends in "the light of autumn" (*AV* 12) and the "ornamental lights of the season" (*AV* 13), supposedly Christmas lights. The poem "Prism" consists of twenty shorter sections and evokes the memories of a life cycle: it begins with "Fragments / of blistered rock. On which / the exposed heart constructs a house, memory" (*AV* 20), referring to the broken materials memory has to work with. Then the speaker tries to retrieve memories of the sister and the mother. Next, she remembers falling in love once, then with "several men" (*AV* 27). At the end, "The great plates [keep] invisibly shifting and changing—" (*AV* 27), forestalling narrative closure. The poem "Landscape" depicts a cycle of different space-times. First, "the sun is setting behind the mountains, / the earth is cooling" (*AV* 40). The second section is set in a landscape of ice where "Time passed, turning everything to ice" (*AV* 42),

followed by a "field of wheat" (*AV* 44) in the third section that a young girl sets on fire in late autumn. Then, the speaker "fell asleep in a river" (*AV* 46), and in the final section, it is time again to remember, as in the first section, that the sun is setting. This requires the speaker to break from her reminiscing mode and to ride "quickly, in the hope of finding / shelter before darkness" (*AV* 48).

7. Glück, *Proofs and Theories*, 74.

8. Sigmund Freud, "Recommendations to Physicians Practising Psycho-Analysis" (1912), in *Standard Edition*, 12:111.

9. Sigmund Freud, "Two Encyclopaedia Articles" (1923), in *Standard Edition*, 18:237.

10. Sigmund Freud, "Remembering, Repeating and Working-Through" (1914), in *Standard Edition*, 12:150.

11. Freud found out that the patient's free associations, forgetting of familiar words or names, slips of the tongue, and dreams were all potentially valuable points of access to the unconscious as the storage place of forgotten memories. Contemporary psycho-analysis places less emphasis on the reconstruction of a person's autobiographical or, as it is called by current memory research, explicit memory, but on changes effected in a person's implicit memory. One cannot hope to reconstruct autobiographical memories accurately, and the experiences crucial in forming the first object relations, and with them, the basic structure of the mind, occur too early to be stored by memory. However, these earliest unsymbolized memories—preverbal experiences and primary relations—are not lost, but retained by implicit memory. In Mauro Mancia's words: "Implicit memory constitutes an unconscious nucleus of the self which is not repressed; this unconscious nucleus influences the person's affective, cognitive, and sexual life even as an adult." Mauro Mancia, "Dream Actors in the Theatre of Memory: Their Role in the Psychoanalytic Process," *International Journal of Psycho-Analysis* 84 (2003): 946. See also Peter Fonagy, "Memory and Therapeutic Action," *International Journal of Psychoanalysis* 80 (1999): 215–23. Freud was not wholly silent about this kind of memory but did not have the findings of neuroscience at his disposal, which might have enabled him to explore it further. In his comparison of the analyst's work to that of the archaeologist, he points out that both "make out what has been forgotten from the traces which it has left behind." But in contrast to the archaeologist, who retrieves "something destroyed," the analyst deals with "something that is still alive." Sigmund Freud, "Constructions in Analysis" [1937], in *Standard Edition*, 23:257–58.

12. Sigmund Freud, *New Introductory Lectures on Psycho-Analysis* (1933), in *Standard Edition*, 22:73.

13. Oscar Sternbach, "Aggression, the Death Drive and the Problem of Sadomasochism: A Reinterpretation of Freud's Second Drive Theory," *International Journal of Psycho-Analysis* 56 (1975): 324.

14. Glück, *Proofs and Theories*, 104.

15. Eliot, *Complete Poems and Plays*, 37.

16. Sigmund Freud, "The Theme of the Three Caskets" (1913), in *Standard Edition*, 12:299.

17. Joyce McDougall, *Theaters of the Body: A Psychoanalytic Approach to Psychosomatic Illness* (New York: Norton, 1989), 39–40.

18. Glück, *Proofs and Theories*, 5.

19. Ibid., 7.

20. Ibid., 25.

21. Jung defines the archetype or "primordial image" as follows: "In this 'deeper' stratum [of the collective unconscious; my insertion] we also find the *a priori*, inborn forms of 'intuition,' namely the *archetypes* of perception and apprehension, which are the necessary *a priori* determinants of all psychic processes. Just as his instincts compel man to a specifically human mode of existence, so the archetypes force his ways of perception and apprehension into specifically human patterns." C. G. Jung, "Instinct and the Unconscious," in *The Portable Jung*, ed. Joseph Campbell (New York: Viking Penguin, 1971), 52. Archetypes, these basic and psychically inherited modes of apprehending one's experience in the world, are ubiquitous, and *"wherever we meet with uniform and regularly recurring modes of apprehension, we are dealing with an archetype, no matter whether its mythological character is recognized or not"* (Jung, "Instincts," 57). At the same time, "archetypes are not determined as regards their content, but only as regards their form and then only to a very limited degree. A primordial image is determined as to its content only when it has become conscious and is therefore filled out with the material of conscious experience. . . . The archetype in itself is empty and purely formal, nothing but a *facultas praeformandi*, a possibility of representation which is given *a priori*. The representations themselves are not inherited, only the forms, and in that respect they correspond in every way to the instincts, which are also determined in form only." C. G. Jung, *The Archetypes and the Collective Unconscious* (Princeton, NJ: Princeton University Press, 1969), 79.

22. Jung, *Archetypes*, 89–90.

23. Ibid., 183.

24. Ibid., 186.

25. C. G. Jung, "The Relations between the Ego and the Unconscious," in *The Portable Jung*, ed. Joseph Campbell (New York: Viking Penguin, 1971), 106.

26. Jung, *Archetypes*, 187.

27. Ibid., 79; Jung, "Instinct and the Unconscious," 52, 57.

28. Jung, "The Relations between the Ego and the Unconscious," 123.

29. Ibid., 127.

30. Glück, *Proofs and Theories*, 105–6.

31. Jung, *Archetypes*, 157.

Epilogue

Plath's, Howe's, Hinsey's, and Glück's poetry is pervaded by a sense that the self must be drawn from sources other than conscious personal memory. The intuitive conviction that unless they write poems, they remain "ignorant of themselves," as Plotinus says, may be the very motor driving their work. Poetic speakers have a crucial function in the practice of poetic memory. A poet and her speakers overlap to varying degrees; the confessional "I" is nearly identical with the poet, the speaker wearing a mask is more detached from her. Regardless of how verisimilar to the poet, all poetic speakers, from the perspective of poetic memory, are modes of testing the limits of the writing self and of re-membering, varying, expanding, or transforming the self.

Plath, Howe, Hinsey, and Glück search different realms for poetic memory. If Wordsworth goes to nature, they too go to various domains uncharted by their culture. If Wordsworth tries to capture intimations of childhood, they too explore varieties of preexisting, detached, or forgotten selves. Plath invokes fields of ruins and devastation and exaggerates her speaker's self-estrangement by assembling eclectic pieces from the historical and popular stores of memory into gruesome figures. Howe searches the wilderness of the American experience as it becomes manifest in the disruptions, incoherences, margins, and blanks of its textual remains. Hinsey reimagines the dimensions that mark and limit experience: space, time, and collective memory. Like Howe, she retrieves forgotten aspects of the self from beloved figures of the past. Glück immerses herself in the unconscious and enriches the self through the rewriting of archetypes.

Subjectivity, as it emanates from Plath's, Howe's, Hinsey's, and Glück's practices of poetic memory, has a strong element of otherness. It is grounded in memory, but not in the personal memory of the "I." These poets transcend what Plotinus calls "their willingness to belong to themselves," which is the determination to cut oneself off from one's true origins and be reduced to the "I" of Plato's sensible world. They seek to transcend the diminished "I" of historic memory by searching for the self's other dimensions in places presumably unrelated to it. One could view their divergent practices of poetic memory as attempts to reverse the self-estrangement described by Plotinus. Plath dramatizes the need for the memory of the other through her invocations of "Daddy," whom she cannot have. She demands that the "old man" surface from the depth of the sea because she yearns for an earlier self. Her pleas to the sea are reminiscent of Wordsworth's immersion in nature; but nature has lost its charms and proves a threat to survival rather than a source of spiritual replenishment. The mnemonic vacuum her speakers struggle with attracts collective memory, which gradually outweighs and eventually swallows personal memory. Subjectivity remains an act of assertion through performance. Because the performance of subjectivity in poetry happens in language, subjectivity, like language, can be reinvented (as "Lady Lazarus" suggests).

Plath identifies the otherness within the self as forms of public discourse and literary memory, and Howe makes it visible as quotation. Subjectivity in her poetry is literally and immediately inhabited by other voices. In contrast to Plath, these other voices are not elements foreign to the self but constitutive of it. Subjectivity in Howe's poetry draws on remembering particularly that other who has been marginalized and forgotten and who, deliberately or not, eludes representation. Subjectivity comprises varying degrees of otherness, from a nameable to an elusive, imaginary other.

As in Howe, subjectivity in Hinsey's poems requires the subject's recognition of his or her affiliation with the past, of his or her past dimension. The poet presupposes that the past is both self and other. More precisely, the past is initially perceived as other and must be searched for its personal significance. Subjectivity depends on the recognition that the past other is intricately entwined with the present self, and Hinsey makes these bonds visible in the way specific people clash with watershed historical events. She also describes moments of recognizing oneself in a person from the past. For Hinsey, the past becomes other through the artificial conceptual separation of time and space. Events in history fall back in our memory because they are not associated with and sufficiently consolidated by space; places and the spatial remains of the past are superficially registered in their present existence rather than imagined in their temporal depth and historical significance. Hinsey uses the poem to create the dimension of time-space; she visualizes time in terms of space and saturates space with time.

Like these other poets, Glück expands ideas of the self by making the (mythical) other the self, or finding the self in the other. Her poetry can be interpreted as exploring the psyche to fathom the other on deeper levels of the self. Enacting a psychoanalytic process, she moves from the personal conscious to the personal unconscious to the collective unconscious. Myth can be viewed as an outside aid guiding the way toward the inner archetypal structure. When the personal and the collective unconscious meet, both are changed through the encounter.

Plath's, Howe's, Hinsey's, and Glück's memory poems have a self-reflexive dimension characteristic of postmodern writing. They reveal the mnemonic processes that went into their writing. They stage the imposition of collective varieties of memory on personal memory in the writing process. They lay open the intertextual processes contributing to their composition through implied reference to the poetic tradition or outright through quotation. Seeking alternative ways to represent the past, some poems remind their readers of editorial rectifications and the assimilation to ideologically coherent forms of memory "suffered" by texts. Some poems reveal their mnemonic or archaeological nature by referring to themselves as fragments from the broken colossus, maps outlining settlements and the wilderness, or "cities of memory." They can also represent the associative process in which formerly repressed or forgotten memories are retrieved.

Mnemonic self-reflexivity figures in the role the poems assign the reader. The reader has to participate in the process of memory constitution. After all, he is the one on whom the poems' memories are bestowed. Plath baffles her readers by confronting them with their own generic expectations of poetry and their own subjection to collective memory. Howe's collagist poetics of memory challenges the reader and requires him to be an active reader: he is forced to add the conjunctions by exercising his memory and is made aware of the otherwise mostly unconscious processes involved in reading poetry. He becomes the next link in the chain of readers and writers invoked in the poems. Hinsey's poetomnemonic palimpsests can be "experienced" by the reading subject. Endowing her reader with a "lantern" to shed light on the dark past ("The Disasters of War") or making him the witness of the past as the speaker's "You" ("The Roman Arbor"), she incites him to discover his affinities with the past. Glück addresses the reader to make him aware of his own psychic and transferential patterns and to facilitate transcending them. Otherwise, he will remain subject to the condition, as Glück describes it in her poem "Nostos," of having looked "at the world once, in childhood. / The rest is memory."[1]

The four poets suggest we think of a poem as a mnemonic topography. It is an object extending horizontally and vertically on the page and deeply, that is, into the third dimension, in language. The poem is a specific, material structure that binds and stores memories and conditions the mnemonic modalities. To Plath, a poem is a construct made from the fragments of the "colossus." From these ruined grounds—a metaphor of collective memory—she draws shards reflecting the chaos and destruction they come from and arranges them into a poem: the result is meant to be gruesome, macabre, exhilarating. To Howe, the poem is a map of consciousness, representing the conscious, the repressed, and the forgotten via print, the disruption of print, the margin, and the blank. To Hinsey, it is a mental city or space in which she inscribes her experience of historical places; it is a structure that allows for the experience and its representation. Glück uses the poem as a space for psychoanalytic association, malleable enough to follow and enable the movements of the mind while promoting thinking toward psychic depth.

Poetry, as a form, generates poetic memory. Even narrative poetry, insofar as it foregrounds poetic form, resists the temporal linearity of historic memory. The poem as a spatial construct is not bound to the consecutive depiction of events in their "real" order; memory starts in the present and is able to pull the distant past near, just as it may distance the recent past. The recursive mode of poetic reading supports the rearrangement of meaning. Peter Brooks, speaking specifically about the lyric, describes the experience of "simultaneity" when reading a poem: "Lyric poetry, we feel, strives toward an ideal simultaneity of meaning, encouraging us to read backward as well as forward (through rhyme and repetition, for instance), to grasp the whole in one visual and auditory image; and expository argument, while it can have a narrative, generally seeks to suppress its force in favor of an atemporal structure of understanding."[2] The poem can generate simultaneity because of its spatial characteristics. The fragmentary and elusive intimations retrieved by poetic memory are not forced into a narratively closed form. Poetic language—riven with metaphor, unrestricted by familiar forms of logic—is especially conductive to the work of poetic memory. It facilitates association, ambiguity, and subtlety and approximates the ineffable. Poems are "saying" not "said." The poem sustains the need of memory to be constantly renewed, if it wants to remain a living thing. Historic memory favors the reproduction of the constructed narrative; poetic memory and the poem want to be reread. Memory poems trigger cohesive thinking without final results. Poetic form is flexible enough to provide poetic memory with varying degrees of structural support. The poem may present itself as prose, in formal prosody, as collage, as dissolving words, or as the blank on the page. Its capacity for openness grants poetic memory breathing space. The poem consolidates memory as little as possible but as much as necessary.

NOTES

1. Louise Glück, *Meadowlands* (New York: Ecco Press, 1997), 43.
2. Peter Brooks, *Reading for the Plot: Design and Intention in Narrative* (New York: Alfred A. Knopf, 1984), 20–21.

Bibliography

PRIMARY TEXTS

Glück, Louise. *Ararat*. New York: Ecco Press, 1990.
———. *Averno*. New York: Farrar, Straus and Giroux, 2006.
———. *The First Four Books of Poetry: Firstborn, The House on Marshland, Descending Figure, The Triumph of Achilles*. New York: Ecco Press, 1995.
———. *Meadowlands*. New York: Ecco Press, 1997.
———. *October*. Louisville, KY: Sarabande Books, 2004.
———. *Proofs and Theories: Essays on Poetry*. Hopewell, NJ: Ecco Press, 1994.
———. *The Seven Ages*. New York: Harper Collins, 2002.
———. *A Village Life*. New York: Farrar, Straus and Giroux, 2009.
———. *Vita Nova*. New York: Ecco Press, 1999.
———. *The Wild Iris*. New York: Ecco Press, 1993.
Hinsey, Ellen. *Cities of Memory*. New Haven, CT: Yale University Press, 1996.
———. *Update on the Descent*. Northumberland, UK: Bloodaxe Books, 2009.
———. *The White Fire of Time*. Middletown, CT: Wesleyan University Press, 2002.
Howe, Susan. *Articulation of Sound Forms in Time*. Windsor, VT: Awede Press, 1987.
———. *A Bibliography of the King's Book or, Eikon Basilike*. Providence, RI: Paradigm Press, 1989. Reprinted in *The Nonconformist's Memorial*, 45-82.
———. *The Birth-mark: Unsettling the Wilderness in American Literary History*. Hanover, NH: University Press of New England, 1993.
———. *Cabbage Gardens*. Chicago: Fathom Press, 1979.
———. *The Captive Morphology*. Santa Fe, NM: Weaselsleeves Press, 1990.
———. *Defenstration of Prague*. New York: Kulchur Foundation, 1983.
———. *The Europe of Trusts*. Los Angeles: Sun and Moon Press; New York: New Directions, 1990.
———. *Federalist 10. Abacus 30* (November 15, 1987). Elmwood, CT: Potes and Poets Press, 1987.
———. *Frame Structures: Early Poems 1974–1979*. New York: New Directions, 1996.
———. *Hinge Picture*. New York: Telephone Books, 1974.
———. *The Liberties*. Guilford, CT: Loon Books, 1980.
———. *The Midnight*. New York: New Directions, 2003.
———. *My Emily Dickinson*. Berkeley, CA: North Atlantic Books, 1985.
———. *The Nonconformist's Memorial*. New York: New Directions, 1993.
———. *Pierce-Arrow*. New York: New Directions, 1999.
———. *Pythagorean Silence*. New York: Montemora Supplement, 1982.
———. *Secret History of the Dividing Line*. New York: Telephone Books, 1978.
———. *Singularities*. Hanover, NH: University Press of New England, 1990.
———. *Souls of the Labadie Tract*. New York: New Directions, 2007.
———. *That This*. New York: New Directions, 2010.

———. *The Western Borders.* Willits, CA: Tuumba Press, 1976.

Howe, Susan, and Susan Bee. *Bed Hangings.* New York: Granary, 2001.

Plath, Sylvia. *Ariel.* London: Faber and Faber, 1965.

———. *The Bell Jar*, 1963. New York: Harper and Row, 1971.

———. *Collected Poems.* New York: Harper Collins, 1992.

———. *The Colossus and Other Poems.* London: Heinemann, 1960.

———. *Crossing the Water.* London: Faber and Faber, 1971.

———. *Johnny Panic and the Bible of Dreams: Short Stories, Prose, and Diary Excerpts.* 1977. Reprint, New York: Harper Collins, 1979.

———. *The Journals of Sylvia Plath 1950–1962.* Edited by Karen V. Kukil. London: Faber and Faber, 2000.

———. *The Journals of Sylvia Plath.* Edited by Frances McCullough. New York: Dial Press, 1982.

———. *Letters Home: Correspondence 1950–1963.* Edited by Aurelia Schober Plath. New York: Harper Collins, 1975.

———. *Winter Trees.* London: Faber and Faber, 1971.

SECONDARY SOURCES

Adamson, Gregory Dale. "Serres Translates Howe." *SubStance: A Review of Theory and Literary Criticism* 83 (1997): 110–124.

Aird, Eileen M. *Sylvia Plath.* New York: Barnes and Noble Books, 1973.

Akhmatova, Anna Andreevna. *Poems of Akhmatova.* Translated by Stanley Kunitz and Max Hayward. Boston: Brown, Little, 1973.

Alexander, Paul. *Rough Magic: A Biography of Sylvia Plath.* New York: Viking Penguin, 1991.

Altieri, Charles. *Self and Sensibility in Contemporary American Poetry.* Cambridge: Cambridge University Press, 1984.

———. "Some Problems of Agency in the Theories of Radical Poetries." *Contemporary Literature* 37, no. 2 (1986): 207–37.

Alvarez, A. *Beyond All This Fiddle: Essays 1955–1967.* London: Allen Lane, 1968.

———. *The Savage God: A Study of Suicide.* London: Weidenfeld and Nicolson, 1971.

Annas, Pamela J. *A Disturbance in Mirrors: The Poetry of Sylvia Plath.* New York: Greenwood Press, 1988.

———. "The Self in the World: The Social Context of Sylvia Plath's Late Poems." *Women's Studies: An Interdisciplinary Journal* 7, nos. 1/2 (1980): 171–83.

Aristotle. "On Memory." In *The Complete Works of Aristotle.* Revised Oxford Translation. Edited by Jonathan Barnes. 714–20. Princeton, NJ: Princeton University Press, 1984.

Assmann, Aleida. *Erinnerungsräume: Formen und Wandlungen des kulturellen Gedächtnisses.* Munich: C. H. Beck, 1999.

———. "Vier Formen des Gedächtnisses." *Erwägen, Wissen, Ethik* 13, no. 2 (2002): 183–90.

Assmann, Aleida, Monika Gomille, and Gabriele Rippl. *Ruinenbilder.* Munich: Wilhelm Fink, 2002.

Assmann, Jan. *Moses the Egyptian: The Memory of Egypt in Western Monotheism.* Cambridge, MA: Harvard University Press, 1997.

————. *Religion and Cultural Memory: The Studies*. Translated by Rodney Livingstone. Stanford, CA: Stanford University Press, 2006.

Augustine. *Confessions*. Translated by F. J. Sheed. Indianapolis, IN: Hackett, 1993.

Axelrod, Steven Gould. "The Mirror and the Shadow: Plath's Poetics of Self-Doubt." *Contemporary Literature* 26, no. 3 (1985): 286–301.

————. *Sylvia Plath: The Wound and the Cure of Words*. Baltimore: Johns Hopkins University Press, 1990.

Bachelard, Gaston. *The Poetics of Reverie: Childhood, Language, and the Cosmos*. Translated by Daniel Russell. Boston: Beacon Press, 1969.

Back, Rachel Tzvia. *Led by Language: The Poetry and Poetics of Susan Howe*. Tuscaloosa: University of Alabama Press, 2002.

Baker, Peter. "Languages of Modern Poetry." *College Literature* 21, no. 2 (1994): 151–54.

Bakhtin, Mikhail M. "From the Prehistory of Novelistic Discourse." In *Modern Criticism and Theory*. Edited by David Lodge and Nigel Wood. 2nd ed. 105–36. New York: Longman, 2000.

————. "The Problem of the Text in Linguistics, Philology, and the Human Sciences: An Experiment in Philosophical Analysis." In *Speech Genres and Other Late Essays*. Edited by Caryl Emerson and Michael Holquist. Translated by Vern W. McGee. 103–31. Austin: University of Texas Press, 1986.

Barthes, Roland. *Image, Music, Text*. Edited and translated by Stephen Heath. 1977. Reprint, New York: Noonday Press, 1988.

Bartlett, Frederic C. *Remembering: A Study in Experimental and Social Psychology*. 1932. Reprint, Cambridge: Cambridge University Press, 1995.

Bartlett, Lee. "What Is Language Poetry?" *Critical Inquiry* 12 (1986): 741–52.

Bassnett, Susan. *Sylvia Plath*. Basingstoke, UK: Macmillan, 1987.

Beckett, Tom. "*The Difficulties* Interview." *The Difficulties* 3, no. 2 (1989): 17–27.

Benesch, Klaus, Jon–K. Adams, and Kerstin Schmidt, eds. *The Sea and the American Imagination*. Tübingen, Germany: Stauffenburg Verlag, 2004.

Benjamin, Walter. "Theses on the Philosophy of History." In *Illuminations: Essays and Reflections*. Edited by Hannah Arendt. Translated by Harry Zohn. 253–64. New York: Schocken Books, 1968.

————. "Das Kunstwerk im Zeitalter seiner technischen Reproduzierbarkeit (Zweite Fassung)." In *Walter Benjamin: Ein Lesebuch*. Edited by Michael Opitz. 313–47. Leipzig: Suhrkamp, 1996.

————. "The Work of Art in the Age of Mechanical Reproduction." In *Illuminations: Essays and Reflections*. Edited by Hannah Arendt. Translated by Harry Zohn. 217–51. New York: Schocken Books, 1968.

Bennett, Paula. *My Life, a Loaded Gun: Female Creativity and Feminist Poetics*. Boston: Beacon Press, 1986.

Bercovitch, Sacvan. *The Puritan Origins of the American Self*. New Haven, CT: Yale University Press, 1975.

Bergson, Henri. *Matter and Memory*. Translated by Nancy Margaret Paul and W. Scott Palmer. 1896. Reprint, New York: Zone Books, 1988.

Bernard, April. "My Plath Problem." *Parnassus: Poetry in Review* 18/19, nos. 2/1 (1993): 340–57.

Bernstein, Charles. "Passed by Examination: Paragraphs for Susan Howe." *The Difficulties* 3, no. 2 (1989): 84–88.

————. *A Poetics*. Cambridge, MA: Harvard University Press, 1992.

Bernstein, Richard J. "Tradition, Trauma and the Return of the Repressed." In *Freud and the Legacy of Moses*. 27–75. Cambridge: Cambridge University Press, 1998.

Birkle, Carmen. *Women's Stories of the Looking Glass: Autobiographical Reflections and Self-Representations in the Poetry of Sylvia Plath, Adrienne Rich, and Audre Lorde*. Munich: Wilhelm Fink, 1996.

Blanchot, Maurice. *The Infinite Conversation*. Translated by Susan Hanson. Minneapolis: University of Minnesota Press, 1993.

Blasing, Mutlu Konuk. *American Poetry: The Rhetoric of Its Form*. New Haven, CT: Yale University Press, 1987.

———. *Lyric Poetry: The Pain and the Pleasure of Words*. Princeton, NJ: Princeton University Press, 2007.

Blessing, Richard Allen. "The Shape of the Psyche: Vision and Technique in the Late Poems of Sylvia Plath." In *Sylvia Plath: New Views on the Poetry*. Edited by Gary Lane. 57–73. Baltimore: Johns Hopkins University Press, 1979.

Bloch, Ernst. "Nonsynchronism and the Obligation to Its Dialectics." *New German Critique* 11 (1977): 22–38.

Bloom, Harold. *The Anxiety of Influence: A Theory of Poetry*. 2nd ed. New York: Oxford University Press, 1997.

———, ed. *Sylvia Plath*. Modern Critical Views Series. New York: Chelsea House, 1989.

———. *The Western Canon: The Books and School of the Ages*. New York: Harcourt Brace, 1994.

Blosser, Silvianne. *A Poetics on the Edge: The Poetry and Prose of Sylvia Plath*. Bern: Peter Lang, 2001.

Bok, Sissela. "Autobiography as Moral Battleground." In *Memory, Brain, and Belief*. Edited by Daniel L. Schacter and Elaine Scarry. 307–24. Cambridge, MA: Harvard University Press, 2000.

Bonds, Diane S. "The Separative Self in Sylvia Plath's *The Bell Jar*." *Women's Studies* 18, no. 1 (1990): 49–64.

Boruch, Marianne. "Plath's 'Bees.'" *Parnassus: Poetry in Review* 17/18, nos. 2/1 (1993): 76–95.

Boym, Svetlana. *The Future of Nostalgia*. New York: Basic Books, 2001.

Brain, Tracy. *The Other Sylvia Plath*. Harlow, UK: Longman, 2001.

———. "'Your Puddle-Jumping Daughter': Sylvia Plath's Midatlanticism." *English* 47, no. 187 (1998): 17–39.

Brennan, Karen, Kathleen Crown, Rachel Blau DuPlessis, Kathleen Fraser, Elisabeth Frost, Jenny Goodman, Donna Hollenberg, Susan Howe, Jeanne Heuving, Laura Hinton, Cynthia Hogue, and Aldon Nielsen. "The Contemporary Long Poem: Feminist Intersections and Experiments. A Roundtable Conversation." *Women's Studies* 27, no. 5 (1998): 507–36.

Britzolakis, Christina. *Sylvia Plath and the Theatre of Mourning*. Oxford: Oxford University Press, 1999.

Broe, Mary Lynn. *Protean Poetic: The Poetry of Sylvia Plath*. Columbia: University of Missouri Press, 1980.

Bronfen, Elisabeth. *Sylvia Plath*. Plymouth, UK: Northcote House (in Association with the British Council), 1998.

Brooks, Peter. *Reading for the Plot: Design and Intention in Narrative*. New York: Alfred A. Knopf, 1984.

Bryant, Marsha. "Plath, Domesticity, and the Art of Advertising." *College Literature* 29, no. 3 (2002): 17–35.

Buber, Martin. *I and Thou*. Translated by Ronald Gregor Smith. New York: Macmillan, 1958.

Bundtzen, Lynda K. "Poetic Arson and Sylvia Plath's 'Burning the Letters.'" *Contemporary Literature* 39, no. 3 (1998): 434–51.

Burgin, Victor. *In/Different Spaces: Place and Memory in Visual Culture*. Berkeley: University of California Press, 1996.

Burkart, Annette. *"Kein Sterbenswort, Ihr Worte!" Ingeborg Bachmann und Sylvia Plath: Acting the Poem*. Tübingen, Germany: Francke, 2000.

Burke, Peter. "History as Social Memory." In *Memory: History, Culture, and the Mind*. Edited by Thomas Butler. 97–113. Oxford: Blackwell, 1989.

Butler, Judith. "Performative Acts and Gender Constitution: An Essay in Phenomenology and Feminist Theory." In *Performing Feminisms: Feminist Critical Theory and the Theatre*. Edited by Sue-Ellen Chase. 270–82. Baltimore: Johns Hopkins University Press, 1990.

Butler, Thomas, ed. *Memory: History, Culture and the Mind*. Oxford: Blackwell, 1989.

Butscher, Edward. *Sylvia Plath: Method and Madness*. New York: Seabury Press, 1976.

———, ed. *Sylvia Plath: The Woman and the Work*. New York: Dodd, Mead, 1977.

Butterick, George F. "The Mysterious Vision of Susan Howe." *North Dakota Quarterly* 55 (1987): 312–21.

Butzer, Günter. *Fehlende Trauer: Verfahren epischen Erinnerns in der deutschsprachigen Gegenwartsliteratur*. Munich: Wilhelm Fink, 1998.

Candau, Joël. *Anthropologie de la mémoire*. Paris: Presses Universitaires de France, 1996.

Caruth, Cathy, ed. *Trauma: Explorations in Memory*. Baltimore: Johns Hopkins University Press, 1995.

———. *Unclaimed Experience: Trauma, Narrative, and History*. Baltimore: Johns Hopkins University Press, 1996.

Chénetier, Marc. "Du Palais à l'hypertexte: les avatars de Mnémosyne. Esquisse d'une réflexion sur les rapports entre conceptions de la mémoire et littérature." *Le Temps des savoirs* 6 (2003): 115–39.

Chiasson, Dan. *One Kind of Everything: Poem and Person in Contemporary America*. Chicago: University of Chicago Press, 2007.

Churchwell, Sarah. "Ted Hughes and the Corpus of Sylvia Plath." *Criticism* 40, no. 1 (1998): 99–132.

Connell, Elaine. *Sylvia Plath: Killing the Angel in the House*. West Yorkshire, UK: Pennine Pens, 1993.

Connerton, Paul. *How Societies Remember*. Cambridge: Cambridge University Press, 1989.

Crown, Kathleen. "'This Unstable I-Witnessing': Susan Howe's Lyric Iconoclasm and the Articulating Ghost." *Women's Studies* 27, no. 5 (1998): 483–505.

Daly, Leo. *Swallowing the Scroll: Late in a Prophetic Tradition with the Poetry of Susan Howe and John Taggart*. Buffalo, NY: M Press, 1994.

Davison, Michael. *Ghostlier Demarcations: Modern Poetry and the Material World*. Berkeley: University of California Press, 1997.

De Certeau, Michel. "Walking in the City." In *The Cultural Studies Reader*. Edited by Simon During. 2nd ed. 126–33. London: Routledge, 1999.

Deleuze, Gilles, and Félix Guattari. *A Thousand Plateaus: Capitalism and Schizophrenia*. Translated by Brian Massumi. Minneapolis: University of Minnesota Press, 1987.

Derrida, Jacques. *Cinders*. Edited and translated by Ned Lukacher. Lincoln: University of Nebraska Press, 1991.

———. "Freud and the Scene of Writing." In *Writing and Difference*. Translated by Alan Bass. 246–91. London: Routledge, 2001.

———. *Mémoires: For Paul de Man*. Rev. ed. Translated by Cecile Lindsay, Jonathan Culler, Eduardo Cadava, and Peggy Kamuf. New York: Columbia University Press, 1989.

———. "Shibboleth." In *Midrash and Literature*. Edited by Geoffrey H. Hartman and Sanford Budick. 307–47. New Haven, CT: Yale University Press, 1986.

———. *Specters of Marx: The State of the Debt, the Work of Mourning, and the New International*. Translated by Peggy Kamuf. New York: Routledge, 1994.

———. "Structure, Sign, and Play in the Discourse of the Human Sciences." In *Writing and Difference*. Translated by Alan Bass. 351–70. London: Routledge, 2001.

Dickie, Margaret. "Seeing Is Re-Seeing: Sylvia Plath and Elizabeth Bishop." *American Literature* 29, no. 2 (1993): 131–46.

Dickie Uroff, Margaret. *Sylvia Plath and Ted Hughes*. Urbana: University of Illinois Press, 1979.

Dickinson, Emily. *The Complete Poems*. Edited by Thomas H. Johnson. New York: Little, Brown, 1960.

Diehl, Joanne Feit, ed. *On Louise Glück: Change What You See*. Ann Arbor: University of Michigan Press, 2005.

DuPlessis, Rachel Blau. *The Pink Guitar: Writing as Feminist Practice*. New York: Routledge, 1990.

Dworkin, Craig Douglas. "'Waging Political Babble': Susan Howe's Visual Prosody and the Politics of Noise." *Word and Image* 12, no. 4 (1996): 389–405.

Eakin, Paul John. "Autobiography, Identity, and the Fictions of Memory." In *Memory, Brain, and Belief*. Edited by Daniel L. Schacter and Elaine Scarry. 290–306. Cambridge, MA: Harvard University Press, 2000.

Eber, Dena Elisabeth, and Arthur G. Neal, eds. *Memory and Representation: Constructed Truths and Competing Realities*. Bowling Green, KY: Bowling Green State University Popular Press, 2001.

Edwards, Derek, and David Middleton, eds. *Collective Remembering*. London: Sage Publications, 1990.

Eliot, T. S. *The Complete Poems and Plays 1909–1950*. New York: Harcourt, Brace and World, 1971.

———. "Tradition and the Individual Talent." In *Selected Essays*. 3–11. New York: Harcourt, Brace and World, 1960.

Emerson, Ralph Waldo. *Emerson's Prose and Poetry*. Norton Critical Edition. Edited by Joel Porte and Saundra Morris. New York: Norton, 2001.

Erll, Astrid, and Ansgar Nünning, eds. *Gedächtniskonzepte der Literaturwissenschaft: Theoretische Grundlegung und Anwendungsperspektiven*. Berlin: Walter de Gruyter, 2005.

Falon, Janet Ruth. "Speaking with Susan Howe." *The Difficulties* 3, no. 2 (1989): 28–42.

Felman, Shoshana. "Education and Crisis." In *Traum: Explorations in Memory*. Edited by Cathy Caruth. 13–60. Baltimore: Johns Hopkins University Press, 1995.

———. *Jacques Lacan and the Adventure of Insight: Psychoanalysis in Contemporary Culture*. Cambridge, MA: Harvard University Press, 1987.

———. *The Juridical Unconscious: Trials and Traumas in the Twentieth Century*. Cambridge, MA: Harvard University Press, 2002.

————. *Writing and Madness.* Translated by Martha Noel Evans. Palo Alto, CA: Stanford University Press, 2003.

Finch, Annie. *The Body of Poetry: Essays on Women, Form, and the Poetic Self.* Ann Arbor: University of Michigan Press, 2005.

Firestone, Lisa, and Joyce Catlett. "The Treatment of Sylvia Plath." *Death Studies* 22, no. 7 (1998): 667–92.

Folsom, Jack. "Death and Rebirth in Sylvia Plath's 'Berck-Plage.'" *Journal of Modern Literature* 17, no. 4 (1991): 521–35.

Fonagy, Peter. "Memory and Therapeutic Action." *International Journal of Psychoanalysis* 80 (1999): 215–23.

Forché, Carolyn. "Twentieth Century Poetry of Witness." *American Poetry Review* 22, no. 2 (March–April 1993): 9–16.

Foster, Edward. "An Interview with Susan Howe." First published in *Talisman: Journal of Contemporary Poetry and Poetics* 4 (Spring 1990): 14–38. Reprinted in Susan Howe, *The Birth-mark: Unsettling the Wilderness in American Literary History*, 155–81.

Foucault, Michel. "What Is an Author?" In *Modern Criticism and Theory*. Edited by David Lodge and Nigel Wood. 2nd ed. 174–87. New York: Longman, 2000.

Frank, Robert Joseph, and Henry M. Sayre, eds. *The Line in Postmodern Poetry*. Urbana: University of Illinois Press, 1988.

Freud, Sigmund. *Beyond the Pleasure Principle*. 1920. Translated by James Strachey. New York: Norton, 1961.

————. *Civilization and Its Discontents*. 1930. Translated by James Strachey. New York: Norton, 1961.

————. "Constructions in Analysis." 1937. In Vol. 23 of *Standard Edition*, 255–70.

————. *Delusions and Dreams in Jensen's "Gradiva."* 1907. In Vol. 9 of *Standard Edition*, 3–96.

————. "The Dissection of the Psychical Personality." In *New Introductory Lectures on Psychoanalysis*. 1933. Translated by James Strachey. 57–80. New York: Norton, 1965.

————. *The Ego and the Id*. 1923. In Vol. 19 of *Standard Edition*, 1–66.

————. *Five Lectures on Psycho-Analysis*. 1910. Translated by James Strachey. New York: Norton, 1961.

————. *Group Psychology and the Analysis of the Ego*. 1921. New York: Norton, 1959.

————. *The Interpretation of Dreams*. 1900. Edited and translated by James Strachey. New York: Basic Books, 1958.

————. *Letters of Sigmund Freud*. Edited by Ernst L. Freud. Translated by Tania and James Stern. New York: Basic Books, 1960.

————. *Moses and Monotheism*. 1939. Translated by Katherine Jones. New York: Vintage Books, 1959.

————. "Mourning and Melancholia." 1917. In Vol. 14 of *Standard Edition*, 237–58.

————. *New Introductory Lectures on Psycho-Analysis*. 1933. In Vol. 22 of *Standard Edition*, 1–182.

————. "Recommendations to Physicians Practising Psycho-Analysis." 1912. In Vol. 12 of *Standard Edition*, 109–20.

————. "Remembering, Repeating and Working-Through." 1914. In Vol. 12 of *Standard Edition*, 145–56.

————. *The Standard Edition of the Complete Psychological Works of Sigmund Freud*. 24 vols. Translated by James Strachey. London: Hogarth Press, 1953–74.

————. "The Theme of the Three Caskets." 1913. In Vol. 12 of *Standard Edition*, 289–302.

———. *Three Essays on the Theory of Sexuality.* 1905. In Vol. 7 of *Standard Edition,* 123–246.

———. *Totem and Taboo.* 1913. In Vol. 13 of *Standard Edition,* vii–162.

———. "Two Encyclopaedia Articles." 1923. In Vol. 18 of *Standard Edition,* 233–60.

Freud, Sigmund, and Lou Andreas-Salomé. *Briefwechsel.* Edited by Ernst Pfeiffer. Frankfurt am Main: Fischer, 1966.

Friedman, Ellen G., and Miriam Fuchs, eds. *Breaking the Sequence: Women's Experimental Fiction.* Princeton, NJ: Princeton University Press, 1989.

Funkenstein, Amos. "Collective Memory and Historical Consciousness." *History and Memory: Studies in Representation of the Past* 1, no. 1 (1989): 5–26.

Gerbig, Andrea, and Anja Muller-Wood. "Trapped in Language: Aspects of Ambiguity and Intersexuality in Selected Poetry and Prose by Sylvia Plath." *Style* 36, no. 1 (2002): 76–92.

Gilbert, Sandra M. "Widow." *Critical Inquiry* 27, no. 4 (2001): 559–79.

Gilbert, Sandra, and Susan Gubar. *The Madwoman in the Attic: The Woman Writer and the Nineteenth-Century Literary Imagination.* 2nd ed. New Haven, CT: Yale University Press, 2000.

Golding, Alan. "Avant-Gardes and American Poetry." *Contemporary Literature* 35, no. 1 (1994): 156–70.

Goody, Jack, and Ian Watt. "The Consequences of Literacy." *Comparative Studies in Society and History* 5, no. 3 (1963): 304–45.

Goya Y Lucientes, Francisco. *The Disasters of War.* Introduction by Philip Hofer. New York: Dover, 1967.

Grabher, Gudrun. *Das lyrische Du: Du-Vergessenheit und Möglichkeiten der Du-Bestimmung in der amerikanischen Dichtung.* Heidelberg: C. Winter, 1989.

Green, Fiona. "'Plainly on the Other Side': Susan Howe's Recovery." *Contemporary Literature* 42, no. 1 (2001): 78–101.

Greenblatt, Stephen. "Resonance and Wonder." In *Exhibiting Cultures: The Poetics and Politics of Museum Display.* Edited by Ivan Karp and Steven Lavine. 42–55. Washington, DC: Smithsonian Institution Press, 1991.

Greer, Michael. "Ideology and Theory in Recent Experimental Writing or, The Naming of Language Poetry." *Boundary* 26, nos. 2/3 (1989): 335–55.

Gregerson, Linda. *Negative Capability: Contemporary American Poetry.* Ann Arbor: University of Michigan Press, 2001.

Gubar, Susan. "Prosopopoeia and Holocaust Poetry in English: Sylvia Plath and Her Contemporaries." *Yale Journal of Criticism* 14, no. 1 (2001): 191–215.

Gusdorf, Georges. *Mémoire et personne.* Paris: Presses Universitaires de France, 1951.

Guttenberg, Barnett. "Plath's Cosmology and the House of Yeats." In *Sylvia Plath: New Views on the Poetry.* Edited by Gary Lane. 138–52. Baltimore: Johns Hopkins University Press, 1979.

H. D. (Hilda Doolittle). *Collected Poems 1912–1944.* Edited by Louis L. Martz. New York: New Directions, 1983.

Hacking, Ian. *Rewriting the Soul: Multiple Personality and the Sciences of Memory.* Princeton, NJ: Princeton University Press, 1995.

Halbwachs, Maurice. *On Collective Memory.* Edited and translated by Lewis A. Coser. Chicago: University of Chicago Press, 1992.

Hall, Caroline King Barnard. *Sylvia Plath, Revised.* New York: Twayne Publishers, 1998.

———. *Sylvia Plath.* Boston: Twayne Publishers, 1978.

Halpern, Nick. *Everyday and Prophetic: The Poetry of Lowell, Ammons, Merrill, and Rich.* Madison: University of Wisconsin Press, 2003.

Hammer, Langdon. "Plath's Lives." *Representations* 75, no. 1 (2001): 61–88.

Hartley, George. *Textual Politics and the Language Poets.* Bloomington: Indiana University Press, 1989.

Hartman, Geoffrey H. *The Longest Shadow: In the Aftermath of the Holocaust.* Bloomington: Indiana University Press, 1996.

———. *Scars of the Spirit: The Struggle against Inauthenticity.* New York: Palgrave Macmillan, 2002.

———. *The Unremarkable Wordsworth.* Minneapolis: University of Minnesota Press, 1987.

Haverkamp, Anselm, and Renate Lachmann, eds. *Memoria: Vergessen und Erinnern.* Munich: Wilhelm Fink, 1993.

Hayman, Ronald. *The Death and Life of Sylvia Plath.* New York: Birch Lane Press, 1991.

Heidegger, Martin. *Poetry, Language, Thought.* Translated by Albert Hofstadter. New York: Harper and Row, 1971.

Heine, Heinrich. *Poetry and Prose.* Edited by Jost Hermand and Robert C. Holub. German Library. Vol. 32. New York: Continuum, 1982.

Herman, Judith Lewis. *Trauma and Recovery: The Aftermath of Violence—From Domestic Abuse to Political Terror.* New York: Basic Books, 1992.

Hinsey, Ellen. "Journey to Berlin: Poetic Journal." *The Literary Review* 44, no. 1 (2000): 62–63.

———. First letter to the author: "Notes on *Cities of Memory.*" August 17, 2003.

———. "The Rise of Modern Doggerel." *New England Review* 19, no. 2 (1998): 138–45.

———. Second letter to the author. February 23, 2005.

Hobsbawm, Eric, and Terence Ranger, eds. *The Invention of Tradition.* Cambridge: Cambridge University Press, 1992.

Hogue, Cynthia. "Towards a Poetics of Performative Transformation." In *Women Poets of the Americas: Toward a Pan-American Gathering.* Edited by Jacqueline Vaught Brogan and Cordelia Chavez Candelaria. 51–67. Notre Dame, IN: University of Notre Dame Press, 1999.

Holbrook, David. *Sylvia Plath: Poetry and Existence.* London: Athlone Press; Atlantic Highlands, NJ: Humanities Press, 1976.

Holler, Paul. "A Conversation with Ellen Hinsey." http://international-poetry.org/hinsey/interviews/holler.html.

Homans, Margaret. *Bearing the Word: Experience in Nineteenth-Century Women's Writing.* Chicago: University of Chicago Press, 1986.

Howe, Susan. "Either Either." In *Close Listening: Poetry and the Performed Word.* Edited by Charles Bernstein. 111–27. New York: Oxford University Press, 1998.

———. "These Flames and Generosities of the Heart: Emily Dickinson and the Illogic of Sumptuary Values." In *The Birth-mark: Unsettling the Wilderness in American Literary History*, 131–53.

———. "Four-Part-Harmony: Robert Creeley and Susan Howe Talk It Out." *Village Voice Literary Supplement* (April 12, 1994): 21–22.

———. *Incloser: An Essay.* Santa Fe, NM: Weaselsleeves Press, 1982. Reprinted in *The Birth-mark: Unsettling the Wilderness in American Literary History*, 43–86.

———. Interview with the author. May 22, 2003.

———. "P. Inman, Platin." In *In the American Tree: Language, Realism, Poetry*. 1980. Edited by Ron Silliman. 555–56. Reprint, Orono, ME: National Poetry Foundation, 1986.

———. "Renunciation Is a P(ei)rcing Virtue." *Profession* (1998): 51–61.

———. "Sorting Facts: Or, Nineteen Ways of Looking at Marker." In *Beyond Document: Essays on Nonfiction Film*. Edited by Charles Warren. 295–343. Hanover, NH: University Press of New England, 1996.

———. "Statement for the New Poetics Colloquium, Vancouver, 1985." *Jimmy and Lucy's House of "K"* 5 (1985): 13–17.

Hungerford, Amy. *The Holocaust of Texts: Genocide, Literature, and Personification*. Chicago: University of Chicago Press, 2003.

Huyssen, Andreas. *Twilight Memories: Marking Time in a Culture of Amnesia*. New York: Routledge, 1995.

Iser, Wolfgang. *The Act of Reading: A Theory of Aesthetic Response*. Baltimore: Johns Hopkins University Press, 1978.

———. *Die Appellstruktur der Texte: Unbestimmtheit als Wirkungsbedingung literarischer Prosa*. Konstanz, Germany: Universitätsverlag, 1970.

Jacobus, Mary. "Freud's Mnemonic: Women, Screen Memories, and Feminist Nostalgia." *Women and Memory*. Spec. issue of *Michigan Quarterly Review* 26, no. 1 (1987): 117–39.

Jakobson, Roman. "Dialogue on Time in Language and Literature." In *Verbal Art, Verbal Sign, Verbal Time*. Edited by Krystyna Pomorska and Stephen Rudy. 11-24. Minneapolis: University of Minnesota Press, 1985.

———. *Language in Literature*. Edited by Krystyna Pomorska and Stephen Rudy. Cambridge, MA: Belknap Press, 1987.

James, Henry. *The House of Fiction: Essays on the Novel*. Edited by Leon Edel. Westport, CT: Greenwood Press, 1973.

Johnson, Greg. "The Eloquent Wrath of Sylvia Plath." *Georgia Review* 54, no. 4 (2000): 750–56.

Jung, Carl Gustav. *The Archetypes and the Collective Unconscious*. Princeton, NJ: Princeton University Press, 1969.

———. "The Concept of the Collective Unconscious." In *The Portable Jung*. Edited by Joseph Campbell. 59–69. New York: Viking Penguin, 1971.

———. "The Relations between the Ego and the Unconscious." In *The Portable Jung*. Edited by Joseph Campbell. 70–138. New York: Viking Penguin, 1971.

Kammen, Michael. *Mystic Chords of Memory: The Transformation of Tradition in American Culture*. New York: Alfred A. Knopf, 1991.

Keller, Lynn. *Forms of Expansion: Recent Long Poems by Women*. Chicago: University of Chicago Press, 1997.

———. "An Interview with Susan Howe." *Contemporary Literature* 36, no. 1 (1995): 1–34.

Kendall, Tim. *Sylvia Plath: A Critical Study*. London: Faber and Faber, 2001.

———. "Sylvia Plath's 'Piranha Religion.'" *Essays in Criticism* 49, no. 1 (1999): 44–61.

Kirsch, Adam. *The Modern Element: Essays on Contemporary Poetry*. New York: Norton, 2008.

Klein, Kerwin Lee. "On the Emergence of Memory in Historical Discourse." *Representations* 69, no. 1 (2000): 127–50.

Knapp, Steven. "Collective Memory and the Actual Past." *Representations* 26 (1989): 123–49.

Koselleck, Reinhart. *Futures Past: On the Semantics of Historical Time.* Translated by Keith Tribe. Cambridge, MA: MIT Press, 1985.

———. *The Practice of Conceptual History: Timing History, Spacing Concepts.* Stanford, CA: Stanford University Press, 2002.

Kracauer, Siegfried. *The Mass Ornament: Weimar Essays.* Translated by Thomas Y. Levin. Cambridge, MA: Harvard University Press, 1995.

Krell, David Farrell. *Of Memory, Reminiscence, and Writing.* Bloomington: Indiana University Press, 1990.

Kristeva, Julia. *About Chinese Women.* Translated by Anita Barrows. London: Marion Boyars, 1977.

———. "Freudian Time." In *The Portable Kristeva.* Edited by Kelly Oliver. 129–31. New York: Columbia University Press, 1997.

———. "The Semiotic and the Symbolic." In *The Portable Kristeva.* Edited by Kelly Oliver. 32–70. New York: Columbia University Press, 1997.

———. "Women's Time." In *The Portable Kristeva.* Edited by Kelly Oliver. 349–69. New York: Columbia University Press, 1997.

Kroll, Judith. *Chapters in a Mythology: The Poetry of Sylvia Plath.* New York: Harper and Row, 1978.

Lacan, Jacques. "The Agency of the Letter in the Unconscious or Reason Since Freud." In *Ecrits: A Selection.* Translated by Alan Sheridan. 161–97. London: Routledge, 1977.

———. *The Ethics of Psychoanalysis.* Edited by Jacques-Alain Miller. Translated by Dennis Porter. New York: Norton, 1992.

———. *The Four Fundamental Concepts of Psycho-Analysis.* 1973. Edited by Jacques-Alain Miller. Translated by Alan Sheridan. Reprint, London: Vintage, 1998.

LaCapra, Dominick. *History and Memory after Auschwitz.* Ithaca, NY: Cornell University Press, 1998.

Lachmann, Renate. *Memory and Literature: Intertextuality in Russian Modernism.* Translated by Roy Sellars and Anthony Wall. Minneapolis: University of Minnesota Press, 1997.

Landrey, David. "The Spider Self of Emily Dickinson and Susan Howe." *Talisman: A Journal of Contemporary Poetry and Poetics* 4 (1990): 107–9.

Lane, Gary, ed. *Sylvia Plath: New Views on the Poetry.* Baltimore: Johns Hopkins University Press, 1979.

Lant, Kathleen Margaret. "The Big Strip Tease: Female Bodies and Male Power in the Poetry of Sylvia Plath." *Contemporary Literature* 34, no. 4 (1993): 620–69.

Lau, Beth. "Wordsworth and Current Memory Research." *Studies in English Literature 1500–1900* 42, no. 4 (2002): 675–92.

Lazer, Hank. *Opposing Poetries: Volume 2—Readings.* Evanston, IL: Northwestern University Press, 1996.

Le Goff, Jacques. *History and Memory.* Translated by Steven Randall and Elizabeth Clamen. New York: Columbia University Press, 1992.

Lehrer, Sylvia. *Dialectics of Art and Life: A Portrait of Sylvia Plath as Woman and Poet.* Salzburg, Austria: Institut für Anglistik und Amerikanistik, Universität Salzburg, 1985.

Leonard, Garry M. "'The Woman Is Perfected. Her Dead Body Wears the Smile of Accomplishment': Sylvia Plath and Mademoiselle Magazine." *College Literature* 19, no. 2 (1992): 60–82.

Lerner, Laurence. "What Is Confessional Poetry?" *Critical Quarterly* 29, no. 2 (1987): 46–66.

Lessing, Gotthold Ephraim. *Laocoon: An Essay upon the Limits of Poetry and Painting (1766)*. Translated by Ellen Frothingham. Reprint, New York: Farrar, Straus, and Giroux, 1969.

Lévinas, Emmanuel. *Entre Nous: Thinking-of-the-Other*. Translated by Michael B. Smith and Barbara Harshav. New York: Columbia University Press, 1998.

Lindberg-Seyersted, Brita. "'Bad' Language Can Be Good: Slang and Other Expressions of Extreme Informality in Sylvia Plath's Poetry." *English Studies* 78, no. 1 (1997): 19–31.

———. "Sylvia Plath's Psychic Landscapes." *English Studies* 71, no. 6 (1990): 509–22.

———. *Sylvia Plath: Studies in Her Poetry and Her Personality*. Oslo: Novus Press, 2002.

Lipsitz, George. *Time Passages: Collective Memory and American Popular Culture*. Minneapolis: University of Minnesota Press, 1990.

Longenbach, James. *Modern Poetry After Modernism*. New York: Oxford University Press, 1997.

———. *Modernist Poetics of History: Pound, Eliot, and the Sense of the Past*. Princeton, NJ: Princeton University Press, 1987.

Luria, Aleksandr R. *The Mind of a Mnemonist: A Little Book about a Vast Memory*. Translated by Lynn Solotaroff. Chicago: H. Regnery, 1976.

Lyotard, Jean-François. *The Postmodern Condition: A Report on Knowledge*. Translated by Geoff Bennington and Brian Massumi. Minneapolis: University of Minnesota Press, 1984.

Ma, Ming-Qian. "Articulating the Inarticulate: Singularities and the Counter-method in Susan Howe." *Contemporary Literature* 36, no. 3 (1995): 466–89.

———. "Poetry as History Revised: Susan Howe's 'Scattering as Behavior Toward Risk.'" *American Literary History* 6 (1994): 716–37.

MacIntyre, Alisdair. *After Virtue: A Study in Moral Theory*. Notre Dame, IN: University of Notre Dame Press, 1981.

Maier, Charles S. "A Surfeit of Memory? Reflections on History, Melancholy and Denial." *History and Memory: Studies in Representation of the Past* 5, no. 2 (1993): 136–52.

Malcolm, Janet. *The Silent Woman: Sylvia Plath and Ted Hughes*. New York: Alfred A. Knopf, 1994.

Mancia, Mauro. "Dream Actors in the Theatre of Memory: Their Role in the Psychoanalytic Process." *International Journal of Psycho-Analysis* 84 (2003): 945–52.

Mann, Thomas. "Freud and the Future." In *Freud: A Collection of Critical Essays*. Edited by Perry Meisel. Translated by H. T. Lowe-Porter. 45–60. Englewood Cliffs, NJ: Prentice Hall, 1981.

———. *Joseph and His Brothers*. Vol. 2. Translated by H. T. Lowe-Porter. New York: Alfred A. Knopf, 1935.

Margalit, Avishai. *The Ethics of Memory*. Cambridge, MA: Harvard University Press, 2002.

Markey, Janice. *A Journey into the Red Eye: The Poetry of Sylvia Plath—A Critique*. London: Women's Press, 1993.

———. *A New Tradition? The Poetry of Sylvia Plath, Anne Sexton, and Adrienne Rich—A Study of Feminism and Poetry*. Frankfurt am Main: Peter Lang, 1985.

Marsack, Robyn. *Sylvia Plath*. Bristol, UK: Open University Press, 1992.

Marsh, Nicky. "'Out of My Texts I Am Not What I Play': Politics and Self in the Poetry of Susan Howe." *College Literature* 24, no. 3 (1997): 124–37.

Martin, Stephen-Paul. *Open Form and the Feminine Imagination.* Washington, DC: Maisonneuve Press, 1988.

Massin, Jean, and Brigitte Massin. *Ludwig van Beethoven.* Paris: Fayard, 1967.

Materer, Timothy. "Occultism as Source and Symptom in Sylvia Plath's 'Dialogue over a Ouija Board.'" *Twentieth Century Literature* 37, no. 2 (1991): 131–47.

Matsuda, Matt K. *The Memory of the Modern.* Oxford: Oxford University Press, 1996.

Mazzaro, Jerome. "Sylvia Plath and the Cycles of History." In *Sylvia Plath: New Views on the Poetry.* Edited by Gary Lane. 218–40. Baltimore: Johns Hopkins University Press, 1979.

McClatchy, J. D. "Old Myths in New Versions." *Poetry* 172, no. 3 (1998): 154–64.

———. "Short Circuits and Folding Mirrors." In *Sylvia Plath: New Views on the Poetry.* Edited by Gary Lane. 19–32. Baltimore: Johns Hopkins University Press, 1979.

McCorkle, James. "Prophecy and the Figure of the Reader in Susan Howe's *Articulation of Sound Forms in Time.*" *Postmodern Culture* 9, no. 3 (May 1999).

McDougall, Joyce. *Theaters of the Body: A Psychoanalytic Approach to Psychosomatic Illness.* New York: Norton, 1989.

McGann, Jerome. *Black Riders: The Visible Language of Modernism.* Princeton, NJ: Princeton University Press, 1993.

McIntire, Gabrielle. *Modernism, Memory and Desire: T. S. Eliot and Virginia Woolf.* Cambridge: Cambridge University Press, 2008.

Melman, Billie. "Gender, History and Memory: The Invention of Women's Past in the Nineteenth and Early Twentieth Centuries." *History and Memory: Studies in Representation of the Past* 5, no. 1 (1993): 5–41.

Merleau-Ponty, Maurice. *Phenomenology of Perception.* Translated by Colin Smith. London: Routledge and Kegan Paul, 1962.

———. *Themes from the Lectures at the Collège de France 1952–1960.* Translated by John O'Neill. Evanston, IL: Northwestern University Press, 1970.

Messerli, Douglas, ed. *"Language" Poetries.* New York: New Directions, 1987.

Metcalf, Paul. "The Real Susan Howe." *The Difficulties* 3, no. 2 (1989): 52–56.

Middleton, Peter. "On Ice: Julia Kristeva, Susan Howe and Avant Garde Poetics." In *Contemporary Poetry Meets Modern Theory.* Edited by Antony Easthope and John O. Thompson. 81–95. Toronto: University of Toronto Press, 1991.

Middleton, Peter, and Tim Woods. *Literature of Memory: History, Time and Space in Postwar Writing.* Manchester, UK: Manchester University Press, 2000.

Miller, Ellen. "Philosophizing with Sylvia Plath: An Embodied Hermeneutic of Color in *Ariel.*" *Philosophy Today* 46, no. 1 (2002): 91–101.

Mink, Louis O. "Narrative Form as a Cognitive Instrument." In *The Writing of History: Literary Form and Historical Understanding.* Edited by Robert H. Canary and Henry Kozicki. 129-49. Madison: University of Wisconsin Press, 1978.

Mitchell, W. J. T. "Spatial Form in Literature: Toward a General Theory." *Critical Inquiry* 6, no. 3 (1980): 539–67.

———. *Iconology: Image, Text, Ideology.* Chicago: University of Chicago Press, 1986.

Möckel-Rieke, Hannelore. *Fiktionen von Natur und Weiblichkeit: Zur Begründung femininer und engagierter Schreibweisen bei Adrienne Rich, Denise Levertov, Susan Griffin, Kathleen Fraser und Susan Howe.* Trier, Germany: Wissenschaftlicher Verlag, 1991.

Montante, Sarah. "Interview with Ellen Hinsey." *Poetry Magazine* 8, no. 1 (2003). http://www.poetrymagazine.com/archives/2003/Feb03/hinsey_interview.htm.

Montefiore, Janet. *Men and Women Writers of the 1930s: The Dangerous Flood of History.* New York: Routledge, 1996.

Moore, Marianne. *Complete Poems.* New York: Macmillan/Penguin, 1994.

Morgan, Robert P. "Musical Time/Musical Space." *Critical Inquiry* 6, no. 3 (1980): 527–38.

Morris, Daniel. *The Poetry of Louise Glück: A Thematic Introduction.* Columbia: University of Missouri Press, 2006.

Mounic, Anne. *Poésie et mythe: Edwin Muir, Robert Graves, Ted Hughes, Sylvia Plath, Ruth Fainlight.* Paris: L'Harmattan, 2000.

Nalbantian, Suzanne. *Memory in Literature: From Rousseau to Neuroscience.* Houndmills, UK: Palgrave Macmillan, 2003.

Naylor, Paul. *Poetic Investigations: Singing the Holes in History.* Evanston, IL: Northwestern University Press, 1999.

Nicholls, Peter. "'The Pastness of Landscape': Susan Howe's Pierce-Arrow." *Contemporary Literature* 43, no. 3 (2002): 441–61.

———. "Unsettling the Wilderness: Susan Howe and American History." *Contemporary Literature* 37, no. 4 (1996): 586–601.

Nietzsche, Friedrich. *The Birth of Tragedy and the Genealogy of Morals.* Translated by Francis Golffing. New York: Doubleday, 1956.

———. "On the Uses and Disadvantages of History for Life." In *Untimely Meditations.* Edited by Daniel Breazeale. Translated by R. J. Hollingdale. 57–123. Cambridge: Cambridge University Press, 1997.

Nora, Pierre. "Between Memory and History: *Les Lieux de Mémoire.*" *Representations* 26 (Spring 1989): 7–24.

———. *Realms of Memory: Rethinking the French Past.* Edited by Lawrence D. Kritzman. Translated by Arthur Goldhammer. New York: Columbia University Press, 1996–1998.

Olster, Stacey. *Reminiscence and Re-Creation in Contemporary American Fiction.* Cambridge: Cambridge University Press, 1989.

Ovid. *Metamorphoses.* Translated by Mary M. Innes. London: Penguin, 1955.

Palatella, John. "An End of Abstraction: An Essay on Susan Howe's Historicism." *Denver Quarterly* 29, no. 3 (1995): 74–97.

Park, Jooyoung. "'I Could Kill a Woman or Wound a Man': Melancholic Rage in the Poems of Sylvia Plath." *Women's Studies* 31, no. 4 (2002): 467–97.

Parmet, Harriet L. *The Terror of Our Days: Four American Poets Respond to the Holocaust.* Bethlehem, PA: Lehigh University Press, 2001.

Peck, John. *Maritime Fiction: Sailors and the Sea in British and American Novels, 1719–1917.* Houndmills, UK: Palgrave, 2001.

———. "Two at the Gap: Jorie Graham and Susan Howe." *Partisan Review* 64, no. 3 (1997): 497–502.

Peel, Robin. *Writing Back: Sylvia Plath and Cold War Politics.* Madison, NJ: Fairleigh Dickinson University Press, 2002.

Perelman, Bob. *The Marginalization of Poetry: Language Writing and Literary History.* Princeton, NJ: Princeton University Press, 1990.

Perloff, Marjorie. "'Collision or Collusion with History': The Narrative Lyric of Susan Howe." *Contemporary Literature* 30, no. 4 (1989): 518–33.

———. "Language Poetry and the Lyric Subject: Ron Silliman's Albany, Susan Howe's Buffalo." *Critical Inquiry* 25, no. 3 (1999): 405–34.

———. *Poetic License: Essays on Modernist and Postmodernist Lyric.* Evanston, IL: Northwestern University Press, 1990.

———. "The Two Ariels: The (Re)making of the Sylvia Plath Canon." *American Poetry Review* 13, no. 6 (1984): 10–18.

Plato. "Phaedo." In *Complete Works.* Edited by John M. Cooper. Translated by G. M. A. Grube. 49–100. Indianapolis, IN: Hackett, 1997.

———. "Phaedrus." In *The Works of Plato.* Edited and translated by B. Jowett. Vol. 3. 359–449. New York: Dial Press, 1936.

Platt, Jonathan Brooks. "Proteus Bound and Unbound: The 1937 Pushkin Jubilee and Literature in the Soviet Schools." *Harriman Review* 14, no. 1/2 (2002): 47–55.

Plotinus. *Enneads V.* Edited by Jeffrey Henderson. Translated by A. H. Armstrong. Loeb Classical Library. Cambridge, MA: Harvard University Press, 1984.

Pound, Ezra. *Literary Essays of Ezra Pound.* Edited by T. S. Eliot. New York: New Directions, 1968.

Proust, Marcel. *Remembrance of Things Past. Vol. 1. Swann's Way.* Translated by C. K. Scott Moncrieff and Terence Kilmartin. New York: Random House, 1981.

Quartermain, Peter. *Disjunctive Poetics: From Gertrude Stein and Louis Zukofsky to Susan Howe.* Cambridge Studies in American Literature and Culture Series. Cambridge: Cambridge University Press, 1992.

Ramazani, Jahan. "'Daddy, I Have Had to Kill You': Plath, Rage, and the Modern Elegy." *PMLA* 108, no. 5 (1993): 1142–56.

Reinfeld, Linda. *Language Poetry: Writing as Rescue.* Baton Rouge: Louisiana State University Press, 1992.

———. "On Henry David (Susan Howe's) 'Thorow.'" *The Difficulties* 3, no. 2 (1989): 97–104.

Ricoeur, Paul. *La Mémoire, l'histoire, l'oubli.* Paris: Editions du Seuil, 2000.

Rose, Jacqueline. *The Haunting of Sylvia Plath.* London: Virago, 1991.

———. "'This Is Not a Biography.'" *London Review of Books* (August 22, 2002): 12-15.

Rosenbaum, Susan B. *Professing Sincerity: Modern Lyric Poetry, Commercial Culture, and the Crisis in Reading.* Charlottesville: University of Virginia Press, 2007.

Rosenblatt, Jon. *Sylvia Plath: The Poetry of Initiation.* Chapel Hill: University of North Carolina Press, 1979.

Rosenthal, M. L. *The New Poets: American and British Poetry Since World War II.* New York: Oxford University Press, 1967.

Roth, Michael S. *The Ironist's Cage: Memory, Trauma, and the Construction of History.* New York: Columbia University Press, 1995.

Saldívar, Toni. *Sylvia Plath: Confessing the Fictive Self.* New York: Peter Lang, 1992.

Salvesen, Christopher. *The Landscape of Memory: A Study of Wordsworth's Poetry.* Lincoln: University of Nebraska Press, 1965.

Schacter, Daniel L. *Searching for Memory: The Brain, the Mind, and the Past.* New York: Basic Books, 1996.

Schacter, Daniel L., and Elaine Scarry. *Memory, Brain, and Belief.* Cambridge, MA: Harvard University Press, 2000.

Schläger, Jürgen. "Seamus Heaney: Natur als Archiv." In *Englische und amerikanische Naturdichtung im 20. Jahrhundert.* Edited by Günter Ahrends. 171–84. Tübingen, Germany: Narr, 1985.

Schneidau, Herbert N. *Waking Giants: The Presence of the Past in Modernism.* New York: Oxford University Press, 1991.

Schweitzer, Viktoria. *Tsvetaeva*. Edited by Angela Livingstone. Translated by Robert Chandler and H. T. Willetts. London: Harper Collins, 1992.

Sebald, Winfried Georg. *Austerlitz*. Translated by Anthea Bell. London: Penguin, 2002.

Selinger, Eric Murphy. "My Susan Howe." *Parnassus: Poetry in Review* 20, no. 1/2 (1995): 359–85.

Schultz, Susan. "Exaggerated History." *Postmodern Culture* 4, no. 2 (January 1994).

Shakespeare, William. *King Lear*. Arden Shakespeare. Edited by R. A. Foakes. Walton-on-Thames, UK: Thomas Nelson, 1997.

———. *The Tempest*. London: Penguin, 1968.

Sielke, Sabine. *Fashioning the Female Subject: The Intertextual Networking of Dickinson, Moore, and Rich*. Ann Arbor: University of Michigan Press, 1997.

———. "'Rowing in Eden' and Related Waterway Adventures: Seaward Visions in American Women's Writing." In *The Sea and the American Imagination*. Edited by Klaus Benesch, Jon-K. Adams, and Kerstin Schmidt. 111–34. Tübingen, Germany: Stauffenburg Verlag, 2004.

Smith, Grover. *T. S. Eliot and the Use of Memory*. Lewisburg, PA: Bucknell University Press, 1996.

Smith, Stan. "Waist-Deep in History: Sylvia Plath." In *Inviolable Voice: History and Twentieth-Century Poetry*. 200–25. Dublin: Gill and Macmillan, 1982.

Smithson, Robert. *The Collected Writings*. Edited by Jack Flam. 2nd ed. Berkeley: University of California Press, 1996.

Smitten, Jeffrey R., and Ann Daghistany. *Spatial Form in Narrative*. Ithaca, NY: Cornell University Press, 1981.

Sontag, Susan. "Looking at War: Photography's View of Devastation and Death." *New Yorker* (December 9, 2002): 82–98.

Sorabji, Richard. *Aristotle on Memory*. Providence, RI: Brown University Press, 1972.

———. *Self: Ancient and Modern Insights about Individuality, Life, and Death*. Chicago: University of Chicago Press, 2006.

Spiegel, Gabrielle M. "Memory and History: Liturgical Time and Historical Time." *History and Theory* 41 (2002): 149–62.

Starn, Randolph. "Memory and Authenticity." *Studies in 20th Century Literature* 23, no. 1 (1999): 191–200.

Steele, Cassie Premo. *We Heal from Memory: Sexton, Lorde, Anzaldúa, and the Poetry of Witness*. New York: Palgrave, 2000.

Steiner, George. "Dying Is an Art." In *The Art of Sylvia Plath: A Symposium*. Edited by Charles Newman. 211–18. London: Faber and Faber, 1970.

Sternbach, Oscar. "Aggression, the Death Drive and the Problem of Sadomasochism: A Reinterpretation of Freud's Second Drive Theory. *International Journal of Psycho-Analysis* 56 (1975): 321–33.

Stevenson, Anne. *Bitter Fame: A Life of Sylvia Plath*. London: Viking, 1989.

Strangeways, Al. "'The Boot in the Face': The Problem of the Holocaust in the Poetry of Sylvia Plath." *Contemporary Literature* 37, no. 3 (1996): 370–90.

———. *Sylvia Plath: The Shaping of Shadows*. Madison, NJ: Fairleigh Dickinson University Press, 1998.

Sturken, Marita. *Tangled Memories: The Vietnam War, the AIDS Epidemic, and the Politics of Remembering*. Berkeley: University of California Press, 1997.

Suleiman, Susan Rubin, ed. *The Female Body in Western Culture: Contemporary Perspectives*. Cambridge, MA: Harvard University Press, 1986.

Sword, Helen. "James Merrill, Sylvia Plath, and the Poetics of Ouija." *American Literature* 66, no. 3 (1994): 553–72.

Taggart, John. *Songs of Degree: Essays on Contemporary Poetry and Poetics.* Tuscaloosa: University of Alabama Press, 1994.

Taussig, Michael. "'Dying Is an Art, Like Everything Else.'" *Critical Inquiry* 28, no. 1 (2001): 305–16.

Tennyson, Alfred Lord. *The Poems of Tennyson in Three Volumes.* Edited by Christopher Ricks. 2nd ed. Harlow, UK: Longman, 1987.

Terdiman, Richard. *Present Past: Modernity and the Memory Crisis.* Ithaca, NY: Cornell University Press, 1993.

Tuhkunen-Couzic, Taïna. *Sylvia Plath: Une Ecriture embryonnaire.* Paris: L'Harmattan, 2002.

Upton, Lee. *Defensive Measures: The Poetry of Niedecker, Bishop, Glück, and Carson.* Lewisburg, PA: Bucknell University Press, 2005.

———. *The Muse of Abandonment: Origin, Identity, Mastery in Five American Poets.* Lewisburg, PA: Bucknell University Press, 1998.

Van Dyne, Susan R. "Fueling the Phoenix Fire: The Manuscripts of Sylvia Plath's 'Lady Lazarus.'"*Massachusetts Review* 24 (1982): 395–410.

———. "Rekindling the Past in Sylvia Plath's 'Burning the Letters.'" *Centennial Review* 32 (1988): 250–65.

———. *Revising Life: Sylvia Plath's Ariel Poems.* Chapel Hill: University of North Carolina Press, 1993.

Van Pelt, Tamise. "Symptomatic Perfectionism: Ideal Ego and Ego Ideal in the Journals of Sylvia Plath." *Literature and Psychology* 43, no. 1/2 (1997): 47–64.

Vendler, Helen. *Coming of Age as a Poet: Milton, Keats, Eliot, Plath.* Cambridge, MA: Harvard University Press, 2003.

———. *Part of Nature, Part of Us: Modern American Poets.* Cambridge, MA: Harvard University Press, 1980.

Wägenbaur, Thomas, ed. *The Poetics of Memory.* Tübingen, Germany: Stauffenburg Verlag, 1998.

Wagner, Erica. *Ariel's Gift: Ted Hughes, Sylvia Plath and the Story of Birthday Letters.* London: Faber and Faber, 2000.

Wagner, Linda W., ed. *Critical Essays on Sylvia Plath.* Boston: G. K. Hall, 1984.

———. "Plath's *The Bell Jar* as Female Bildungsroman." *Women's Studies* 12, no. 1 (1986): 55–68.

Wagner-Martin, Linda W. *Sylvia Plath: A Biography.* New York: Simon and Schuster, 1987.

———, ed. *Sylvia Plath: The Critical Heritage.* New York: Routledge, 1988.

———. *Sylvia Plath: A Literary Life.* New York: St. Martin's Press, 1999.

Wang, Qun. Review of *Cities of Memory,* by Ellen Hinsey. *Magill's Literary Annual* (1997): 152–55.

Werth, Wolfang. *Ikonographie des Entsetzens: Die Todeslyrik der Sylvia Plath.* Trier, Germany: Wissenschaftlicher Verlag, 1990.

Wertsch, James. *Voices of Collective Remembering.* Cambridge: Cambridge University Press, 2002.

White, Hayden. *Tropics of Discourse: Essays in Cultural Criticism.* Baltimore: Johns Hopkins University Press, 1978.

Williams, Megan. "Howe Not to Erase(her): A Poetics of Posterity in Susan Howe's 'Melville's Marginalia.'" *Contemporary Literature* 38, no. 1 (1997): 106–32.

Wills, Clair. "Contemporary Women's Poetry: Experimentalism and the Expressive Voice." *Critical Quarterly* 36, no. 3 (1994): 34–52.

Winnicott, D. W. *Playing and Reality.* 1971. Reprint, London: Routledge, 2005.

Winter, Jay. *Sites of Memory, Sites of Mourning: The Great War in European Cultural History.* Cambridge: Cambridge University Press, 1995.

Wittgenstein, Ludwig. *Philosophical Investigations.* Translated by G. E. M. Anscombe. Cambridge, MA: Blackwell, 1997.

Wood, David John. *Critical Study of the Birth Imagery of Sylvia Plath, American Poet, 1932–1963.* Lewiston, ME: Edwin Mellen Press, 1992.

Woolf, Virginia. *A Room of One's Own.* New York: Harcourt, 1929.

Wordsworth, William. *The Early Letters of William and Dorothy Wordsworth (1787–1805).* Edited by Ernest de Selincourt. Oxford: Clarendon Press, 1935.

———. *Selected Poems and Prefaces.* Edited by Jack Stillinger. Boston: Houghton Mifflin, 1965.

Wurst, Gayle. *Voice and Vision: The Poetry of Sylvia Plath.* Geneva: Slatkine, 1999.

Wyschogrod, Edith. *An Ethics of Remembering: History, Heterology, and the Nameless Others.* Chicago: University of Chicago Press, 1998.

Yates, Frances A. *The Art of Memory.* London: Routledge and Kegan Paul, 1966.

Yenser, Stephen. *A Boundless Field: American Poetry at Large.* Ann Arbor: University of Michigan Press, 2002.

Yezzi, David. "Confessional Poetry and the Artifice of Honesty." *New Criterion* 16, no. 10 (1998): 14–21.

Young, Allan. *The Harmony of Illusions: Inventing Post-Traumatic Stress Disorder.* Princeton, NJ: Princeton University Press, 1995.

Young, James E. "'I May Be a Bit of a Jew': The Holocaust Confessions of Sylvia Plath." *Philological Quarterly* 6, no. 1 (1987): 127–47.

Index

Akhmatova, Anna, 170–171; "Requiem," 171

Almack, Edward: *Bibliography of the King's Book*, 72, 99

amnesia, 13, 29, 174n12; infantile, 4

anamnesis, 3, 19n5

Andreas-Salomé, Lou, 161

Antony (in *Julius Caesar*), 102

archetype, 15, 18, 179–180, 182, 204–209, 211n21, 213, 215. *See also* collective unconscious; unconscious

Assmann, Aleida, 66n19, 152, 157, 175n29

Atherton, Hope, 115, 116

Augustine (Saint): *Confessions*, 64

authenticity: acting versus, 56, 68n40; literature and, 79–80, 101; memory and, 11, 128n46, 143–144

authorship: Glück's, 18; Hinsey's, 164–165; Howe's, 76, 80, 81, 83, 92–95, 123, 127n24; Plath's, 33, 42

autobiography, 29, 78, 85, 203

Axelrod, Steven, 43, 67n25

Bachelard, Gaston, 35–36, 137

Bartlett, Frederic, 148, 175n32. *See also* schema

Beethoven, Ludwig van. *See* "March 26 1827" (Hinsey)

Benjamin, Walter, 17, 139–141, 148, 157; Messianic history, 140, 148; monad, 148; "Theses on the Philosophy of History," 148; tiger's leap, 140–141

Blanchot, Maurice, 140

Blasing, Mutlu Konuk, 19n7, 68n40

Bloch, Ernst, 147

Bloom, Harold, 88

Britzolakis, Christina, 33, 42

Brooks, Peter, 216

Buber, Martin: *I and Thou*, 165

Burke, Peter, 163

Butler, Judith, 59, 65

Caruth, Cathy, 115, 118–119, 129n68

Charles I (king), 71, 77, 98, 99, 122–123. *See also* "A Bibliography of the King's Book or, Eikon Basilike" (Howe)

Coleridge, Samuel Taylor, 89, 110

collective memory, 10, 12, 15, 16, 23–24, 29, 34–36, 39, 40, 43, 45–46, 48, 49, 50, 51, 52–53, 58–59, 60, 64–65, 66n1, 66n19, 110, 124, 135, 145, 161, 213, 215–216

collective unconscious, 179, 205–207, 211n21, 215. *See also* archetype; unconscious

confessional poets, 16, 18, 23, 24, 65, 213

Cowen, Wilson Walker: *Melville's Marginalia*, 74

death, 8; *ars moriendi*, 55, 57; conversation with the dead, 87; death drive/thanatos, 179, 189, 190, 191–193, 195, 198, 199, 202, 206, 208, 209; in dream of the burning child (Freud and Lacan), 117; Glück on, 179, 181, 182–184, 185, 188, 190, 193, 194–195, 199–200, 202, 203, 205; Hinsey on, 135, 136, 137, 139, 145, 150, 167, 170, 171, 174n10, 175n14; Howe on, 74, 80, 98, 104–107, 113, 117, 120; Lévinas on, 152; *memento mori*, 63, 179, 182, 183, 205; memory redeems, 170; Plath on, 29, 33, 36, 40, 53, 54, 58, 63, 66n4

Deleuze, Gilles, 91

Demeter (mother of Persephone), 193, 197, 198, 200–204, 205

About the Author

Uta Gosmann received her Ph.D. in American literature from the University of Bonn and the University of Paris 7—Denis Diderot. She was awarded fellowships from the German Academic Exchange Service (DAAD) for graduate study at SUNY Buffalo and Yale University. Her critical writing and translations of poetry have appeared in publications in Europe and the United States, including *Common Knowledge* and *Akzente*. She is a psychoanalyst in training and lives in New Haven, Connecticut.